WHO

Joshua Lionel Cowen, the founder of **Lionel** trains, also claimed to have invented the flashlight, the doorbell, and the electric fan.

Prior to revolutionizing America with his "57" varieties, H. J. **Heinz** was among the first party of Westerners to be admitted to the Forbidden City of Peking.

Mary Kay had to support her ailing father during the Depression—and utilized those working skills into becoming a cosmetics entrepreneur.

Major league baseball player A. G. **Spalding** turned his love for athletics into a sports equipment franchise.

And seventy more true stories of the people behind the brand names . . .

Made in America

The True Stories
Behind the Brand Names
That Built a Nation

JOHN GOVE

BERKLEY BOOKS, NEW YORK

MADE IN AMERICA:
THE TRUE STORIES BEHIND THE BRAND NAMES
THAT BUILT A NATION

A Berkley Book / published by arrangement with
the author

PRINTING HISTORY
Berkley edition / March 2001

The Penguin Putnam Inc. World Wide Web site address is
http://www.penguinputnam.com

ISBN: 0-425-17883-8

BERKLEY®
Berkley Books are published by The Berkley Publishing Group,
a division of Penguin Putnam Inc., 375 Hudson Street,
New York, New York 10014.
BERKLEY and the "B" design
are trademarks belonging to Penguin Putnam Inc.

PRINTED IN THE UNITED STATES OF AMERICA

10   9   8   7   6   5   4   3   2   1

*to my father, who never would have
believed I'd get interested
in anything like this*

Contents

Acknowledgments

W riting a book is supposed to be an arduous task,
but in my case it was surprisingly easy—made so
by numerous people whom I would like now to thank.

First are my subjects themselves, all 115 or so of them,
though regrettably, only seven remain alive to savor the
honor. They get the prime acknowledgment simply for
having lived the lives they did. I was merely the enthralled
scrivener of their tales. Often inspiring, sometimes momentous, and more than occasionally weird, the stories in
this book are theirs, not mine.

Thanks also go to people who led me to these tales: to
Linda Griffin of Brunswick for the beautifully illustrated
book on the history of that company; to Mrs. Agnes Asta
for her reminiscences about her late brother-in-law Chef
Boyardee; to Elmer Sanborn, proud eighth cousin twice
removed of coffee baron James; to Kevin Jones of Hormel
Foods for clarifying the Dinty Moore story for me; to Joe
Cavanaugh of the Dr Pepper Museum for reconciling the
myriad conflicting accounts in the Dr Pepper story; and
to Anita Wazniuk of the McDonald's Museum for telling
me which McDonald brother was which in their photo.

To Pamela Scholl, for review and comment on the
chapter on her great uncle, the foot doctor to the world;
to Jackie Love of the Hoover Museum for help on the
Hoover vacuum cleaner story; to Michele Aldrich of Otis
Elevator; Elizabeth King of Johnson & Johnson; Diane
Backus of Kellogg's; Ron Krajnovich of Maytag; Ed
Rider, archivist of Procter & Gamble; Robert Chandler of
Wells-Fargo; and Barbara Zibell of Wrigley's—all for ed-
itorial assistance.

Special thanks go to my agent, Paige Wheeler, who

amazed me one day last August with the news that my book had been sold. Finally, thank you to Christine Zika of Penguin Putnam for her thorough review of the manuscript.

Introduction

One day last year I was standing in a long checkout line at the supermarket. There were tabloids on display, and I could have relieved my boredom by reading about the Dubuque swamp monster or Madonna's Venusian love child, but instead my eyes were drawn by a certain item in my shopping cart. It was a coffee can with the portraits of two distinguished-looking gentlemen from, I would guess, the 1870s, their visages ensconced in quaint little oval frames with labels. "Chase," read one; "Sanborn," read the other.

Who *were* those guys? I asked myself. How did they get into the coffee business? Did they get along? Did they have any hobbies? Did they know the Hills brothers?

Beside it was a little box of Band-Aids. Who were Johnson & Johnson? Brothers? Father and son? Unrelated people?

Campbell's mushroom soup, Chef Boyardee ravioli, Reynolds Wrap—practically everything in my cart had somebody's name on it. Newman's Own salad dressing was the only product whose maker I knew anything about.

Finally, it was my turn to be checked through. I asked the clerk, "Who was Mr. Kroger, anyway?"

"He isn't here anymore," she quipped. At least, I think she was quipping.

Driving home in my *Chevrolet,* I passed billboards touting *Procter & Gamble* products, *Kellogg's* cereals, *Kimberly-Clark*'s Kleenex, and *Dr Pepper.*

After stopping for lunch at a *Wendy's,* I decided I would find out something about these people who were making all these things for me. Using my *Hewlett-Packard* DeskJet printer, I ran off letters onto *Weyer-*

haeuser paper and made phone calls to dozens of these companies.

My quest, which began as idle curiosity, quickly became an obsession. Every day I rushed home to riff through my mail, like a kid hoping his Captain Midnight secret transmitter ring had arrived. I was young again.

No two days at the mailbox turned out the same. Some days my eyes bugged as I beheld beautifully illustrated books that I couldn't have bought for twenty dollars in a store; other days, all I got was a couple of sheets from some company telling me how great their products are. So I surfed the Net, got books out of libraries, went to museums, interviewed people—in some cases the subjects themselves. One way or another, I managed to collect 74 stories of 116 people, more or less.

And the stuff I found out! The people who gave their names to the familiar brands of American commerce, so I learned, represent every character type you can imagine. There were geniuses, and there were fools who got lucky. Some grew obscenely wealthy, but there were sad stories of economic ruin. Some had rich and varied lives outside their work; others were (sometimes literally) consumed by their work. Some lived in response to their noblest impulses, while others led lives filled with lust, betrayal, and greed.

A surprising number didn't actually have any connection with the companies that took their names. I learned how America's premier luxury car came to be named for a French explorer and a popular candy bar for a president's daughter. Two of my subjects turned out to be entirely fictional. And, incredibly, two others were real people, but nobody really knows who they were.

Like the people we know, some American entrepreneurs fascinate more than others. Not many moved history the way the Du Ponts did, and few are as ingratiating as Ben and Jerry, as flamboyant as Isaac Singer, or as weird as King Gillette, but all are interesting in some way. Important factors were fame and fortune—forces that often contort people into weird and fascinating shapes.

So be prepared to be surprised fairly often. I certainly was. Some of these people are not at all what I'd expected them to be. In fact, my biggest obstacle in selling this book was convincing people the stories were real. I swear they're true, or at least consistent with the information I was given.

But my biggest surprises—there were two of them—weren't about any of the individuals or the scarcely believable events in their lives; they were about the nature of America and its system of commerce. I will tell you what they were in the afterword. You can skip to there if you're curious, or you can try to figure out what they were as you read along.

In either case, I hope you enjoy as much as I did finding out about Harry Heinz, Louis Chevrolet, William Wrigley, and the others who made the lives we live possible.

Anheuser-Busch

E berhard Anheuser (1805–1880), son of a merchant in the Rhine Valley, emigrated to America in 1843 and settled in St. Louis, where he came to make a rather good living as a soap maker. A few years later, going from one suds business to another, he joined up with Nicholas Schaffer to form a brewery that soon became so prosperous that the two could declare, "It's Miller time" and vacation in Europe for months at a time. No wonder: beer in those days could be made for a dollar a barrel and sold for eight.

For years, Anheuser and Schaffer lived what their rival, Frederick Miller, would call the "high life," but in 1854, Eberhard's wife, Dorothea, died. With six children to raise, he suddenly found himself in a far more settled existence, and family responsibilities became the center of his life.

One of his children was a stunning blonde nicknamed Lilly, who worked in his office. It was there that a young brewery supply salesman came to peddle his wares, and not incidentally to woo his client's daughter. The salesman was successful in both ventures, and in March 1861, Eberhard walked sixteen-year-old Lilly down the aisle of the local German Lutheran church to give her away to the young salesman—Adolphus Busch.

Adolphus Busch (1839–1913) was the twenty-first of twenty-two children born to Ulrich Busch, who, like John Jacob Anheuser, Eberhard's father, came from the Rhineland. After attending schools in Mainz, Darmstadt, and Brussels, Adolphus worked as a lumberjack, floating logs down the Rhine for his father's lumber business, and later became an apprentice in his uncle's brewery, and then a shipping clerk in Cologne.

The twenty-four Busches lived a no doubt crowded yet reasonably contented existence, until the late 1840s, when social unrest spread throughout Europe. High inflation, political upheaval, a succession of bad harvests, and general all-around misery forced many Germans, several of whom we will meet in this book, to try their fortune in the New World. In 1857, following the lead of three of his thirteen brothers, Adolphus came to St. Louis, where, as we already know, he sold brewing supplies, and got married.

The month after his marriage, the Civil War broke out. In Missouri, the slavery issue was especially contentious, and every able-bodied male that could be found, including brewmeisters, was recruited for the Union cause. I can't quite picture Anheuser and Busch as Civil War soldiers—one of them a wealthy executive in his late fifties, the other a dapper, baby-faced, five-foot-five-inch boy-man with a foppish goatee and a thick German accent. But they did their jobs and were among five thousand Unionists who with Sherman and Grant successfully fought off a rebel attack and quelled subsequent street rioting.

Returning to private life, Eberhard and his young son-in-law established a partnership. Busch himself was himself a promising brewmeister, and ardently he set to the task of improving Anheuser's beer, a beer that by all accounts was abominable. It contained alcohol, but that was its only redeeming feature.

Over the next few years, Busch became a true student of the brewing art, and he made no fewer than twenty-two trips to the old country to learn the old world's brewing secrets. On one occasion, he visited a brewery in České-Budějovice, near Pilsen. The town, called Budweis by the Germans, made an exceptionally fine beer. His alleged appropriation of the name and the process provoked a controversy that continues to this day.

Busch's Budweiser is a lager beer made from bottom-fermenting yeasts. With a recipe that hasn't changed for 123 years, he used the finest German hops, and added rice, far costlier than corn, as an auxiliary ingredient.

In 1880, Anheuser, who had developed throat cancer three years earlier, died, and Busch bought up all the stock of his heirs, for as much as $60,000 a share. Now with exclusive control, and with a product heads above the competition, Busch was well positioned to exploit his advantage. He built a seventy-acre brewery complex with 110 buildings and six thousand workers. He laid his own railroads, bought a controlling interest in the company that made his railroad tank cars, constructed a network of ice-houses to store his beer, and even built glass plants to make his bottles.

He was so proud of his creation that he hired guides to give factory tours. No doubt the guides were told to show visitors what he wanted them to see and never to take them into the bowels of the brewery. There, visitors would have felt like Dante descending through the nine circles of hell. They would have seen huge copper vats of boiling wort, turned in revulsion as workers' eyes were gouged out by exploding glass vessels, heard the deafening machinery, choked on the smoke and fumes, and most of all, felt the unremitting heat that killed ten boiler stokers in one summer alone.

The workday began in darkness and would not end until fourteen hours later (again in darkness), except on Sunday, when it was mercifully shortened to six hours. Working there was fiendishly oppressive for the workers, and the appearance of Mr. Busch, with his pointed goatee and his "manners of a gentleman" must have suggested the Prince of Darkness himself, when viewed across the smoke and flames of the kettle rooms.

But he was rarely at the brewery. Instead, he and the Busch family were living an opulent life, even by Gilded Age standards, in sumptuous homes in St. Louis, Pasadena, upstate New York, and Germany.

The St. Louis home he called Grantmoor. Built on

property once owned by his commanding general, it was elaborate and elegantly furnished, though it was architecturally overpowered by the huge castlelike brewery buildings next door. During the months when windows were open, the sight, sounds, and smells of the brewery probably were to Adolphus's liking, but not to Lilly's, so the Busches spent most of their summers in the Pasadena home, now the site of Busch Gardens, on Millionaires Row. The German home, called Villa Lilly, was a base for travel to the finest Paris restaurants and the elegant spas of Carlsbad.

The contrast between Busch's life and that of his workers offends modern sensibilities, but the workers, mostly German expatriates, were accustomed to living under the thumb of despots, and seemed to accept their lot. In fact, they adored their leader and greeted his returns from European pleasure domes to his marbled St. Louis mansion with cannon shots, and he, also accepting his status as a given, waved in his carriage like a conquering monarch.

The workers may have sympathized with his private problems, for his family life was filled with disillusionment and tragedy. Adolphus and Lilly had thirteen children, almost all of whom were disappointments to them— some by dying too soon, others by not dying soon enough.

Three sons died as young men—curiously, all of appendicitis. One may have had his appendix intentionally ruptured by a girlfriend's hat pin. A fourth son, Augustus, left home to become a cowboy.

Of the daughters, three did not survive infancy. Nellie, the oldest surviving one, married a musician, whom she divorced to marry a second husband, who committed suicide. Daughter Clara married a German prince, an intimate of the kaiser. This connection to the archenemy who was killing our doughboys in the trenches of Europe, together with the Busches' continuing pleasure jaunts to Eurospas, didn't win them any points with the folks back home, but worse was yet to come. Another daughter, with the curious name Edmee, married one of her cousins, a

German from Wiesbaden who was in the import business. The marriage furthered the impression in the hearts of America that the Busches' primary allegiance was to the old world. Wilhelmina, born in 1884, was the couple's last child. She eloped with a German soldier, and her enraged father never forgave her. Known as the "last Bavarian Queen," she became as notoriously spendthrift as her father and was noted for her lavish parties in the immediate aftermath of World War I, as American sons were laid to rest to the soft blare of bugles in Arlington.

Family and PR problems aside, Adolphus had a rich social life, including mistresses, one of whom continued to arouse Lilly's jealousy even when the couple were in their seventies. Other Busch passions were cars, cards, and hunting.

Busch was a fierce competitor and didn't like to lose. He and fellow brewmeister Captain Frederick Pabst had an ongoing rivalry that made news in 1893 when their beers competed for the Blue Ribbon at the Columbian Exposition in Chicago. Busch lost, and was so outraged that he dogged one of the judges all over Europe to beg him to reconsider. The chuckling Pabst rubbed salt in the wound by calling his beer "Blue Ribbon" and ostentatiously emblazoning the prize on his cans, where it remained for over one hundred years. Adolphus must have been absolutely livid.

As obsessed as he was, Busch was not all beer; he became involved in other business ventures, principally banks and hotels; the elegant Adolphus Hotel is still *the* hotel in Dallas. He became so interested in cars that he bought exclusive rights from Rudolf Diesel to produce diesel engines in America.

Busch died at seventy-four on a hunting trip within a few miles of his birthplace in the Rhineland. Son Augustus ("Gus"), the one who had become a cowboy, came back home, took over the brewery, and his descendants remain in charge to this day.

The cause of Busch's death was cirrhosis of the liver.

From drinking too many Buds? No, it was probably wine that did him in. He drank lots of it, and was known to be a connoisseur. He would bet people a hundred dollars or more that he could identify any wine in his huge cellar by winery and vintage—and he usually won.

As for Budweiser, he never liked it. He called it "schlop."

Baby Ruth

This popular candy bar was named not for Yankee star Babe Ruth, as many suppose, but rather in honor of Ruth Cleveland (1891–1904), first of the five children of President and Mrs. Grover Cleveland and, except for the Kennedys, possibly the most beloved of all White House children.

Ruth's birth was a turning point in the life of Grover Cleveland, actually *Stephen* Grover Cleveland, who until age forty-seven had been a bachelor. After her birth, Grover described himself as a man who "puts aside as hardly worth a thought all that has gone before—fame, honor, place, everything." Quite an assertion from someone who had become one of America's most prominent and influential men—mayor of Buffalo, governor of New York, president of the United States.

Cleveland, you may recall, was the president who served nonconsecutive terms. He was both the twenty-second and the twenty-fourth president, his service interrupted by the term of number twenty-three, Benjamin Harrison.

It was during the Harrison "interregnum," when the family was living at 618 Madison Avenue in New York, that Baby Ruth was born. Grover was fifty-four at the time, rather late to start a family, but he continued to have children through age sixty-seven, when the last of Ruth's siblings was born.

Ruth's mother, Frances Folsom Cleveland, was a daughter of Grover's former law partner. She had known Grover from earliest childhood; in fact, the first baby carriage she rode in was a gift from "Uncle Cleve." Her father died when she was twelve, and Grover became an unofficial surrogate parent; nine years later, he became her husband. In that stern and unforgiving age, the incestuous overtones of the Clevelands' relationship could not have gone unnoticed. And it was not the first time that Grover's sexual mores had come under scrutiny: his fathering of an illegitimate child had nearly cost him an election.

But Frances was a lovely lady, and she became greatly loved as first lady. At twenty-one, she was the youngest presidential wife ever to serve in that role. Inexplicably, this most winsome and feminine of young women went by the nickname "Frank."

Like many men who marry late, Cleveland doted to excess on his children, particularly his first, his "Baby Ruth." To visitors, he would say, "Frank, bring Ruth in here. Never mind the state of her frock. Bring her in." But the attention didn't spoil her. Ike Hoover, who served as the White House electrician for forty-two years, said the Cleveland daughters (there were three of them) were the most loved and best behaved of all the presidential children he'd known. Ruth so enchanted the people that they almost literally stormed the gates of the White House to see and touch her. On one occasion, doting visitors passed her from hand to hand, to the point where Mrs. Cleveland and Ruth's nurse lost sight of her. From that point on, visitors had limited access to the White House, which till then had been open to the public. "The White House belongs to the Nation. The Nation has the right to come in," Grover said. "No," said Frank, and the policy of restricted access has prevailed ever since.

There were unforeseen consequences to the policy of exclusion. The more privacy one has, the Clevelands learned, the greater the potential for rumors, in that most suspicion-prone age. "She [Baby Ruth] must be deaf, or dumb, or both," was one ludicrous rumor. "A half-wit. Why else would they hide her so?" went another. A rumor that she had deformed ears was bruited about. Grover himself took abuse from the press as well. He was called an alcoholic and a wife beater. According to one story, he threw Frances out of the White House into a storm, and she had to issue a statement to the press denying the rumors. Secret Service protection went from three to twenty-seven for the beleaguered president. It was a strange contrast to Harrison, who had walked on Washington streets freely, with no protection at all.

Of all presidents, it seems Baby Ruth's dad had the worst press relations. Harassment became so vicious and persistent that the family spent little time in the White House. They lived most of the time on a farm in Georgetown, and spent their summers in Maine.

Scandals and rumors, combined with the 1893 financial panic and ensuing depression, caused Cleveland to lose the 1896 election to McKinley, and the family moved to Princeton, New Jersey. There, Ruth spent happier times. She attended a private school run by a Miss May Fine and in her free time was an avid bicyclist. But her greatest treasure was a black-and-white pony, which she hitched to a tan go-cart for the amusement of her friends, one of whom was Eleanor, daughter of future president Woodrow Wilson, who became the university's president in 1902, when Grover was lecturer. Eleanor's memoirs describe Ruth as theatrical and talented at writing plays. She might have become an actress, but her own life's play had a tragic end: in January 1904, at age twelve, Ruth died of diphtheria. The Clevelands and the nation were decimated. Grover sold his Cape Cod property because of the many happy memories he wanted to forget. She is buried in the family plot in Princeton Cemetery.

In the 1920s the Curtiss Candy Company named a candy bar in her honor. The design on the wrapper was patterned after the medallion struck in her honor at the 1893 Columbian Exhibition. Out of respect for her untimely death, the basic design has not changed since.

Ben & Jerry's

 ❦

Ice cream may be a "fun" food, but the ice cream industry is surprisingly competitive, even brutal. Small players running onto the field of play are likely to be beaten up by bullies, and that is what happened repeatedly to the pair of intrepid entrepreneurs featured in this chapter. Their recent buyout by Lever Brothers came as a surprise to those who were following their careers—and to many it was a disappointment. Their whole lives had been spent in getting up after being knocked down by the big boys, and it looked to many like Lever had delivered the knockout punch. Ben and Jerry reportedly got $114 million from the deal, but only time will tell what happens to the company, its product, and its mission.

"Ben" and "Jerry" are Bennet Cohen and Jerry Greenfield. They were born in Brooklyn in 1951, within a week of each other, and were raised in Merrick, Long Island. Ben's dad (an accountant) and mom were named Irving and Frances, and he has a sister, Alice. Jerry's parents were Malcolm and Mildred, and he has a sister, Ronnie, and a brother, Geff.

Ben and Jerry, who met and became friends at Calhoun High School, were both bright, but they had starkly contrasting personalities: laid-back Ben, hard-driving Jerry.

For Ben, Colgate was the college of choice, "because it had fireplaces in the dorm rooms," he explained. The summer after his freshman year, he unknowingly started down his destined life path by getting a job selling ice cream from a truck. The next year he dropped out of Colgate and went to Skidmore in Saratoga Springs, New York. He liked it better there, because of its more open curriculum, although he probably missed his fireplace. Apparently he didn't like it enough at "Skid," though, because he moved on once more, this time to Greenwich Village, where he became a potter and a pottery wheel salesman, and moonlit by admitting patients to Bellevue Hospital and driving a cab.

Meanwhile, "Type A" Jerry went to Oberlin College in the Ohio town of the same name, where he was "pre-med." In 1973, he moved in with "Type B" Ben in the Village and took a lab job studying mitochondria. Shortly afterward, the restless Ben moved on, this time to the Adirondacks, where he became a crafts teacher. Jerry stayed on in New York, where he met his future bride, a nursing student named Elizabeth Skarie. She and Jerry took off to Chapel Hill, North Carolina, where he got a job in biomedical research at UNC Hospital. He made his living chopping off the heads of rats, throwing them into liquid nitrogen, and chiseling out their brains.

The next year Jerry and Elizabeth split up, maybe because she tired of hearing about his days at work. Later, in 1977, they got together again and married. The year 1977 was one of reconciliation, because Ben and Jerry also rejoined, this time in Saratoga, where they set up an ice-cream stand. But soon an enemy loomed: Baskin and Robbins. Driven out, the disgusted entrepreneurs moved on to Vermont—"the only state without a Baskin-Robbins franchise" was their muttered rationale—and in an abandoned gas station in Burlington started up operations again, on, May 5, 1978.

Their business prospered. They grew and grew, first moving to an abandoned textile mill, then to a vacant space in a building that was basically a truck repair shop. Next it was on to the big time: a "virgin" plant of their own design in St. Albans, Vermont. Before they knew what was happening, B&J had become a $35 million company.

Though successful beyond their dreams, all was not

smooth for B&J. With their drive-out from Saratoga at the hands of the fierce Baskin-Robbins fresh in their minds, they were soon faced with another, deadlier, more implacable—and far more unlikely—foe: it was "Poppin' Fresh," the Pillsbury Doughboy.

What could the irrepressibly giggling Doughboy possibly have against B&J? Some explanation is called for here. Pillsbury had recently become the proud new owner of Häagen-Dazs, a pseudo-Danish outfit from the Bronx (the Bronx!) whose efforts to sound Nordic had people in Denmark fuming. At first, their pretentious competitor was a source of äamusement to the boys as well, who joined in the ridicule, but things soon turned ugly. B&J's distributors were telling them that the Doughboy had given them an ultimatum: "Deliver Häagen-Dazs and only Häagen-Dazs or we'll find somebody else," were the threatening words from the lovable Poppin' Fresh. Ben & Jerry's believed that Pillsbury was trying to squeeze out small competitors, and, knowing an affectionate poke to the company mascot's tummy wouldn't do the trick, they spent much of their time and fortune in courthouses defending their honor in a lawsuit.

But it wasn't just the courts. B&J mobilized the public as well. They took to the streets of Minneapolis, the very fort of the enemy, passed out leaflets pleading their case, and carried placards reading WHAT'S THE DOUGHBOY AFRAID OF? The public, even Pillsbury employees, and—get this—even Charlie Pillsbury, heir apparent to much of the family fortune, agreed with them. Thousands of cards and calls came to the Doughboy pleading for B&J's case.

The end result had a good side. The case made publicity: articles in every major newspaper made the names "Ben and Jerry" familiar to millions throughout the land who had never heard of them before. "New England's Own Cold War," cried out one editorial extolling the entrepreneurs and dissing the Doughboy. They got a million dollars' worth of publicity that they couldn't have bought otherwise.

But to them, that wasn't the point. The point was, they had fun. Fun, in fact, describes the company's whole approach. "If it's not fun, why do it?" is their motto. When it came time to hire a new CEO, they held a "YO! I Want to Be a CEO Because . . . in 100 Words or Less" contest. This is not management as taught at Harvard Business School.

Their unconventional approach has paid off. Their charmingly silly, vaguely antiestablishment antics and outrageous puns have no doubt won them as much consumer acceptance, and free publicity, as their paid advertising. Who else can make us chuckle at the Stop & Shop? "Cherry Garcia ice cream? Bovinity Divinity? Why can't all companies market like that?" we ask, sighing on reflection that not everyone can be a clown.

As buffoons, they have no equal in the marketplace, but apply some cold cream and a few vigorous strokes of Kleenex to their clown makeup and you will find the faces of two men who take their business very seriously. Their Willie Wonka–style factory produces the best product in Icecreamdom, and that does not happen in a company that is casually run. You would never guess from their court-jester style that they put in a good many seven-day weeks of sixteen-hour days, and that Jerry once collapsed from exhaustion in the parking lot.

They are also serious about their social and environmental responsibilities. Their philosophy seems to be genuine, and it comports well with that of the consumers in their market niche.

Their surprising success has made them folk heroes to some, including President Ronald Reagan, from whom they got an achievement award, presented in the White House Rose Garden, in 1988.

Despite their overall success, their career has been spotted by occasional failure. Lemon Peppermint Carob Chip and Honey Apple Raisin Oreo were flavors not many ordered twice.

Betty Crocker

Betty Crocker (1921–), according to General Mills, "has spent her life talking to consumers who cook. After all these years, people still relate to her. To her credit, she has worked hard to stay in touch with how changing lifestyles affect cooking and eating preferences."

This is typical of the tone of General Mills in the information they put out about her. I'm convinced they believe she was a real person. They talk about the "Betty Crocker Cooking School of the Air," which they tell me was broadcast over a group of radio stations that would later become NBC. The show continued for twenty-four years, and reached an audience of as many as a million listeners.

During the forties, Betty Crocker was the most recognizable female name in America, except for Eleanor Roosevelt. "Eleanor was 'First Lady of the Nation,' " so General Mills says, "and Betty was 'First Lady of Food.' " Her fame came partly from her contributions to the war effort: a radio program, *Our Nation's Rations,* and a book, *Your Share,* to help homemakers make the most of their rationed foods.

"In the early 1950's," continues her General Mills biography, "Betty Crocker became a television personality in a variety of programs on CBS and ABC. Television audiences across the country saw her teach George Burns and Gracie Allen how to bake a cake."

"Betty" founded seven model Betty Crocker kitchens in different regions of the country, established the Betty Crocker awards and scholarships program for talented cooks and homemakers, and published the *Betty Crocker*

Picture Cookbook, of which 27 million copies have been sold.

Despite her wholesome, homemaker-next-door image, she has had seven face-lifts—major makeovers, really—many of them radically changing her appearance, and making her look younger and younger each time. Amazingly, in her most recent incarnation, she looks twenty years younger than she did in her first, which appeared in 1936.

The idea of Betty Crocker was created in 1921. She was named for William G. Crocker, who had recently retired from the General Mills board of directors. He was the son of George Crocker, who was active in the founding of many flour mills, including General Mills and Pillsbury. Her first name was chosen because it seemed to evoke the homemaker-next-door image that the company wanted.

The current likeness of Betty Crocker, unveiled on her seventy-fifth birthday, in 1996, looks like a real person but is actually a computer-generated composite of seventy-five women, selected by the company on the basis of cooking and homemaking skills and commitment to family and community.

Birds Eye

Clarence Birdseye (1886–1956) was the inventor of marketable frozen food. True, there had been frozen food before, but it was abominable. Today we know, but we didn't then, that food's cellular structure breaks down during freezing and, when thawed, melts into mostly water, with a tasteless, pulpy vegetable mass at the bottom. Among the many who tried their hand at the frozen food business and failed was Richard Nixon, who in 1940 made "Citra-Frost," a reconstituted orange juice that turned into such a fiasco that it cost him his life savings and drove him into politics.

It was Birdseye who found the secret. In his travels in Labrador, he came upon it by accident, noting that fish that were *fast*-frozen tasted okay, and those that were *slowly* frozen didn't. He went into business, and the timing couldn't have been better. The economy was good, improvements in refrigeration technology were starting to make fast freezing possible, and the increasing presence of women in the workforce meant that they had less time for meal preparation and needed "convenience" foods. Frozen food became the best thing since sliced bread, and like Joseph Campbell and H. J. Heinz the generation before him, Clarence Birdseye revolutionized the way we shop and cook.

But who was this guy with that curious name Birdseye?

He was born in Brooklyn and was one of eight children of Clarence and Ada Underwood Birdseye. At one time Clarence, Sr., a lawyer, was a justice on the New York Supreme Court.

Young Clarence went to Amherst College in Massachusetts, where he majored in natural sciences. Forced to quit because of money problems in 1910, he got a job with the U.S. Department of Agriculture, collecting biological specimens in the arid Southwest.

In 1915, he married Eleanor Gannett of Washington, D.C. The couple went to Labrador, where for two or four years (accounts differ) Clarence pursued a living as a fur trapper, traveling by dogsled. No word on how Eleanor enjoyed her new life. But there is a hint: in 1922, they moved to Manhattan.

There, Clarence worked on perfecting the fast-freezing techniques that he had discovered by accident in the frozen north. Later they moved to Gloucester, Massachusetts. There, Clarence founded a company that packaged frozen foods in old candy boxes. The little company was to become General Foods, one of the largest corporations on the New York Stock Exchange.

In addition to pioneering in frozen foods, Clarence was at the forefront of food dehydration. Removal of food's water weight makes it far more portable, a fact important in the nation's war efforts, and blessed by every Boy Scout who has ever had to backpack a week's supply of food rations into the wilderness.

Clarence had other interests besides food. He took out three hundred patents on all sorts of things, including infrared lamps and a new kind of whaling harpoon.

He and his wife, Eleanor, who had five children, also became experts in wildflowers and in birds of the Western United States.

Although his name was spelled as one word, "Birdseye" (and pronounced BIRDS-ee), the frozen food line was both spelled and pronounced Birds Eye.

Borden

Gail Borden (1801–1874) was the oldest of seven children born to Gail Borden Sr. and his wife, Philadelphia Wheeler Borden. Like Abe Lincoln, he was born in a log cabin, and this was only the first in a long list of similarities in the lives of these two remarkable men. Is this another one of those "eerie Lincoln parallels" stories that came into vogue after the Kennedy assassination? Not really, but the two men's characters, life histories, and even their physical appearance were remarkably similar.

The log cabin in which Gail was born in Norwich, New York, is still standing, and in fact is still used as a private home, though it has been modernized. Gail and his family lived in that cabin until 1815, when they took a flatboat down the Ohio to Covington, Kentucky, where Gail helped his father, a surveyor, plot the town.

The next year the Bordens moved from Kentucky to Indiana. It was 1816, the same year that Thomas Lincoln moved his family between those same two states. Gail's family all survived, but Abe's mother, Nancy, was to die two years later—ironically, for our story—from drinking bad milk.

Like young Abe, Gail learned the three R's at home, with only about a year and a half of formal schooling. Despite his modest academic experience, Gail became a schoolteacher while continuing his surveying, a field young Lincoln also undertook at one time. He worked briefly on a flatboat crew on the Mississippi. As if emulating him, Abe did the same thing a few years later.

Gail moved to Mississippi, where he met and married sixteen-year-old Penelope Mercer in 1828. Soon after settling down, the couple heard about a pioneer expedition to settle Texas and decided to give it a shot. The next year, along with Gail's father and his three brothers, they joined Stephen F. Austin and ended up playing major roles in the history of that region.

At the time, Mexico welcomed Anglo-American settlements. Texas was so barren that the Mexicans didn't want it, and Anglos under Mexican political control could be a buffer against foreign ambitions. In 1833, to establish the colonial government, Austin, Sam Houston, Jim Bowie, Gail Borden, and others assembled to draft the first Texas constitution. It called for a degree of independence that was unsettling to the Mexicans, who were already nervous about the number of Anglo-Americans coming in: twenty thousand families, far more than they'd expected. Mexico abruptly ordered an end to immigration and imposed harsh restrictions on those already there, causing settlers to abort plans already in the works to develop the region. The settlers' hopes were raised the next year, when Santa Anna took over the Mexican government in a coup, but he turned out to be even worse than the guy he'd overthrown. Relations became more and more strained, and Austin went to Mexico City for months at a time to negotiate, but ended up in Santa Anna's prison. This left Borden in charge, and he became unofficially the acting president of Texas, answering letters, meeting dignitaries, and generally managing things. In 1836, matters came to a head when Texas declared independence, and the Texas War was on. Thus Gail Borden, like Abe Lincoln a few years later, found himself (in a sense) presiding over a nation at war.

While his three brothers left to fight, Penelope and Gail stayed behind, and Gail edited a newspaper. When he heard the news of the massacre at the Alamo, where four thousand Mexican troops killed all two hundred Texas volunteer defenders, including Davy Crockett, his paper was the first to print Sam Houston's rallying cry, "Remember the Alamo."

Gail Borden.

With the coming of peace, he returned to surveying and was the first to make a topographical map of Texas. Then he applied his surveying talents to "plotting" Galveston and Houston, and even today the basic form of both cities is Gail Borden's design.

His urban planning chores over, he served as tax collector for the Port of Galveston. It was an important post, since nearly one-third of the budget of the new Texas Republic came from the city's import duties. Soon he and Sam Houston had a falling-out, and Borden was effectively fired, but he didn't go quietly: the stubborn Borden for a time refused to hand over some $27,000 in tax receipts.

In 1839, he joined the Galveston City Company, an outfit that sold lots and developed communities on them, sort of like Florida developers do today. During his twelve years with GCC, he saw the population rise from 1,300 to 4,200, and as land values rose, he became wealthy. In 1848, his taxable assets included 8 lots in Galveston, over 13,000 acres outside the city, 350 head of cattle, 10 horses, 2 carriages and, alas, 5 slaves.

In 1844, Penelope died of yellow fever, a disease that would also claim two of his six children. With a houseful of children to raise, the oldest being only thirteen, Borden was anxious to remarry, and he soon took a second wife, a widow by the name of Mrs. Stearns. Very little is known about her; even her first name is in dispute. By some accounts it's Azuba, by others Augusta.

For a wedding present, Gail made his bride a movable round table, surrounded by a stationary outer ring. The inner table turned, like a lazy Susan, so food dishes could be passed among guests by a flick of the wrist. "Inventions" like this had become an amusement for Borden, who was now blessed with enough money and time to pursue hobbies.

The inventive impulse grew, and soon he was the town's "crackpot" inventor, most notably for his "terraqueous machine." For months he secreted himself in his shed, Noah-like, sheltered from the jeers of the neighbors as he pursued his mysterious invention. One night, about midnight, he invited a number of favored friends to show them the invention. But first, they had to sample food he had prepared. It was recycled food, another scheme of his. "These are articles on this table," he explained, "from which, if you knew what they were in their original condition, you would turn with loathing and horror. I have passed them, however, through certain processes by virtue of which they are delicious. Out of the offal of the kitchen and the streets, I have created a food for the poor that will cost almost nothing. I have transmuted the dirt itself into delicacies."

After the horrible meal, the guests were taken into the shed and, stumbling in the darkness, were led to seats in what appeared to be some kind of queerly altered wagon. When all were seated, horses led the thing and its wary passengers to the beach, where a stiff wind was blowing. The horses were unhitched, and Borden hoisted a sail. As the wind filled the sail, the strange craft began to move. Along the beach it rumbled, faster and faster, and some of the women began to scream. Grousing about the weakness and aversion to adventure of the female sex, Borden reluctantly applied the brakes before the most exciting part of the demonstration: the entry into the water. You see, the bottom of the wagon had been altered to make the craft amphibious, and the spectacular water entry was to have been the high point of the adventure. But even without its denouement, it was a night not soon forgotten by the shaken guests. One asked if the "terraqueous machine" could fly, too. Borden answered in the negative, ignoring the sarcasm. "But I will one day," he added, probably meaning it.

During this prosperous period, Borden paid particular attention to his higher duties: among them, serving as a deacon and choirmaster in the Baptist church. He was not the most ecumenical of souls: he distrusted Catholics and once considered writing a booklet on the "errors" of their faith that he would distribute to Catholic children. When told that the priests would object, he proposed to write tracts to convert the priests.

He also briefly practiced medicine by prefixing "Dr." to his name and becoming a homeopathic physician, concocting herbal remedies for the ailing of Galveston. He noted that people never got yellow fever in the winter and thought that if they could be kept under refrigeration all year round, the disease could be controlled. He envisioned entire refrigerated underground cities—and this long before the advent of mechanical refrigeration.

His head was swimming with ideas, rushing about as frantically as his body rushed about town. He was seen every day, this shabbily dressed, tall, gaunt Ichabod Crane of a man, walking with a forward stoop, as if spending his life struggling against a stiff wind. He walked at a rapid pace that matched the speed of his talk. Meeting a new acquaintance, he would ask questions in rapid fire, not waiting for the poor person to respond to one before asking the next.

People chuckled and shook their heads, but everybody loved the guy. There wasn't a soul in any town he lived in who wasn't crazy about him. He would enthrall the young with tales from his Texas past and the old with his visions of a future very different from what anyone else imagined.

Some of his plans dropped from sight, though; among them his steam-powered rowboat and the terraqueous machine, after it capsized on a subsequent outing, nearly drowning its captain.

Now he turned his attention to the "meat biscuit," a boiled-down extract of meat mixed with flour. A much-improved outgrowth of the garbage-to-food dishes offered to the terraqueous machine riders the year before, this was a concentrated and palatable protein source resistant to spoilage. It would be useful for the army, he thought, but they rejected it, for what some thought was opposition from meat packers. It was devastating news to Borden, who thought the meat biscuit would be the food of the world's poor. "I shall be styled the World's cook. The acme of my highest aspirations for worldly fame," he declared. The venture was financially devastating as well. He'd invested thousands of dollars, building a factory, making thousands of biscuits that he traveled the world to sell, even to the Crimea to show to Florence Nightingale. To finance his venture he had sold his lots one by one, and he was now living off loans that he wondered how he could ever repay. He sent away his family to live with relatives, because he couldn't support them.

Debt-ridden and desperate, Gail Borden was now well into middle age, and we have not yet gotten to the part of his story for which he would be remembered. The turning point leading to his dairyman career occurred in 1851. While returning from England, biscuits in hand, he saw several infants on his ship die from drinking milk from sick cows. Such scenes were not uncommon. Hundreds of women, and thousands of children died every year in New York alone from the milk/manure mixtures peddled on the streets. Descriptions in exposés of "stablehands propping up diseased cows for one last milking before the wretched animals died" may have been exaggerations but not by much.

Borden was so moved by what he saw that he chucked the biscuit idea and directed the rest of his life to purifying milk. It recalls a poignant incident in Lincoln's early life when he saw a master beating a slave and said, "Someday I'm going to do something about that."

Borden first tried boiling the milk, but this gave it a

scorched taste. Then he remembered that in his childhood he had seen women in the religious group known as Shakers heating milk in vacuum pans, at 160 degrees. He went to a Shaker village, got some vacuum pans, found the process worked, and began peddling his purified milk on street corners.

His milk sold well, but the money he made didn't cover his costs. He was already impoverished by the meat biscuit fiasco; all he needed was more debt from a new, even riskier venture. Meanwhile there were family troubles. The second Mrs. Borden—Azuba, or whatever her name was—disappeared. She may have died, or perhaps she just packed up and left. In any event, she vanished as abruptly and mysteriously as she had come. And to add to his money woes, his daughter Phila married a widower who died soon afterward, leaving her with four children to raise.

Luckily, he got financial backing from a wealthy merchant, Jeremiah Milbank, whom he met on a train, and in Burrville, Connecticut, he built a plant the foundation of which still exists, and started producing purified milk. A little roadside plaque commemorates the site, but calls it the place where the first condensed milk was produced. It remarkably understates its significance, because it really was the birthplace of the modern dairy industry. Before Borden, dairy farmers sold their milk directly to stores or consumers. Borden's idea was to buy raw milk from many farmers and process it centrally. He imposed strict standards of cleanliness on his suppliers, and he hermetically sealed the milk to protect it from later contamination. By doing so, he totally changed the way we process that fragile fluid and transformed it from the food of babes, sold almost entirely for consumption by infants, into a safe and vital staple of the world's diet. The fact that it was "condensed" was quite incidental.

For years, business remained precarious, but with the Civil War, Borden no longer had to worry about sales; while Lincoln agonized in Washington over how to win the war, Borden struggled in Burrville to make enough milk to keep Union troops alive. Civilian sales increased, too, and the endorsement of Lincoln's wife, Mary, didn't hurt.

Once again, Borden was wealthy. He and his third wife, Emaline Church, whom he had met in Connecticut and married in 1860—surprisingly, after signing a prenuptial agreement—lived in style in New York State. Though he'd lived for many years in the South, and had held slaves, he sided with the North in the war. "I did not vote for Mr. Lincoln, but I would vote for him today—aye, and fight for him, too," he wrote. The war made the Borden home a house divided. Gail's son John Gail fought with New York's 150th Infantry, while son Lee enlisted in the Texas 35th Cavalry.

After the war, Mr. Borden took his first and only vacation to return to Texas. Fearing he would be received as a traitor for helping the North win the war, he was surprised and pleased to be welcomed back as a beloved native son. And it was there that he died, in a town that is now called Borden, but his body was returned to his birth state of New York for burial. His epitaph reads, "I tried and failed, I tried again and again, and succeeded."

It would have been a fitting one for Lincoln as well.

Brunswick

❦

John Moses Brunswick (1819–1886) was born in Switzerland and at age fifteen came to New York, where he worked for a butcher. After a few months, he took off to Philadelphia, where he found the work he really wanted, in the carriage industry. After four years of apprenticeship, he became a journeyman and moved to Harrisburg, to work for a carriage maker named Greiner. There, John married Greiner's daughter Louisa, probably in 1839, and the next year the couple moved to Cincinnati, where he worked for a number of carriage companies, until he was thrown out of work in the panic of 1841.

The more or less desperate Brunswick took work as a steward on a riverboat for a while. Whenever the boat was docked and he didn't have any chores, he would observe traders buying and selling at the wharf. He learned the values of goods, sensed that he had an aptitude for sales, and went into the business. By 1845, he had made enough money by trading to be able to start his own carriage company.

His little firm prospered, and he became a widely admired self-made man, active in Jewish organizations and businessmen's social clubs. At one club event, he was shown a billiard table, and that was the turning point in his life. It was the most gorgeous thing he had ever seen, and he couldn't take his eyes off it. He knew he could make tables like that—and he knew it was his destiny to do so.

His decision to get in the billiard table business was a timely one. Billiards up until that time had not been widely played. Games of all sorts were considered at least vaguely sinful; then, too, the primitive equipment didn't make the game very enjoyable. Besides, there were no real sports then, as we think of them. The two top "sports" were footracing and rowing.

Suddenly, in the 1860s, the popularity of billiards soared. Recent inventions (slate tabletops by John Thurston, and leather-tipped cues by a Frenchman named Mingaud) increased the appeal of the game. It became a rage, even as a spectator sport. Four hundred people would pay five dollars (a week's salary for a workman) to see a match that featured great players, like Phelan and Seereiter, playing for an incredible $15,000 purse. They are long forgotten, of course, but they were the Michael Jordan and Mark McGwire of their day.

Along with the game, the billiard table business boomed. In fact, demand was so great that John enticed several of his brothers to come to America and join him. (Actually they were half brothers, since John's mother had died in childbirth.) The company, curiously styled "J. M. Brunswick and Brother," employed seventy-five men in 1858 and had a book value of $200,000. Some of the tables it produced with elaborate carving and inlay are now coveted museum pieces.

While the business boomed, the Brunswick family life had its share of tragedy and disappointment: two sons died young, in separate accidents, probably both by drowning. Then relationships with John's half brothers deteriorated. One, Emanuel, went to Chicago to form a competing company. Two others, Joseph and Hyman, operated billiard parlors. The last, Solomon, became a poet.

Still prominent and much admired, John ran for a seat in the Ohio Legislature, and won. While still running his company, he became an able representative. He introduced a bill that became known as the "Dram Shop Act," making bar owners liable for accidents caused by their drunken customers. Ironically, in addition to tables,

Brunswick made bars for upscale taverns and restaurants. Some beautiful and elaborate ones still exist.

Although the Brunswick Company is best known for its bowling equipment, that part of the business didn't start until four years after the founder's death.

Buick

꧁꧂

The story of David Buick has to be the saddest in this book. A brilliant inventor and tireless worker, he might have led a life as grand as that of Henry Ford or the Dodge brothers, but he ended his life nearly as a pauper. On his lonely ride to work in the trolley, the sad old man could look out the window and see luxurious Buick cars passing by and—for whatever satisfaction it might have given him—know that they were "his" cars. Did tears well up in his eyes in sadness? Or did his heart burn with anger? Did he wonder what would happen to his wife, Catherine, and his four children, who would inherit nothing upon his death? Or did he simply avert his eyes and read the morning paper?

If he were alive today, Mr. Buick might at least take satisfaction in knowing that of the several hundred American makes that were in business when he was, his car is one of only four that still survive. Yet *he* is nearly forgotten. Not one in a thousand Buick owners even knows his first name, or perhaps even realizes that he was a *person*. Even fewer know his sad story.

David Dunbar Buick (1854–1929) came to America at the age of two from Arbroath, a tiny but historic village on Scotland's North Sea coast. He began his career as many of us have, as a paper boy, in his case for the *Detroit Free Press*. After a stint as a farm laborer, he took a job with the Flower Brothers Machine Shop. It seems to have been an incubator for auto pioneers: Henry Ford later worked there.

It was at Flower Brothers that David met William Sherwood, with whom he formed a partnership in a plumbing products business. In their shop, located at Champlain Street and Meldrum Avenue in Detroit, Buick developed a process for bonding enamel onto steel. This was the seminal event for a major industry that includes products you now see everywhere. The tub and lav in your bathroom, your kitchen sink, the enameled surfaces of appliances, enamelware pots and pans—all were made from the process Mr. Buick developed in that shop. Although it had actually been invented in Europe, Buick discovered it independently and held the American rights.

In 1899, David and his son Tom sold the enamelization patent for $100,000 to what became the American Standard Company, whose logo you see on the majority of the country's toilets and urinals. Using their profits, they made themselves what every other man of means and mechanical inclination seemed to be making in those days—a car. They produced their first one at 39 Beuebein Street, now the site of a parking garage for the Detroit Renaissance Center.

They wanted to mass-produce it, but they couldn't possibly scrape up the money to finance a manufacturing operation. A guy named Brioschi seemed interested at first, but he was lured away by Jonathan Maxwell, who seemed to have a more promising vehicle.

Finally, Buick did obtain funding and began making cars in Flint. In July 1904, David's son Tom drove the first Buick car to Detroit. It went so fast, he said, that he whizzed right past the six-mile-per-hour speed-limit sign. The new company started out as small as the first Buick was slow: the first year, with twenty-five workers, they made only six cars. But over time, it grew and prospered.

Later the Flint Wagon Works bought out Buick's assets and set up a plant next door to their wagon factory. David received his buy out from Flint not in cash, but in the form of debt notes in the new Buick company. He had to renew these every year. In 1908, he learned a lesson in life: read what you're signing. One year, he signed a form that he thought was a standard renewal, but through a clerical error, it effectively deprived him of all ownership rights in the company. With the stroke of a pen, he was ruined.

He made a series of vain attempts to recover. He went to California, where he bought into a gold mine and later formed an oil company. Both ventures failed. Then he came back to Detroit to start a carburetor company with his son. That, too, failed. Next he made himself a partner in a car called the Dunbar. Same story. He even went into Florida real estate—and failed.

He ended up as a clerk and instructor in the Detroit School of Trades.

Buster Brown

B uster Brown (1902–) is one of three fictional characters in this book. He was the creation of Richard F. Outcault, who also drew the "Yellow Kid," the world's first comic strip. Outcault's son, daughter, and Boston bulldog became models for the cartoon characters Buster, Mary Jane, and Tige.

But how did B. B. get into shoe business? In 1878, George Warren Brown, a shoe manufacturer, left his native New England to found a shoe company in the Midwest. A company executive, John A. Bush, decided that the popular cartoon character Buster Brown would be a great "mascot" for their product—a play on the name Brown. The Brown Company contracted with Outcault for a promotion campaign.

Over the years, Brown hired a succession of midgets (and others) to be Buster Brown models. The most famous was five-year-old Milton Berle, whose mother, for a dollar-fifty a day, dressed him in a Little Lord Fauntleroy suit and foppish hat. According to Milton, he had the tar kicked out of him by local bullies, who thought his mode of dress wasn't appropriate for the neighborhood.

What Mr. Brown failed to do was to get *exclusive* rights to the Buster Brown trademark. Once Buster caught on, you saw him everywhere: there was Buster Brown candy, Buster Brown chewing gum, Buster Brown soap, even Buster Brown horseshoes—some thirty products. And Brown couldn't do anything about it.

Though the strip was abandoned in 1926, Buster Brown lives on not only in his shoes, but in the English language. The mild epithet "Buster" as in, "Watch your step, Buster," is thought to have originated in the cartoon strip.

Cadillac

Owners of America's premier luxury automobile might be surprised to learn that their car was named for the man who founded Detroit. He was Antoine Laumet de La Mothe Cadillac (1658–1730), and he was born in Gascony, in the Pyrenees region of France in a house that reportedly is still occupied. His father, Jean Laumet, came from a family of merchants, and he was wealthy enough to send young Antoine to college, probably to a Jesuit school in Montauban.

At the behest of his patron, Louis XIV—the "Sun King"—Antoine went to Canada, where he served as commander of a fort at Port Royal. Louis may have sent him there just to get rid of him. The governor of Port Royal, de Ménneval, didn't much care for him: "This Cadillac, the most malicious person in the world, is a wild man driven from France for who knows what crimes," he wrote. Perhaps he had in mind Cadillac's brandy trading with the Indians and other profiteering ventures, which he undertook when he should have been attending to the king's business.

But not everyone was down on poor Cadillac. He was lauded by his boss, Frontenac, as a man "of distinction, of great capacity, and worth . . . adroitness, firmness, and tact." Though seedy in character, he had a great redeeming feature: a unique familiarity with the geography of the North Atlantic coast. He could—and did—prepare charts to enable French assaults on New York and Boston and to defend Maine, which the English were attempting to seize.

He used his "great capacity and worth, . . . adroitness, firmness, and tact" for personal advantage, specifically, to win the hand of the young Marie Thérèse Guyon, whom he married in June 1687. True to form, he fabricated his ancestry and reduced his age by four years to make himself more enticing to young Marie.

Soon afterward, Antoine declared his wish to become a lawyer, but his nemesis, Governor de Ménneval, was unrelenting in his antipathy, and would have none of it, calling Antoine "a rascal and a mendacious spirit entirely capable of embroiling these poor people in a thousand chicaneries and suits in order to profit therefrom."

Continuing his adventures, young Antoine turned his sights to the Great Lakes. He apparently was the first to realize the strategic significance of "the strait" (*d'étroit,* in French) that connects Lakes Erie and St. Clair. Returning to France, he proposed to the colonial minister, Pontchartrain, that he establish a fort there. In the summer of 1701, he went to what became Detroit with his royal charter and about fifty soldiers and as many settlers, and built a citadel he called Fort Pontchartrain. In the fall, Madame Cadillac joined him. In a tone that casts doubt on the tale's authenticity, she declared, no doubt in a Lillian Gishesque hands-over-heart pose, "I know the dangers and the hardships of the voyage and the isolation of the life to which I am going, but I am eager to go."

He ran the settlement for ten years, then in a turn of events difficult to understand, he was sent to Louisiana, where he served as governor from 1710 to 1717.

Judging from his portraits, he was an intimidating figure, resembling Captain Hook in Disney's *Peter Pan;* and he had a personality to match. Fierce and arrogant, even by the standards of his day, he was resented in both Detroit and Louisiana and derided as a visionary, but he had a vision appealing to modern sensibilities: he promoted schools, hospitals, and churches, and approved of intermarriage with the Indians in order to blend in with the native population. He was recalled to France and after a six-month stay in the Bastille (no one seems to know on what charge) spent his final years in the Languedoc region of southern France.

Despite having thirteen children, Antoine Laumet de La Mothe Cadillac has no direct living descendants. Yet his name lives on in his car, thanks to auto pioneer Henry Leland. Perhaps Leland chose the name because Cadillac had not only founded the motor city, but had spoken so highly of it: "The climate is temperate and the air purified through the day and the night by a gentle breeze," he proclaimed. "The skies are always serene and spread sweet and fresh influence that makes one enjoy a tranquil sleep." Modern-day Detroiters may consider their founder's assessment a bit romantic and may even chuckle or wince, but Cadillac is beloved in Detroit, living eponymously in a park, a square, and gardens in the city he founded.

Before the Cadillac venture, which began in 1903, Leland had worked in partnership with Henry Ford in one of the two enterprises in which Ford failed prior to starting his own motor company. The Cadillac was, and is, a car of exceptional quality and among its distinctions was that it was the first car to have a self-starter. To this day the name Cadillac evokes an image of supreme elegance and excellence, a distinction that must annoy the ghost of Antoine's nemesis, Governor de Ménneval.

Campbell's

J oseph Campbell (1817–1900) was raised in Bridgeton, Cumberland County, New Jersey, and as a young man became an employee of a produce wholesaler in Philadelphia. In 1869, he entered into a partnership with Abraham Anderson, a tinsmith who built iceboxes, but who was also interested in food preservation. The partners established a factory that used tin cans, rather than jars for canning food. They were among the first to do so commercially, although the technology had been developed by Nicholas Appert in France sixty years before for preserving rations for Napoleon's troops.

Campbell and Anderson succeeded in their business, but didn't get along well. Campbell, who had originally been a purveyor of jams and jellies, saw his product line expanded in their joint venture to include vegetables and condiments, but he wanted even greater diversification; Anderson didn't. They had a falling-out in 1877.

Anderson acted for a while as what we would call a "consultant." Among his clients was the young Henry John Heinz, who was just starting out in his horseradish business in the appropriately named town of Sharpsburg, Pennsylvania. He apparently received good advice, because Heinz became Campbell's chief competitor.

Campbell, meanwhile, formed a partnership with three other men, including a merchant named Arthur Dorrance. Dorrance, who took control of the company after Campbell's retirement in 1894, introduced the company's first soup, "beefsteak tomato soup." Later, more flavors were offered, and the soup was condensed, using the process Gail Borden had developed, to reduce weight and thus lower shipping costs.

Joseph Campbell, "Mr. Soup," in fact never made a single can of it.

In 1898, one company executive went to a Cornell–Penn football game and was struck by the colors of the Cornell players' red-and-white jerseys. At his suggestion, Campbell's adopted these colors for their labels. The design of their logo (the colors and the distinctive script of the name "Campbell's") was adopted about 1900, and changed very little until 1999. All this happened after Campbell had retired. Though millions instinctively associate his name with soup, Joseph Campbell in fact never made a single can of it.

Chase & Sanborn

E xcept for the gaudily commercial Hershey, Pennsylvania, there may be no town in the United States that is prouder of its most successful native son than Harwich, Massachusetts. The one so honored is Caleb Chase (1831–1908), cofounder of one of Americas's most successful coffee companies. The Harwich Chases trace their roots back to the 1600s, and Caleb loved the place. Though he owned a gray-stone mansion on Beacon Street in Brookline, a Boston suburb, he couldn't wait to return to Harwich each summer to stay in his cottage, which he called the "Good Cheer." It's now an Irish pub that goes by the unimaginative name "The Irish Pub." He returned there every summer until he died.

Chase did much for the town. He endowed its library and town hall, gave money to pave most of its roads, donated buildings, and built a home for the Baptist minister. He left his footprints everywhere. There is a Caleb Street and a Chase Street; and there are schools, insurance companies, libraries, and stores that bear the Chase name.

The last of seventeen surviving children born to Job and Phebe Chase, young Caleb attended the village school and worked in his father's general store. At twenty-three, he left home to go to Boston to work in a dry-goods firm, then for a grocery company, and finally with coffee dealers named Carr and Raymond, with whom he became a partner in 1864.

His wife, Salome Boyles Chase, was an avid reader and founded the "Sunshine Club" for promoting reading. It was a sort of combination "Literacy Volunteers" and book club.

The Chases traveled extensively and attended Queen

Victoria's jubilee celebration at her personal invitation.

Salome and Caleb had no children, but Caleb's brother Erastus had several, and the couple treated their many nephews and nieces like their own children. Emily, one of Erastus's daughters, survives, in a manner of speaking. She is a ghost in a Harwich bed-and-breakfast where I once stayed. I slept in her room and heard mysterious knockings, but to my disappointment did not actually see the wispy blond apparition that other guests have described.

Caleb became a colonel in Massachusetts's Ancient and Honorable Artillery Company.

In contrast to Harwich, the tiny village of Wales, Maine, hardly remembers its most famous son at all. He was James Solomon Sanborn (1835–1903), son of Henry, a farmer, and his wife, Ann. His career was quite different from his partner's: he worked in a machine shop for four years, then got into the seed business, selling from village to village out of a wagon. He was a gifted raconteur, regaling his audience with tales of the history and folklore of Maine while selling them seeds. After nine years of this, he moved to Boston and over the next ten years ran an increasingly successful business importing tea, coffee, and spices.

Like Chase, he traveled extensively and adventurously, including a trek through Central America on muleback to remote coffee-growing regions, where he would buy the output of whole plantations and have it carted from the mountains to the seaport in hundred-pound sacks on the backs of laborers paid six and a half cents a day. One plantation owner was Justo Barrio, who was also president of Guatemala when Sanborn visited him in 1885. The very next day, February 28, Barrio issued a decree, "La Union," famous in Central American history. It was followed by an attempt to unify all the Central American countries under a single flag by military force, similar to what Bismarck had done in Germany and Garibaldi in Italy, but unification failed in Central America, and Sanborn's friend Barrio was killed. The timing of the La Union decree was coincidental, although Barrio was known to favor coffee growing as the principal means to achieve economic progress in the region.

In his later years, Sanborn became involved in farming and publishing. He raised French coach horses at his summer home in Poland, Maine (where Poland Spring water comes from), and managed a weekly newspaper, the *Maine Farmer*.

He was an immense man. One time in Guatemala he had to sleep outdoors because he was too fat to fit through the hotel door. Ironically, he married a woman named Small—Harriet Small, specifically—in 1856. They had four children. One daughter, Helen, inheriting her father's gift for storytelling, became a writer, and the two boys, Charles and Oren, followed their father in the coffee business.

Mr. Chase and Mr. Sanborn met in Boston under circumstances lost to history and founded their company in 1878. They were the first to sell coffee in sealed tins. Sales took off after 1893, when they won the contract to supply 700,000 pounds of coffee to the Columbian Exhibition in Chicago. At one time C&S was the nation's second-largest-selling brand.

Did they know the Hills brothers? This, you may recall, was one of the questions that so intrigued me when I first became entranced by the C&S coffee can in my shopping cart. The answer: maybe, maybe not. The Hills brothers (Austin and Reuben were their names) were from the same part of Maine as Sanborn, but they spent their lives in California, having been dragged there by their father, who had failed to find gold during the gold rush but was making a living building ferryboats. They got into the coffee business by buying the Arabian Coffee and Spice Mills in San Francisco. To this day, Hills Brothers coffee cans have retained on their label a robed, turbaned figure to connect to their company's origins and to evoke a Middle Eastern mystique.

C&S coffee cans also have a story to tell. If you have an old empty one in your basement that you use for storing nails or soaking paintbrushes, go down and take a look at it. The founders' portraits appear on it, with little identifying tags, so you know which is which. The problem is, the tags are wrong. The gentleman identified as Chase is really Sanborn and vice versa. Though the can has recently been redesigned, millions of mislabeled cans were sold over a period of many years before anyone noticed.

Chef Boyardee

❦

"**O**h, he was a wonderful man, a very generous man, to his family and to everybody," gushed Mrs. Agnes Asta, in praise of the world's most famous chef. The impression is not surprising: it comports well with the smiling, betoqued, avuncular figure on the familiar orange-and-green ravioli cans. But Mrs. Asta was in a special position to know what kind of man Hector (that was his name) was. She worked for him in his cannery in Milton, Pennsylvania, for many years and knew him better than most: she was also his sister-in-law. "He loved the opera and knew many arias by heart," she continued. "And he loved playing bocci with his friends on Sunday afternoons." And, of course, Hector loved to entertain, and was especially fond of cooking for his guests.

He first learned to cook at age ten from his parents, Joseph and Mary, who ran a restaurant in Piacenza, near Milan. His older brother, Paul, had already emigrated to New York, where he became the maître d' at the Plaza Hotel. He and one of his old *paisans* from Milan, Enrico Caruso, encouraged Hector to come over, too. So at age seventeen, Hector stepped off the gangplank and began pounding the pavement, as they say, to find work as a cook. He soon found it, and his reputation rose rapidly as he gained experience in one great restaurant after another. He was at New York's Ritz-Carlton, then moved on to The Greenbrier in West Virginia, where there is now a noted culinary arts school. In December 1915, he prepared meals for President Woodrow Wilson and his new bride, who had come to The Greenbrier for their honeymoon. It must have been a surreal "immigrant makes it in America" moment for young Hector: eighteen years old, in this country only about a year, probably barely speaking English, and here he was preparing meals for the world's most important couple—and on their honeymoon, no less.

In 1917, Hector moved to Cleveland, where he became chef at the Winton Hotel at 1012 Prospect Street. The restaurant still exists, though it's now a Lebanese bistro called the Middle East Restaurant.

In 1923, he married Mrs. Asta's sister, Helen Wroblewski, and the couple had one son, Mario, currently retired and living in Maryland after a career in the ornamental tile business.

In 1924, the chef and his wife opened their own restaurant, Il Giardino d'Italia. It was such a success that people began ordering "takeout," an uncommon practice then. After he solved various problems of maintaining product quality during the canning process, he entered into an agreement with a food processor to can and sell his sauces.

His products were distributed to stores and became an almost instant success. Although this occurred during the Depression, the company expanded its operations to larger quarters three times within ten years, and Hector's products came to be distributed nationwide.

In 1938, the chef and his company moved into an abandoned silk mill in Milton, Pennsylvania, where during World War II they supplied field rations for the armed forces. He received the coveted "E for Excellence" pennant for his contribution to the war effort.

Chef Boyardee is credited, by his company at least, with popularizing Italian food in America. Before the 1930s, only Italians and people well off enough to dine in restaurants even knew what it tasted like.

He also developed a process for making animal feed from restaurant scraps, and he briefly owned a steel company, Milton Steel.

In 1985, he died in Parma, Ohio, at age eighty-eight and is buried in All Souls Cemetery.

Chevrolet

L ouis Joseph Chevrolet (1879–1941) was born in La Chaux de Fonds, Switzerland, where his father, Joseph, was a watchmaker. He inherited his dad's mechanical aptitude and displayed it in his early teens by inventing a pump for use in the wine industry. In his spare time, he raced bicycles and filled his case with twenty-eight race trophies. He also repaired and eventually actually built bicycles.

Photo courtesy of Corbis.

Louis Chevrolet actually resented having his name used for Chevrolet cars.

Louis came to America in 1900, hoping to put his mechanical talents to use in the burgeoning horseless carriage trade. But it wasn't as easy as he'd thought, and he had to take a job as a chauffeur in Montreal for a few months to make ends meet. When he finally got into the car business, it was with a long succession of companies. Apparently a difficult employee, he worked for eight different car makers in as many years.

His real forte was car racing, a logical field for a bicycle racer. He became famous when he defeated Barney Oldfield, driving a mile in 52.8 seconds. That was almost seventy miles an hour, an impressive speed for

1905. Through the years, he established numerous other racing records at tracks throughout the country, crowding his already full trophy case.

He even competed in the Indianapolis 500. In 1911, the first running of that race, he qualified at 93 mph, 20 mph faster than the speed of the eventual winner, Ray Harroun. The car he used (made by Buick, incidentally) broke down. If it hadn't been for that, he would probably have been the first Indy 500 winner.

But he wanted to be a car maker as well as a racer, so he collaborated with Will Durant, who agreed to bankroll his venture. In November 1911, after working for six months as feverishly as he had raced, Louis wheeled out from Schulte's Garage on Grand Avenue in Detroit the first of the 130 million Chevrolets that were to grace the American road. The first Chevrolets were pricey: they sold for over $2,150, when a Model T could be had for $490, but they were quality machines, and Louis was a perfectionist.

Satisfied that he had designed a car he could be proud of, he and his young bride, Suzanne Treyvoux, daughter of a Manhattan furrier, went to France for an extended rest and entrusted mass production to Durant. Durant purchased a forty-acre parcel directly across the street from Ford's Model T plant and posted a conspicuous sign to announce it as the future site of Chevrolet Motor Car Company. To the puckish Durant, this was great fun. He delighted in getting his competitor riled up and must have lain awake nights imagining Henry's response when the sign first appeared. Unfortunately, labor unrest forced a change in plans, and the "Chevy" plant was actually built in Flint.

Production soon commenced, but when Louis returned, he went into a rage. He learned that Durant had bastardized his design and was making cars on the cheap to compete with Ford. But what most appalled him was that Durant was calling the cars "Chevrolets." Louis took pride in his family name—never mind that it probably came from the term *chèvre à lait* ("milk goat")—but Durant was bent on capitalizing on Louis's racing fame. After a heated argument in which Louis vented his rage and Durant expressed his disgust at Louis's cigarette habit (he was rarely seen without one dangling from his lower lip), Louis left Durant's company (later to be called General Motors) to go to Indianapolis, where he started making a car called the Frontenac, named for the man who, you may recall, had been Cadillac's boss.

Louis's principal backer in this venture was an old buddy from his bicycle-racing days, Albert Champion, who had won fame and fortune with his invention, the ceramic spark plug. The relationship was not to last long. After learning that Albert was going to make spark plugs for GM, too, Louis fiercely pummeled him and said if he ever saw him again, he'd kill him. His backer quickly and wisely fled.

Despite the loss of Champion's money, Louis continued making Frontenacs. They were racing cars, and good ones—they won two successive Indy 500 runs—but Louis was ever impatient to try new ventures, so he went into partnership with his brother Arthur and a third man, Glenn Martin. Martin had once been a Ford dealer but was now a major player in the budding aircraft industry. The brothers designed for Martin an aircraft engine they called the Chevrolair. Louis, who should have learned by this time to avoid getting into partnerships, quarreled with Arthur over who should receive credit for the design. They parted ways in 1926. Louis took jobs with Stutz Bearcat and raced motorboats in his spare time, while Arthur ended up working in a shipyard in Slidell, Louisiana, where soon after his separation from Louis, he committed suicide.

With Suzanne, Louis enjoyed a brief retirement in Florida, but needing money, or perhaps just something to do, he returned to Detroit to take a job in a Chevrolet plant, where he worked side by side with young high-school dropouts who may have wondered if he was any relation to the guy who founded their company. In June 1941, after his fame as a racer had fled, and after a cerebral hemorrhage and a leg amputation as well, the man whose name has been emblazoned on more cars than that of anyone else in the world died. And hardly anyone noticed.

Chrysler

Walter P. Chrysler's boyhood made him the envy of every other kid of his day. His father, Hank, was a locomotive engineer, and young Walt sometimes got to ride in that huge, muscular machine as it ground its way across the plains, chugging and lugging its hundreds of tons of freight. He pulled the whistle cord, stoked coal into the firebox, oiled the bearings—did everything boys of his day only dreamed of.

The locomotive was to become his lifelong obsession. At age eighteen, he made from scratch an operating miniature steam locomotive, twenty-eight inches long. Just as Michelangelo saw a *David* in every block of marble, Walter Chrysler saw a locomotive in every piece of steel. "I saw a solid piece of iron," he explained, "and started to drill and chip and file." This strange amalgam of mechanical genius and sensitive artist was perhaps America's most unlikely and unusual auto magnate. As competent and successful as he was at running an auto empire, he always seemed a stranger in carland.

The strange double life of Walter Percy Chrysler (1875–1940) was not long in years, but it straddled eras and regions that were so diverse that he seems to have lived the lives of more than one man. Custer's Last Stand occurred within his lifetime—and in his part of the world—and throughout his boyhood, Indian attack remained the greatest fear the Chrysler family faced in tiny Ellis, Kansas. Yet the close of his life occurred well into the modern age. He left in his wake the Chrysler Building—New York's most beautiful structure, in the opinion of many—and the Chrysler car, a machine that laid the foundation for today's auto design.

Walter was the third of four children—two girls and two boys. He was later to father a similar family—two girls and two boys—with son Walter Jr. having the same place in the birth order that Walter Sr. had in his. History repeats, and history persisted in repeating: Junior was to follow Senior into the company presidency.

The Chrysler family had come from Germany and landed originally in Plymouth, Massachusetts, then moved on to New York. If you drive a Plymouth or a Chrysler New Yorker, now you know who named these car models and why.

The lad had an insatiable curiosity that could not be satisfied by the schools in Ellis, so he carried on a voluminous correspondence with *Scientific American*. His many inquiries can be found in the magazine's archives of the 1880s.

Walter started his career as a machine-shop apprentice at five cents an hour. He spent the next several years drifting from job to job, getting from one to the other by hopping a freight. It may sound like a hobo's life, but if you wanted to make it in his place and time, you did it by hopping freights. As he roved, he showed each employer a drive, integrity, and mechanical aptitude that made him quickly rise in favor.

Throughout this period, he continued a weekly correspondence with his Ellis sweetheart, Della Forker, daughter of a local merchant. In 1901, they were married in the Ellis Methodist Church and began their married life in Salt Lake City.

In 1908, Walter saw his first car and fell in love with it. Predictably, it was a Locomobile—of all cars, the one with the name most resembling "locomotive." Della was unhappy with the purchase. Its $5,000 price sucked the family's finances dry, and, at least in the beginning, nobody even got to ride in the thing. For the first three months, it was never out of the barn. Apparently, Walter had bought it solely to take it apart and see how it worked. Eventually, however, he acceded to the family's wishes, put it back together, and took them for occasional outings.

By this time he was "Superintendent of Motive Power" for the Great Western Railway and lived in Oelwein, Iowa. He spent most of his time on the road, and didn't see much of his family, which now consisted of two girls, Thelma and Bernice, and in 1910, his first son, Walter, Jr.

They moved to Pittsburgh, where Chrysler became the works manager of the American Locomotive Company, but he stayed only briefly before Charley Nash, president of GM at the time, hired him to pull the Buick division out of its slump.

In 1913, while Ford was producing a thousand cars a day, Buick was turning out only forty-five. Buick workers, holdovers from the Flint Wagon Works, were still making cars the way they had made carriages in the 1880s. Chrysler, who had a natural instinct for rooting out inefficiency, got the company to make cars as cars should be made, and he turned the company around.

Flushed with success, Chrysler asked Nash to double his pay to $25,000. Nash's jaw dropped, but after some intense negotiations, he finally agreed. On the way out of his office, Chrysler said, "And by the way, next year I want fifty thousand" and closed the door without waiting for a response. He got that raise, too.

Later, Chrysler was the head of all of GM, but hearing whistles in the distance, he decided that at forty-five he had achieved his life goals, and retired to Europe, where he could live in ease while Della could pursue her interest in music.

But Walter P. Chrysler was not the retiring type, and soon he was brought home by the pleas of John North Wyllis, whose company was failing. Walter saved it, partly by reducing the salary of his boss, who may have regretted his choice of rescuer.

This Superman of cars also helped rescue Jonathan Maxwell's company, and in a far more important mission converted the company into the Chrysler Corporation. He chucked the Maxwell and developed the Imperial (which he thought evoked Americans' latent desire for the trappings of European royalty). Three years later he bought out Dodge Motors from the brothers' widows.

Walter had no hobbies, but he did love music. He was one of three boys in the town of Ellis who was made to take piano lessons. He also learned to play drums, tuba, and clarinet, and he played in local bands wherever he went. His tastes may have been pedestrian, in contrast to Della's love for the opera, but they were in their own way refined, sincere, and strong. Such an artistic sense is rare for someone whose real home is the nuts and bolts of giant machines, but both loves were combined in this one remarkable man. "There is in manufacturing a creative joy that only poets are supposed to know," Mr. Chrysler said. "Someday I'd like to show a poet how it feels to design and build a locomotive."

As I said, he was not your usual auto magnate.

Dinty Moore

The real Dinty Moore, according to the Hormel Company, the current owner of the rights to the name, was a bellboy at a hotel in St. Louis around the turn of the century.

I say, the *real* Dinty Moore, because there was also a *fictional* Dinty Moore. He was a character in the comic strip Bringing up Father, which featured the more familiar figures Maggie and Jiggs. The strip originated in 1913 and remained popular through both World Wars.

But the St. Louis bellhop has a rival: the second contender was a New York restaurateur, who—upon seeing cans of "his" beef stew on the shelves and his name in the comics—sued for the rights, but lost. The loss was perhaps unjust, because George McManus, the cartoonist who created the Dinty Moore character, had in fact eaten at *this* Dinty Moore's restaurant on a number of occasions, and the St. Louis bellhop story may have been a fabrication to convince the court that he had not appropriated the restaurateur's name. Adding to the evidence in Moore's favor is the fact that the fictional Dinty Moore himself operated a bar and grill. A recurring plot featured Jiggs using any conceivable excuse or concocting any stratagem to sneak away to Dinty Moore's to escape Maggie's nagging and enjoy Dinty's corned beef and cabbage.

In any event, in 1936, the Hormel Company got the rights to the name and started calling its stew "Dinty Moore." They entered the stew business chiefly to make use of some surplus metal cans they had on hand. The product became so popular that the reverse of the situation followed during the Second World War, when there was a surplus of stew and a shortage of cans.

The company was kind enough to send me a couple of coupons. The stuff's actually good, and the company also sent recipes. There are all kinds of things you can do with it. It can be made into beef Stroganoff, beef pot pies, and ethnic dishes of all sorts.

Reprinted with special permission of King Features Syndicate.

Dinty Moore (left) inquires about the health of his friend Jiggs.

Dodge

It would be hard to imagine two brothers closer than John and Horace Dodge. "If you don't hire my brother," said young Horace to one shop foreman, "I don't want to work for you, either." Years later, in their heyday, the auto magnates were known by their employees as the "Gold Dust Twins," because it seemed they were almost constantly together. In fact, they were so conscious of their brotherhood that they refused to answer mail addressed to the Dodge brothers unless the *b* in "brothers" was capitalized.

Their loyalty to each other was all the more remarkable in view of their strong-willed, ill-tempered, even violent natures. Indeed, at one time they were as famous for their barroom brawling as they were for their cars. For his amusement, John made one barkeep dance on a table at gunpoint, and celebrated his triumph by throwing glasses and smashing the mirror. On another occasion, the boys got into a fight and severely injured a crippled man. Beating a man who had wooden sticks for lower legs may have been an extreme example of their rowdiness, but make no mistake: the Dodge boys were ram-tough.

They were the sons of Daniel Dodge, who operated a foundry in Niles, Michigan. John Francis Dodge (1864–1920) and his brother Horace Elgin (1868–1920) both showed mechanical talent, and they went to work for their father. Later, they worked as boilermakers and (with a partner) as "bicycle engineers," marketing their bikes under the name Evans & Dodge.

In 1901, they entered the auto industry by making transmissions for Ransom E. Olds for use in his merry

Oldsmobiles. The Brothers (note that I'm careful to capitalize the *B*) and their 150 employees made three thousand of these gearboxes over the next two years. They worked almost every day—and night—and survived by wolfing down meals and taking catnaps on benches in the shop, with only an occasional holiday spent at home.

In 1903, impressed with their competence, Henry Ford contracted with the Brothers to make engines, transmissions, chassis, and axles for his cars. One might ask, what else is there? And indeed it's a good question. The fact is that Ford's factory was really only a glorified assembly plant, where Dodge drive trains were bolted onto carriage bodies that Henry bought from a local wagon maker. Ford's $1,160,000 car production in 1904 was made using only $10,000 worth of his own production machinery. It was the Dodge Brothers who did all the heavy lifting to make Ford's tin lizzies run.

The Brothers may have been deprived of their true place in history, but they certainly were not deprived of wealth. By 1905, they were making $800 *a day* in profit from their Ford contract—plus stock dividends. But they knew they could be doing even better on their own, and in 1913 they broke off from Ford, doubled the size of their plant in Hamtramck, and became real car makers.

And innovators as well: Dodge cars, made entirely of steel, were the first that didn't look like motorized buggies. Their styling and their reputation for quality and reliability made them a hit in the marketplace.

The Brothers thought in truly original ways. For a while the company even rejected the concept of model year, and incorporated improvements continuously as they were developed. They even sold replacement parts to owners so they could continually "upgrade" their cars.

Henry Ford didn't react kindly to this development. With a megalomaniacal wish to dominate the industry and with no little pique at being betrayed by a loyal supplier, he declared that he would no longer pay significant stock dividends. The Brothers, who had retained their Ford stock, sued for their dividends, since it was from these that they financed their venture. Without them, their enterprise was threatened with ruin. Fortunately, they won their suit.

Quickly on the heels of this settlement, the Brothers once again were at daggers drawn with Ford. While Henry went on a quixotic mission to negotiate peace with the kaiser on the eve of World War I, the Dodges, feisty as ever, responded to President Wilson's pleas for support in the war effort. In a period of only four months, the Dodge boys, who had no experience with gun manufacture, erected a munitions plant, equipped it with 129 machines, some of which had to be invented for the purpose, and began production of recoil mechanisms for large guns, which they sold to the army at no profit.

After the war, the company once again turned attention to its cars, and by 1920, the year of the Brothers' death, Dodge was the nation's number-four automaker.

The Brothers' personal lives were as full of drama as their business careers. At age twenty-eight, both John and Horace took brides. John married a dressmaker named Ivy Hawkins, and the couple had three children over the next six years—Winifred, Isabel, and John Duval. The first of the family's tragedies occurred in 1901, when Ivy died of tuberculosis. John remarried two years later, to Isabelle Smith, a woman he did not love, but who was a good friend of Horace's wife, Anna. Anna and Isabelle felt a special connectedness: they were exactly the same age—down to the day.

The marriage to Isabelle was secret, kept that way for reasons mysterious to her but clear to the rest of the family: it allowed John to carry on a passionate affair with his true love, his secretary, Matilda Rauche. After four unhappy years, John finally obtained a divorce from Isabelle, whom he had always introduced as "my housekeeper," no doubt much to her irritation, and promptly married Matilda ("Tilly"), who, incredibly, had learned nothing during those four years about the marriage to Isabelle or the subsequent divorce. In fact, it was only on the day of the wedding that Tilly met John's children by his marriage to Ivy.

With Tilly, John fathered a second family, almost identical to the first—first two girls and then one boy, spaced about two years apart. The second carbon-copy family came almost exactly twenty years after the first.

Tilly's parents were not informed of the wedding until it was almost a fait accompli, and they were furious. The turn of events was also distressing to the Dodges' mother, Maria, who was now an invalid and had gotten much friendship and care from Isabelle. She could not stomach Matilda, whom she saw as a gold-digging interloper, and she refused to live in the luxurious house that John had built for the family, even though many features had been designed just for her. Instead she chose to live with her sisters until her death in 1907.

Matilda tried her best to befriend Maria, but to no avail. For the former secretary to make herself a suitable wife for one of the world's richest men was a fruitless struggle. She dropped her nickname "Tilly" and insisted on "Matilda." She took elocution lessons, studied piano, and learned French, but she never became the American countess she aspired to be. But she did at least become every boss's dream secretary: she saved "everything"— Christmas cards, receipts and recipes over a period of sixty years—and saved them so methodically that she could find anything instantly from among thousands of documents stored in dozens of rooms.

Horace's domestic life was far simpler than John's. In 1896, he married Anna Thomson, daughter of a Scottish sail maker. John and Anna got married almost literally on their lunch hour. They took the ferry to Windsor, Ontario, where they wed. John returned to complete his regular workday, while Anna came home to spend the afternoon teaching piano students. It seemed a casual start for such a serious commitment, but the marriage was long and happy. There were two children, Horace Jr. and Delphine.

If Horace's domestic life was quieter than John's, he more than made up for it in his rich avocational life. One of Horace's favorite hobbies was "sheriffing," and he got himself appointed undersheriff of Wayne County (the county that includes Detroit). Cops-and-robbers shoot-outs were great fun for the exuberant auto tycoon, and he did not shrink from even the most perilous and demanding duties of the position. Nor did he shrink from its softer ones: at Christmas, he brought gifts to the prisoners and deputies. He even made friends with some of the robbers he apprehended and offered them jobs.

Another favorite recreation was polo, but played with cars instead of horses.

But his greatest love was music. He was obsessed with it: once while vacationing in Michigan's upper peninsula, he chartered a train just to attend a concert in Detroit, after which he immediately returned to rejoin his hunting buddies. Horace and Anna were the greatest patrons the Detroit music scene has ever had. Anna was one of a group of women who had donated $1,000 to found the Detroit Symphony Orchestra. When the orchestra fell on hard times in 1917, Horace actually *bought* it. Outright ownership of an orchestra by a private individual is apparently unique in musical history, but it saved the orchestra, which even today remains among the world's finest.

As late as 1965, Anna remained a star attraction and the grande dame of Detroit society, and photographers who popped a few flashbulbs at Henry Ford II on symphony opening night, lit the dark when Anna got out of her limousine to enter the concert hall. Anna was herself an accomplished musician, whose talent in her youth attracted Horace, a struggling self-taught amateur at the piano and violin.

Despite their success as businessmen and their generosity to charities and the arts, and despite their political connections, the Dodge Brothers were generally snubbed by Grosse Pointe society because of their humble origins. Horace and Anna nevertheless built an elegant home, named Rose Terrace, on the shore of Lake St. Clair, upon which he floated an equally resplendent yacht. John began construction of a $3 million to $4 million 110-room mansion that was intended to be the world's grandest private residence. Not too shabby for a kid who had walked to Niles Elementary School barefoot, even in November, because he couldn't afford shoes.

John may have built his mansion just to give the Grosse Pointe snobs their comeuppance. The rustic life actually had more appeal for him. He lived on a farm in Rochester, Michigan, with a relatively modest eighteen-room house. By this time George and Margaret, Matilda's parents, had cooled off from the wedding snub and come to recognize their good fortune: being in-laws of one of the world's richest men has its advantages, even if they only worked as servants. Every morning that John was there, Margaret prepared his breakfast of baked beans and mackerel in a spicy tomato sauce—a morning meal that never varied.

John dabbled in politics and was a delegate to the 1916 Republican National Convention. He also became a recognized authority on the life of Alexander Hamilton.

Both sons of the founders caused trouble to the family. John Duval Dodge (called "John Devil Dodge" by wags) was expelled from a succession of schools, married a young Detroit girl, and took off to Texas. John disowned him, and left him to live on a $150-a-month allowance in his will. Horace Jr. was also a rambunctious youth—and adult—going through five unhappy marriages before his death at age sixty-three.

Inseparable in life, the Brothers were inseparable in death as well: both died in 1920 in the great influenza epidemic.

Dow Jones

❧❦❧

Charles Henry Dow (1851–1902), scion of a prosperous dairy-farming family, was born in Sterling, Connecticut, near the Rhode Island border. His father, also named Charles, died when the boy was six. Young Charlie, who grew up as an only child, a decidedly rare circumstance in those days, went to the town school and later took a job with a local newspaper. He moved from one job to another (he claims he held some twenty of them in his youth), and finally found himself as an editor for the *Springfield Republican,* in Springfield, Massachusetts, at age twenty. He stayed in the position for two years, before moving once again, this time to take a job with the *Providence Journal,* where he became acquainted with another young reporter, Eddie Jones.

Edward Davis Jones (1856–1920) came from Worcester, Massachusetts. He attended Brown but did not graduate. Intent on a career in journalism, he quit school, against the wishes of his parents.

Some years later, the two met again in New York and, with a third guy (Charles Bergstresser), formed Dow Jones & Company.

The company was really just a messenger service at first. They would get news of breaking events over the telegraph, write them up in a bulletin format every eight minutes(!), and distribute them to subscribers (brokers and investors) by runners. This operation started in November 1882 in an austere, bleak office at 15 Wall Street. Today a nice brass commemorative plaque marks the spot and tells passersby that it was there that Dow Jones & Company began a daily journal, the *Afternoon News Letter,* that seven years later evolved into the *Wall Street Journal.*

*Charles Dow and Edward Jones were as different
as different could be.*

Except for the two-cent price, Volume 1, Number 1, dated
July 8, 1889, looks very much like the issue printed this
morning, with nearly the same layout and fonts.

Their enterprise was, of course, eminently successful.
It has a daily circulation of nearly 1,800,000, higher than
that of any other newspaper in America.

In 1884, they devised the concept of an "industrial average." To show how times have changed, only one of
the original companies, General Electric, remains on the
average. The Dow Jones Industrial Average lives on to
this day as the most-watched indicator of stockmarket performance.

Though the company prospered, relations among the
partners soon became strained. Dow and Jones could
hardly have been more different. Dow—introverted, austere, scholarly—was decidedly uncomfortable on Wall
Street, which he thought of as little better than a casino,
and sometimes said so in print. He and his wife, Lucy,

eventually retired to a secluded and modest Brooklyn neighborhood to seek the lowest profile possible.

Jones, in contrast, was thoroughly at home on The Street. The flamboyant, red-haired gadabout and his wife, Jeannette, loved the good life and reveled in parties at the homes of Park Avenue's rich and famous. Dow "didn't approve," and he must have made it clear that he didn't. Resentment grew.

Another twist: Dow and Bergstresser had married cousins (Lucy and Helen Russell); Jones saw himself as the odd man out and believed (probably rightly) that the two others were conspiring against him. But there was more at work. Jones had a Jekyll and Hyde personality, aggravated by alcohol. When the message boys did their work well, he would compliment and reward them lavishly; when one of them screwed up, he would go berserk, driving everyone from the office in terror with his rantings, swearing he would dock the offender's pay. He never actually did this, but his volatility made the messengers' lives decidedly unpleasant. Finally, Dow put Bergstresser in charge of the message boys.

That may have been the last straw for Jones. He quit in January 1899. Dow died three years later, but Jones lived for another twenty-two years.

Dr Pepper

~❦~

C harles Taylor Pepper (1830–1903) was the tenth child of John and Mary Pepper, who came from a distinguished Southern family that later included Claude Pepper, the late senator from Florida and champion of Social Security.

Charles was born in Big Spring, Virginia, got his medical degree from the University of Virginia, and practiced in a town that was so rustic that they actually called it Rural Retreat. He was widely loved for his generosity and often dispensed prescriptions free of charge to the needy in his small town, where he was the town druggist as well as physician. Dr. Pepper and his wife, Isabella, whom he married in 1858, were a religious couple, active in charitable and civic affairs. Mrs. Pepper, born Isabella McDowell Howe, was a descendant of Lord Howe, who commanded the British army in North America and tried to crush Washington and his troops during the Revolutionary War.

"All that is very interesting," you may say, "but how did Dr. Pepper get started in his soft-drink business?" He never did. That's a whole different story.

The drink was invented in Waco, Texas, in 1885 by Charles Alderton, a druggist at the Old Corner Drug Store, at Fourth and Austin avenues. He didn't name his tonic, but people came to refer to it as "Waco." It became immensely popular in town, but Alderton thought it could be even more so if it had some name that would imply that it had positive health benefits. It was common practice then to name tonics and pills "Dr. This" or "Dr. That," to foster this illusion. So he named it "Dr. Pepper." (In later years the period was dropped, and it is now Dr Pepper.)

Courtesy Dr Pepper/Seven Up, Inc.

Charles Taylor Pepper, "Dr. Pepper," never knew how he would be immortalized.

But why Dr *Pepper,* and not, say, Dr Johnson or Dr Byskowicz? For that, there are conflicting accounts. The traditional legend attributes the naming to Wade Morrison, Alderton's boss. Morrison had worked as an assistant to Dr. Pepper in his drugstore in Virginia. He was once sweet on Dr. Pepper's daughter, so he asked Alderton to honor her by naming the drink after her dad. Others dispute this account, saying the daughter was much too young to have been romantically involved with Morrison. Some also point out that there was another doctor by the name of Pepper in the area at the time. "There have been so many stories that have been printed over the years that we really probably will never know the correct history," writes Joe Cavanaugh, director of the Dr Pepper Museum. (Yes, there is a museum of Dr Pepper memorabilia. It's in Waco.)

Dr. Pepper, whether Charles Taylor Pepper or the mysterious other doctor, probably went to his grave never dreaming that his name would live for generations after him printed on millions of bottles and cans of soda pop.

Dr. Scholl's

Dr. Scholl as he looked in 1918. He cheated death on August 11, 1936, and lived another thirty-two years.

William Mathias Scholl (1882–1968), whose yellow packages of foot-care products we see every time we go to a drugstore or supermarket, was the son of Peter and Clara Scholl, and was born on a farm near La Porte, Indiana. His father, a Civil War veteran, was a wheelwright as well as a farmer. After he bought the farm, Peter founded a moderately successful dairy business. Young William inherited his father's drive, but it was his grandfather, also named Peter, who gave him his first exposure to the world of feet and set him walking on the path he would take the remainder of his eighty-six years. Grandpa Scholl was a shoemaker, and he taught his young grandson something of the trade. At an early age, William displayed a remarkable talent for stitching leather (the principal shoemaking skill), so at age sixteen, he walked the twelve miles to Michigan City, where he apprenticed himself to a bootmaker.

In those days, even the best shoes rarely fit well, and he saw many painful and debilitating foot problems. Solving these problems became his mission in life, and he enrolled in the "Chicago Summer School of Medicine," now part of Loyola University, and obtained his M.D. degree in 1904. Above and beyond his medical studies, he made detailed anatomical and physiological studies of the foot. He later authored a book, *The Human Foot—Anatomy, Deformities and Treatment,* which became a standard textbook of podiatry.

The first, most obvious problem he identified was weak arches, and he patented his first invention, an arch support that he marketed as the "Foot-Eazer." This was the first of some four hundred Dr. Scholl's products. It came out in 1904, when the doctor was twenty-two. Within six months, he had made over $800, and he decided to manufacture the product rather than practice medicine.

His business grew rapidly, and soon he was renting space in a building occupying an entire city block and stamping out his Foot-Eazers rather than making them one by one, as he had originally done. Apparently mechanically gifted, the doctor designed most of his own mass-production machinery.

It was at this time that he enticed his brother Peter, who was then a clock maker, into the business, and the company expanded into its most familiar product line: those things that you stick on over calluses to protect them from abrasion and allow them to heal.

In 1906, he persuaded a second brother, Frank (called F. J.), to enter the business. William used F. J.'s merchandising skills (he had previously owned two clothing stores) to set up what became a chain of "foot comfort stores" that sold Dr. Scholl products. The first was built in 1913, near St. Paul's in London. By the early thirties, there were fourteen stores in London, and fifty-seven on the continent, in eleven countries.

The first of many Dr. Scholl's stores in the U.S. was opened in Chicago, in 1922. Proprietors of these stores had to pass rigorous tests. One of those who became "Dr. Scholl certified" was Ronald Reagan's father.

In 1912, the doctor founded in Chicago a foot-care school that since 1986 has been called the William M.

Scholl School of Podiatric Medicine. It now graduates half the country's annual turnout of podiatrists, and it contains a fascinating museum on Dearborn Street that is open to the public.

The company even got into shoe manufacturing, and built shoe factories in Wisconsin and Ohio. They also manufacture support hosiery, and have a subsidiary, Avro, that made adhesive tapes for Dr. Scholl's products.

Dr. Scholl became a wealthy man, yet he led a remarkably austere life. When in Chicago, he lived in a one-bedroom apartment in an athletic club. When at his family farm, he lived in a structure he made out of two old railroad freight cars.

He did own a luxurious home, Casa del Lago, on the Lake Michigan shore, but he rarely used it, except to entertain. He built it during Prohibition, and designed it to include a secret room, where he kept a bar, to which he invited the local policemen to enjoy a beer. It would have horrified his German-Catholic father, who had taught his children to be teetotalers.

Although the doctor apparently took an occasional nip, he was always a devout Catholic and became a commander of the Papal Order of the Knights of the Holy Sepulcher in 1931.

He was very health conscious, and did a routine of daily exercise at a gym and took a brisk, three-mile walk to work.

Dr. Scholl was twice engaged. His first fiancée was apparently turned off by his obsession with work. In 1933, his second fiancée was killed in an auto accident in which he was the driver. He never got over it, and perhaps out of respect for her, he never married.

Although he was never a father, he did "inherit" his brother Peter's four children when Peter died suddenly. William was also generous to Peter's family and put most of his nephews and nieces through college.

He treated his employees well, too, and they held him in the highest regard. He was among the first to grant paid sick leave, paid holidays, and the five-day workweek. Every year, he hosted an employee picnic at his farm near La Porte, where whole pigs were roasted on spits above massive trenches full of charcoal.

The doctor had detractors. Some questioned his credentials, others his business ethics. Legislation was introduced (and in some states passed) to outlaw the examination of the foot by anyone other than an M.D. or a podiatrist.

In his later years, he developed health problems, though he still remained active in the business. He was affected by a peculiar condition, in which he could not maintain his head erect, even with the aid of a neck brace, but he recovered. It was never diagnosed. Later he suffered a paralyzing stroke, and he had to learn to write with his left hand, and cried in frustration when he lost the ability to do even that.

He died in Chicago in 1968. On his deathbed, he acknowledged that his last thirty-two years had been a gift: in 1936, he had booked passage on the *Hindenburg,* bound for Lakehurst, New Jersey. He canceled at the last minute, and one can only imagine his response when he picked up the newspaper the next morning.

Du Pont
❧

The Du Pont family became rich and famous in two widely different industries: gunpowder and fabrics. How that happened is an interesting story, but not nearly as interesting as their political and military exploits in revolutionary France and America.

The central figure was E. I. Du Pont (1771–1834), born in Nemours, France, on the eve of the French Revolution. The "E.I." stands for Eleuthière Irénée, rare French names derived from Greek words for liberty and peace, gifts his parents wished for their troubled land.

He styled his name to include his place of birth, to avoid confusion with any other Eleuthière Irénée Du Ponts who may have been around. Hence his (and his company's) name: E. I. Du Pont de Nemours.

Irénée, as he came to be called, learned gunpowder making at the hands of Antoine Lavoisier, who, you may remember from high school, was the father of modern chemistry.

Irénée's father, Pierre, held high positions in the French government. Louis XVI appointed him inspector general of commerce and later counselor of state. In the first position, he was entreated for favored-nation trade status by the U.S. ambassador to France, Benjamin Franklin, whom he came to know well and to whom, incidentally, he bore a striking resemblance, both physically and career-wise: both men achieved note in three fields—public service at the highest levels of government, private dalliances with the most beguiling ladies of the court, and magazine publishing.

Irénée's mother, Marie, was a beautiful and vivacious woman whose passions included amateur theater and hot-

70

air ballooning. She died when Irénée was thirteen, and the morning after her death, in one of the most poignant scenes in the family history, Pierre forced Irénée and his brother Victor to pledge never-ending mutual loyalty. Perhaps he felt a special need to force-bond the two boys, for they were so different. Victor, five years the elder, was quite like his father, intelligent, ambitious, and public-spirited; yet at times he was dissolute, wandering drunkenly from one party to another dressed in silver-trimmed velvet finery. Victor's ways became so costly and embarrassing that Pierre finally shipped him off to America, with a note to Ben Franklin, saying, in effect, "keep an eye on my boy."

Irénée, in contrast, was a quiet and studious lad, forced into shyness by a conspicuous birthmark on his left cheek that seemed to curse him with self-consciousness. Despite this, he wooed and won a lovely young mademoiselle, Sophie Dalmas. Sophie's status as a commoner displeased Pierre, but the marriage was long and happy. The couple settled down, and in that same year, 1791, Irénée started a publishing business, first of scientific tracts, but later of political pamphlets.

Try to picture yourself as a life insurance salesman, carrying a policy on this guy. Here he was manufacturing gunpowder by day and producing political pamphlets during the French Revolution by night. More hazardous endeavors are scarcely imaginable, but incredibly, he, and all the other Du Ponts, survived and even prospered. In fact, they became major players in the political upheavals convulsing France. They were royalists, but what we would call moderates: they wanted to see the life of the peasants ameliorated and hoped that it might happen without bloodshed. As all moderates do, they had enemies on the right and left, and matters became increasingly perilous. The family publishing business was destroyed by royalist troops. Then Pierre was nearly drowned in the Seine by an angry mob. Then they saw hundreds of their fellow citizens being guillotined, including their country's king and queen. Finally, Pierre barely escaped exile to Devil's Island.

Taking the hint, the Du Ponts fled the volcanic France for America, but it turned out that the ocean voyage was more perilous than life under the Reign of Terror. The "thirty-day" voyage turned into ninety-three days of floating hell. After repeatedly getting lost, they ran out of food and survived only by boiling the ship's rats. Fights broke out between passengers and crew, and the Du Ponts took turns keeping nightwatch over their meager provisions at swordpoint. The gasping Du Ponts—there were eighteen of them at this point, including a weeks' old infant—arrived at Newport, Rhode Island, to begin a new life in a new world in a new century. It was January 1, 1800.

A curious incident marked their first day in the new land. Ravenous, they entered uninvited into a private home and helped themselves to a New Year's feast the servants had prepared for the owners, who were out at the time. After gorging themselves, they left a gold coin to the stunned help. Cheeky, those Du Ponts.

This incident points to a curious contradiction in this remarkable family. Though filled with notions of *égalité* and *fraternité,* they arrived with the assumption that they were special. Pierre came with the thought of buying enough land in Virginia to create his own duchy—"Pontiania," he would call it—a little independent realm of his own on American soil. Pierre was, so to speak, unclear on the concept of America, and it took the family lawyer, Alexander Hamilton, to gently take him aside and, arm around neck, set him straight.

Though thwarted in his desire to become an American duke, Pierre and his sons became as thick in military and political machinations here as they had been in France. Their friend Thomas Jefferson, then secretary of state, warmly welcomed them in person, as did George Washington by mail.

In stark contrast was the reception accorded by current president John Adams, who was not at all cordial. As far as he was concerned, the French were not welcome here. The last thing the fragile and barely formed U.S. government needed was to be infected by the revolutionary fever gripping France.

Adams's assessment must have been galling to the Du Ponts, whose government nearly went bankrupt to support the rebel colonies, and especially to Victor, who must have seen firsthand the privations the French troops had suffered to help the independence cause.

Perhaps in disgust, Pierre and Victor returned to France, where Pierre took a post as Napoleon's head of welfare, doing what could be done for the poor and homeless of Paris, and later became, briefly, president of the National Assembly. Victor had a more interesting mission: he accompanied an attaché traveling from Paris to Madrid, bearing a demand that Spain secretly cede the Mississippi Valley to France. Spain was under France's thumb at the time, and Napoleon saw an opportunity to seize land on the North American continent. With control of the Mississippi Valley, and with a substantial French presence in Canada, the United States would be virtually surrounded by French sympathizers. His plan was to send thirty-five thousand troops to Haiti and from there invade the U.S. He gave Victor the lucrative contract to provision these forces, but plans fell apart when yellow fever decimated them, sometimes killing hundreds in a single day.

While Victor's loyalty to his new country was questionable, he did at least have the decency to tell Jefferson, now the president, of Napoleon's plans. Suddenly awake to the threat of French ambitions, Jefferson astounded the country with a plan for an alliance with the British—this a mere twenty years after the end of the war for independence. Pierre, for his part, offered sound counsel to the new president: to foil French ambitions, the U.S. should buy the Mississippi Valley from France. After reflection,

Jefferson realized the sense of this plan, and the Louisiana Purchase, as it became known, was consummated, doubling the size of the country at a cost of three cents an acre. In retrospect, very cheap, but controversial at the time: the $27 million price tag was more money than even existed in U.S. currency then.

The Louisiana Purchase didn't quell French ambition. Napoleon still lusted after the American continent and was up to mischief even during the Madison years, despite his busyness with European conquest. With the American Revolution barely won, Napoleon sought to exploit the hostility between the U.S. and England. It was during the War of 1812, with the British again at America's throat, that Thomas Jefferson, now ex-president, implored the Du Ponts to start making gunpowder.

Gunpowder was already being made in America, but its quality left something to be desired, and Jefferson knew the Du Ponts knew how to make it right. On the Brandywine River near Wilmington, E. I. established a gunpowder factory that would soon become the largest in the world. He moved his household there also, which then consisted of himself, wife Sophie, and four children—Alfred, Victor, Henry, and Alexis Irene—and built a home, a surprisingly elegant and comfortable home for 1803. In response to the revolutionary notion of *égalité,* that all involved in an enterprise should be exposed to equal risk, the home, now a museum, was as close to the powder works as the workers' hovels were.

Most of the funding for the powder works came from investors in France, notably from Talleyrand, Napoleon's foreign minister. The French had more than a profit motive: Du Pont powder would be used to sink British ships and give the French a strategic advantage. Also, having a Frenchman making gunpowder in Delaware might be to their advantage should the French decide to conquer America.

The first Du Pont powder ever fired in combat was used in the War of 1812—in Algeria, on "the shores of

Tripoli"—and our victory, and hence our sustained independence, can be attributed in great measure to the Du Ponts.

After the war, the company continued to prosper, its blasting powder used to clear the way for building America's highways, railroads, and canals.

Powder making was a perilous business, and the Du Ponts took every precaution to protect their employees. Milling was done in a number of widely separated, remotely controlled powder houses, with thick walls on three sides, and the fourth side, the one facing the river, left open to vent any explosions that might occur. Du Pont apparently originated this eminently sensible powder house design, now standard in the industry. Despite all precautions, in their 120 years of operation 228 explosions did occur, sometimes blowing dismembered limbs and even whole bodies across the Brandywine to drape the branches of the trees along the opposite bank. Incredibly, it was not until after one such disaster, in which forty workers were killed, that smoking was prohibited at the powder works.

Though the business prospered, Irénée himself made little, but instead poured all profits, even much of his own salary, into expansion. He was well liked by his employees, who called him "Mr. Irénée," but hated by a partner, with whom he had a falling-out and who fled by night, taking much of the company's cash with him.

In contrast to the adventurous and fiery career of his brother, Victor had chosen the very pastoral life of raising merino sheep and running a woolen mill. Who would have guessed the brothers' careers would turn out the way they did: the quiet, studious Irénée making gunpowder and the flamboyant Victor raising sheep.

Despite their contrasting careers, the brothers' lives ended in the same way. On a trip to Philadelphia in 1828, Victor collapsed from a heart attack on a street and was carried to the United States Hotel, where he died. Six years later, Irénée, also while visiting in Philadelphia, collapsed on the street and was taken to that same hotel, where he died, at nearly the same age and of the same affliction.

Elizabeth Arden

Elizabeth Arden (1878–1966) was perhaps the first person in history to become a household name throughout the world in her lifetime. Before her death, her products were marketed in every country, even in the mountain fastnesses of Tibet. At the time, Coca-Cola was the only other product that had that distinction. She had become what she wanted to be, queen of the world.

It was a most unlikely destiny for the daughter of a truck farmer from Ontario. Born Florence Nightingale Graham, she took the name "Arden" from Tennyson's poem "Enoch Arden." It also is the first five letters of the word "ardent," and that may not be a coincidence, since ardor was her most salient trait. As for "Elizabeth,"

1. It was the name of a famous, ruthless, and frigid queen—all three adjectives and the noun were apt.

2. The first name of her beauty shop's previous tenant, Elizabeth somebody, was already gold-lettered on the door. Leaving it and replacing only the second name saved her some money. "Darling, even queens can't be queenly all the time," she might have said in her defense.

She came to New York in 1908, unaccompanied and penniless, against the vehement but ineffectual protests of her father. She went into partnership with the aforementioned "Elizabeth somebody," but the relationship fizzled (for reasons that will become apparent as you get to know her), and our heroine was soon left sole proprietor of a heavily mortgaged beauty shop.

By a mix of talent, grit, and luck, she made it a success and quickly built herself a substantial queendom, with several pink castles, worked by several dozen serfettes.

By 1915, she could even take a European tour. Arden, who you will recall had taken her name from Tennyson's tale of a sailor lost at sea, used the *Lusitania* as her vessel of choice. It was sunk by the Germans, with twelve hundred of its two thousand passengers drowned, but fortunately not on the voyage Elizabeth took. For her, it returned afloat, with her and two prizes: a kind of makeup called mascara, which she introduced to America, and a fiancé named Tom Lewis, whom she introduced to her friends.

Tom and Elizabeth seemed a happy couple, and the charming, outgoing Tom seemed the ideal prince consort. For fifteen years, he worked nearly as intensely as she in "affairs of state," so to speak, and had a good market sense. Makeup, with its bad-girl mystique, he noted, was becoming a symbol of rebellion to twenties teens. He convinced Elizabeth to expand, and sales doubled every two years. Tom, though playing no part in the trend, saw the opportunity, gave the right advice (not easy to do with Elizabeth), and got credit for the results.

Cosmetics were, and are, a hugely profitable industry. Arden took three cents' worth of water, grain alcohol, boric acid, and perfume and made them into a skin tonic she sold for $2.50. But she was not obsessed with profit; rather, her passion was for pleasing the customer at all costs. A lady from Bangor, Maine, wanted *just the right* shade of lipstick. At a cost of $300, Elizabeth had workers tool up the machines to squeeze out the shade the lady wanted, yet charged her only the usual seventy-five cents.

The graciousness she extended to her customers was not often received by her help. She was indeed the employer from hell. Many a customer saw a tear-streaked "treatment girl" run from the salon, pursued by its enraged owner, yelling, "*Gaahd*, how could you be so stupid?"

There must have been something about the salon that

made her that way, because once away from it, this strange woman mellowed into a powder puff. She would select a favorite treatment girl as a companion and whisk the no doubt trembling thing away to tour the capitals of Europe, first class. In their train compartment, world-famed cosmetics queen and girl-next-door teenybopper would giggle and titter and pajama-party the night away like school chums. But back at work, she reverted to her old self, as if the hot pink walls emanated rays that hit her like moonlight on a werewolf. She ruined one of those walls by hurling jars of cold cream at some luckless offender, then yelling, "Look what you've done!"

But her fiercest wrath was reserved for her husband. After a brief honeymoon, the purportedly happy couple came to dread their time alone, when there was nobody to act as a buffer between them. Many tempests threatened to wreck the Ardens, but in one way the stormy, sterile marriage suited Elizabeth: it enhanced her mystique as virgin queen. As for Tom, the marriage was made quite tolerable indeed by Elizabeth's frequent absences, which allowed the charming, wealthy bon vivant to pursue his hobby of philandering. But unfortunately for Tom, Elizabeth eventually caught on, and her detective reported on Tommy's dalliances with a long succession of treatment girls. So it was good-bye, Tom: he got home one day to find his bags neatly packed and waiting for him outside their penthouse door. Silently, and perhaps without a grimace of surprise, he took them, left, and never returned.

But the thing that most galled Elizabeth was learning that her brother William, who had become Tom's co-worker, was also a cowomanizer, and the two were covering for each other. She never forgave William either. Years later, when he died, Elizabeth cattily announced, "My sister's brother passed away."

But Elizabeth's greatest challenge was not her husband or brother, but the owner of a salon called Maison de Beauté Valaze, which opened at 15 East Forty-ninth Street in 1915. She was Helena Rubinstein, and the conflict between the two strikingly contrasting yet strangely similar women would fascinate the *Vogue* and vichyssoise set, and ultimately enthrall the whole country as much as the doings of movie stars and politicos.

Helena Rubinstein, a Cracow merchant's daughter who had started her business in Melbourne, Australia, of all places, came with her husband, a journalist named Edward J. Titus, to New York from Europe, where she had already established several thriving salons.

She built her New York salon with the cushy, velvet-walled Versaillian opulence to which she had become accustomed, and pictured it in a full-page ad in *Vogue*. It lured many ladies away from the House of Arden, but the aroused Elizabeth soon matched it with resplendently renovated E.A. salons, complete with flame-red doors (still there, incidentally), as if to show her determination and rage.

Tommy helped Elizabeth in her struggles, at least until he found his bags at the door, but Helena's husband was not at all supportive. In fact, he was disgusted with his rouge-aholic wife and threatened to leave. In 1928, the distraught Helena decided to sell out her American operations, apparently with the hope that it would leave her free to save her marriage. It didn't work: Edward divorced her anyway.

To Elizabeth, of course, there couldn't have been better news. "That dreadful woman," as she called her, was gone, and Elizabeth Arden was alone—the world's undisputed cold-cream queen. She could hear trumpet fanfares at her every entrance, and she reveled in them.

Yet her triumph was incomplete. As valiantly as she tried to conceal her Toronto truck-farm heritage, she couldn't. She needed help to social-climb and found a useful ally in Bessie Marbury, an intimate of the Vanderbilts, the Morgans, and most of the rest of "the 400" who inhabited the most posh apartments on Fifth and Park avenues. Bessie was a pathologically obese woman, who required the help of two canes to lumber about. She and her companions, Mrs. William Vanderbilt and Anne Morgan, daughter of J. P., were front-edge liberals who made lesbianism fashionable to New York society, it is said. There were rumors that Elizabeth was herself a latent (or maybe not so latent) lesbian.

But there were males in Elizabeth's life, too. Just as Queen Elizabeth I had her Burghley and her Essex, our Elizabeth had a number of courtiers, some long-lasting, others ephemeral, some platonic, some not.

The most important of these paramours was Michael Evlanov, a Russian prince, who, impoverished after the 1917 Revolution, became a scenery maker under the Bolshoi Ballet's director, Diaghalev. She first lured Prince Mike into redoing her salons, and then enticed him to her own boudoir. He responded with gusto and treated her as no one had ever treated her before. There were flowers (another of her passions) every day. She responded by having all her linens embroidered with the Evlanov crest. "Now I'll be noble," she no doubt thought, "not that far from being queenly," as she scarcely believed a real prince was down there, on his knees, begging for her hand. But the euphoria was not to last, for during the honeymoon, the relationship abruptly changed, when Michael left her and took up with a male lover.

Soon husband number two found his bags neatly packed for him. Then, like the Russian empress Catherine the Great, Elizabeth was to move on to horses as her source of ultimate solace. Ironically, it was as a horse fancier, rather than beautician, that she made the May 6, 1946, cover of *Time*.

Racehorses (her "darlings") soon became a second obsession. The sport of kings was natural for a passionate woman with royalist aspirations. In that world she could pursue her urge to compete while indulging the mothering instincts that she could only suppress in the face-powder world. Pursuant to her belief that women should be treated like horses and horses like women, she made her equines' stalls look like boudoirs, with perfumed cashmere blankets and pink-painted stable walls.

Her two obsessions became related in a surprising way. "Mrs. Mudpack," as the stable hands secretly and unaffectionately called her, massaged the horses' legs with her finest cold cream, and found that it really worked, and E. A.'s Eight-Hour Cream serendipitously came into use in stables throughout the country as a horse-muscle liniment.

Elizabeth was called back from the stables when 1929 "happened," but the stockmarket crash had curiously little effect on her business. Her controlling personality simply didn't let it. She did clever things to maintain sales, like selling lipstick in sets of seven shades so women could color-coordinate makeup and clothes.

Not so for Helena Rubinstein. Maybe Elizabeth gloated when she noticed that H.R. stock plummeted, but the euphoria turned to horror when she realized that Helena had sold out at sixty dollars a share the year before, and now had an opportunity to buy back a controlling interest for only one-twentieth that amount. Helena did just that and was now millions ahead. Once again in charge of her company and her life, she even married a prince—interestingly a *Russian* prince—somebody named Archil Gourielli-Tchkonia.

So the conflict between the two cosmetic queens was on again in earnest. In the old days, it had been waged by advertising, but that was far too tame. Now it was open warfare. Elizabeth stole the best and the brightest nobles from Helena. "Get him!" she would say. "I don't give a damn what it costs, or what that dreadful woman thinks." Over the next few years, she stole eleven H. R. executives and made them hers.

If you wonder why anyone would come to the Arden court for any amount of money, consider that Helena was a mean queen, too, and Elizabeth could ooze charm when she wanted to. Besides, new E. A. workers were guaranteed a year's pay, even if they lasted only a week. As long as a new hire said, "Yes, Miss Arden," and didn't do something stupid, like giving sensible advice, the worker was momentarily safe.

Seeing her courtiers picked off one by one, Helena's alarmed staff were frantic, but the Jewish queen merely smirked. "Capture but one of the Ardenites," she might have said, "that will suffice," and in an episode worthy of the Book of Judges, she got him. The captive was Tom Lewis, "Mr. Elizabeth Arden," still smarting from his ignominious eviction. How Helena must have chortled, imagining Elizabeth's fury.

So Helena lived out her life, and in her final years, the petite (four feet eleven inches) woman was reportedly worth $100 million. She spent her widowhood moving from one of her palatial estates to another. In 1964, the ninety-four-year-old wrote her memoirs, reportedly in her own hand, and in the following year died. Only a year later, Elizabeth would also die, bringing to a close the careers of these fierce rivals, who yet had so much in common.

Both were foreign born. Both took their first husbands at age thirty-seven. Both took as their second husbands effete Russian princes, in both cases to enhance egomaniacal desires for pseudoroyal status.

Both were Capricorns and shared the traits of the cantankerous, little-loved caprine beast: they were ruthless, head butting, and domineering, little brooking questioning or dissent.

Both started out as skin-cream peddlers, though they had nearly flawless complexions and of all women had the least need for the products they produced. Even more curiously, both were marketing products designed to make their customers alluring to men, while they themselves were uninterested in the opposite sex.

Both vigorously suppressed their maternal instincts, yet each doted on a favorite niece, who became a trusted confidante, handmaiden, and surrogate child.

How did these two intense, headstrong women get along? The answer to that is the most bizarre twist in this tale: though they lived and moved in the tiny, ingrown world of big cosmetics, where everybody knew everybody else, and where players constantly mingled, often in the same room, and though they operated their empires only a few blocks apart for more than fifty years, the two women never met. Nor did they ever refer to each other by name. It was always "that woman down the street" or "up the street," depending.

"It's a pity they never met," said Pat, Elizabeth's niece, to Helena's niece, Mila. "They would have liked each other."

Ford

In June 1863, while Union and Confederate forces were converging on Gettysburg to engage in a battle that would determine America's destiny, Mary O'Hearn Ford of Dearborn, Michigan, was making her own contribution to reshaping the world, giving birth to her first surviving son, whom she would name Henry.

The birth of Henry Ford (1863–1947) took place in a surprisingly comfortable home, a homestead still open to visitors of the Ford Museum in Dearborn. Mary and her husband, William, had come from Ireland, from a county called Fairlane, and settled in Dearborn, where Henry and his seven siblings were born.

He got what little education he had at Dearborn's Scotch Settlement School, where he sat next to his best friend, a kid named Edsel Ruddiman, whose unusual first name would live after him in two wildly disparate ways— as a car that became a national joke, and as a beloved and hugely troubled heir apparent to a family fortune who would die before his time, largely as a result of his father's doing.

Young Henry was not good in school, but he was a mechanical genius. He took apart every machine he could get his hands on and put it together again. Watches, clocks, engines—nothing in the house was safe. At sixteen, against the wishes of his father, who had hoped he would take over the family farm, he went to Detroit to continue his tinkering by working at the Flower Brothers Machine Shop.

As a young man Henry was quite good-looking, and his good looks attracted Clara Jane Bryant, a farmer's daughter, at a harvest-moon dance in 1887. The two were married on her twenty-second birthday the following year.

By this time Henry had become chief engineer for the local electric plant. While not tending the generators, "crazy Henry," as he was called, worked on his own project—a car. In a famous meeting in 1889, Henry's boss introduced him to the electric company's president, Thomas Edison, who looked at what he was doing, slapped Henry on the back, and said, "Young man, you have the right idea." Despite the legendary quality of the tale, Ford always insisted that Edison gave him the push he needed to stay enthused, and without that chance meeting, he may very well have chucked his dream.

At the time he was living at 58 Bagley Street, now in the heart of downtown Detroit, then a bucolic setting. In a rare bit of homage to our industrial heritage, a plaque marks the site where the first Ford car was made, a lot now occupied by a humdrum office building. In 1896, the car was finished and was rolled out for the world to see. It was the "baby carriage," as he called it, not just because it looked like one, but because it really was one: the passenger on its first outing was two-year-old son Edsel. And Henry probably considered the car his baby, and it must have churned his innards to mush to have to sell it, but he needed the $200. Later he bought it back (for many times that, I'm sure) and placed it in the foyer of his museum. Now it is enshrined in a thick glass case that makes it look like an icon in a reliquary, and the ungainly machine even seems to have a mystic aura about it that excites a feeling of near reverence, for the visitors know that the progeny of that machine changed the American landscape like nothing else, before or since.

Of course, Henry did not invent the car. In fact, for a "pioneer," he was rather late on the scene. The first American cars had been made by the Duryea brothers seven years earlier, and a total of four thousand cars, by nearly that many carmakers, had already been produced by 1896. The leader of the pack was Ransom E. Olds, who by the century's turn was in full mass production and was selling

750 cars a year in Manhattan alone. The American auto industry was surprisingly robust surprisingly early.

But at least Henry can claim that he was the first *in Detroit* to make cars. In 1901, he and a partner, Henry Leland, formed the Detroit Automobile Company and made some cars, mainly for racing, but soon the two Henrys parted ways—Leland to make Cadillacs, Ford to make Fords.

The first true Ford cars were made in 1903. Using money obtained mainly from the guy who made Daisy rifles, Ford hired ten employees and bought a building on Mack Avenue and painted FORD MOTOR COMPANY on its front. It's now the site of a Pepsi bottling plant.

As you know, he bought engines from the Dodge brothers, and bolted them onto bodies from a local carriage maker. The last step in the process was screwing on the radiator cap with the distinctive logo used to this day—"Ford" written in a script that actually resembled Henry's Success was astounding and almost immediate. By 1908, Henry had made cars called Model A, Model B, etc. and was now up to "Model T" and was pulling down a salary of $36,000 a year.

In 1909, Ford received something of a scare when he was sued by George Selden, a lawyer tinkerer who had built a gasoline-powered engine, which he patented in 1895. Selden claimed exclusive rights to virtually anything that moved under gasoline power. He never made any cars but instead hid in the bushes with his patent. His plan was to let others assume the risks and do the work, then pounce to claim a share of the profits. Fortunately, Selden's claims were thrown out. Henry resumed making his Model T's, and fifteen million of them were to roll off the assembly lines, sometimes at the rate of one every ten seconds, before finally being discontinued in 1928.

Fords were by far the nation's biggest-selling car, yet few people knew anything about Henry himself until 1919. That was the year he started paying his workers $5 a day, when the industry's going wage was about $1.50.

He became an overnight celebrity. Deluged with applications and hounded by reporters, he had to wear disguises and leave his office by crawling out the window. He was now a folk hero, and tales of Henry Ford, the benevolent capitalist baron, abounded. The most touching story is that of Norval Hawkins, a desperate ex-con who was hitchhiking on Ford's way to work. Henry picked him up, hired him, and put him in charge of creating a network of sales agencies. Hawkins became as obsessed with his dealerships as Ford was with his cars, and by 1920, he had formed eleven thousand of them, selling over a million cars a year, and played a major role in the company's success.

Henry, now the beloved commoner king, loved going onto the assembly lines to hear the grinding and clanking of machines and smell the smoke and grease. In a *Time* magazine article in 1999, Lee Iacocca tells how as a young worker, he saw Ford roam the assembly lines, backslap his awestruck workers (of which he himself was one), roll up his sleeves, and work with greasy wrenches to show them how to do their jobs. In fact, he became so popular that he was even touted as a candidate for president in 1920, until Coolidge dissuaded him from running. By that time, he was already something of a politician, having run for a Michigan Senate seat, which he almost won, in 1918.

Foreign affairs especially interested him. When he expressed concern over the impending world war, someone mockingly suggested that he charter a "peace ship" to negotiate a settlement. Not sensing the joke, he said, "Why not?" and chartered a Scandinavian ocean liner, the *Oskar II*, and rounded up a group of peace activists and journalists to accompany him. Once under way, he became dispirited by the bickering among the activists, and forgetting about saving the world, he went to the only place on the ship where he was comfortable, the engine room, and watched the machinery in fascination. The mission ended in humiliating failure, except perhaps for a few tips on how marine engines work.

But there was a further plus. He learned something about how the world works. After the war, Henry came to understand how vulnerable American industry is to supply interruptions, so he built a new mega-complex at River Rouge, with the view of making it entirely self-sufficient, producing its own wood, steel, and glass. At its opening in May 1920, the blast furnaces roared, lit by Edsel's three-year-old son, Henry II. Beginning the next day, the River Rouge's forty-two thousand employees worked in its ninety buildings to crank out ten thousand cars a day at its peak. To satisfy the pathologically neat Henry, nearly one out of eight of the employees was a janitor.

Neatness was only one fetish. Sometimes one wonders how Henry Ford became so successful, or even succeeded at all. Ford Motor Company was a strange place.

- He set up a firing range in his office, where he and his aides amused themselves at lunch taking target practice.

- Impatient with recordkeeping, he once threw all his accountants' ledgers out the window and told them to get a barrel; when people pay for their cars, he said, put the money in the barrel; when people need to be paid, take money out of the barrel.

Some of his *personal* idiosyncrasies were just as exotic.

- He was a teetotaler, forbade tobacco in his factories, and even became a vegetarian in later life. At George Washington Carver's instigation, he took to picking weeds out of the company lawn and eating them in sandwiches.

- He believed that shampooing in rusty water would prevent hair loss.

- He was so superstitious that it was hard to get him out of the house on Friday the thirteenth.

- Chickens scatter at the approach of a car, he said, because they were kicked in the ass in a previous life. He saw this as proof of reincarnation.

Henry's eccentricities and the peace mission fiasco made him an object of ridicule to some, but he still fired the popular imagination. Scenes from his personal life enthralled newsreel viewers in the 1920s. He took camping trips with Edison and Harvey Firestone. The threesome, who had become lifelong friends, took as their guide the country's leading naturalist, John Burroughs. Ford, who had inherited a love of nature from his father, just ate it up. Recreational camping was almost unknown then, and seeing these guys pitching tents and chopping firewood must have amused moviegoers as much as the film they came to see.

His *really* private life was the subject of public interest, too. His marriage was fairly solid, but he did allow himself a mistress—Elizabeth Cote, a cousin of Tyrone Power and a woman as opposite as could be from his wife, the homemaker-gardener Clara. "Billy," as Elizabeth was called, was described as a tomboy who never grew up. She was a champion harness racer and the first female licensed airplane pilot in Michigan. By her, Henry may have had an illegitimate son.

The Ford family lived on a fifteen-acre estate he called Fairlane, at the site of his family farm. There, for $2 million, he built a huge stone castle, with game rooms, a bowling alley, a theater equipped with a $30,000 organ, and garages for eighteen cars. Yet, characteristic for Henry, he was proudest of the estate's powerhouse, and he maintained the generators himself, just as diligently as he had done in his Edison Electric days.

The timing of his extravagance couldn't have been worse; the Great Depression followed immediately, and it was devastating to the auto industry—sales plummeted from over five million a year to fewer than two million. It was also a turning point for Henry's image. He hated FDR and his New Deal social programs, and did not even believe in private philanthropy. He had open contempt for people he deemed whiners, and even believed that the Depression was a good, character-building experience for America.

Henry did not like unions either—at all. Walter Reuther and a guy named Richard Frankenstein organized the United Auto Workers and were bloodied up by the goons of Ford's antilabor henchman, Harry Bennett. Bennett's guards were everywhere. They sat in the company's washrooms to keep the employees from even talking about organizing. Many a worker suspected of being pro-union went home at night to find his apartment ransacked by Bennett's goons. Employees at lunch shouted baseball scores to assure the network of spies that they weren't talking about unionizing. Those who talked too softly—about anything—were deemed seditious and were fired, usually on a charge of fighting, and were roughed up to make it convincing. When newsreel footage of labor unrest at Ford showed a minister's back being broken and a young woman vomiting blood after being kicked in the stomach, the people decided it was too much, and public opinion turned against Ford with a vengeance. Bennett, who (it should not be surprising) kept lions and tigers as pets in the backyard of his Ypsilanti home, took his work seriously and thus obtained the unstinting loyalty of his patron; he rose to become a surrogate son, replacing Edsel.

Henry's treatment of Edsel was almost unremittingly harsh. Viewed by his father as a son who couldn't measure up, he is seen by history as the man who saved the company from ruin by pointing out to Henry that nobody was buying tin lizzies anymore. By so doing, Edsel brought the company into the modern age and—in the cruelest of all of car lore's ironies—Edsel (whose name evokes laughter even today because of the hideous lemon-sucking front end of the car that bore his name) became chief of design, and actually did a commendable job at it until he died of stomach cancer in his early fifties.

But Ford's ugliest trait was his anti-Semitism. He bought an innocent and nondescript local newspaper, the *Dearborn Independent,* and turned it into a vehicle of hate that focused almost exclusively on the Jews, whom he believed were bent on world domination. He even wanted to exhume and study the body of John Wilkes Booth, somehow hoping to prove his bizarre contention that Jewish bankers were behind Lincoln's assassination. His acceptance of the Supreme Order of the German Eagle from Hitler's emissaries did not improve his standing with the Jewish community.

I wonder what the country would have been like if he had accepted his invitation to run for president—and won. It would have been an interesting four years.

Gallo

E rnest and Julio Gallo make a quarter of all the wine in this country. Twenty-five percent is a commendable market share for any company, but astounding for a business that has over five hundred competitors in the U.S. alone. Despite their success and fame, hardly anyone knows much about the two men whose name, Gallo ("rooster" in Italian), has been imprinted on those millions of wine bottles.

Theirs is a tale rich in biblical overtones—a journey to a promised land, toil in the vineyards, wandering in the desert, a blood sacrifice, and a betrayal of brother by brother. It ended with our heroes as virtual Elijahs in the wilderness, hidden behind stone walls and gates guarded by fierce dogs. It was not merely eccentricity induced by old age that drove them there; they got there for a very good reason, which will become clear as their story unfolds.

Ernest and Julio were the sons of Giuseppe Gallo and his wife, Assunta, who emigrated from the Piedmont region of Italy to California in the 1890s. Eager to Americanize themselves, the couple went by the very prosaic names Joe and Susie.

Both parents had come from families of winemakers. Susie had watched her parents in the old country making wine the old-fashioned way, crushing grapes with their feet, and her father came over on the boat with grapevine cuttings in his hands, to plant his family and his grapes in this great new land. The Gallo side of the family also came from generations of winemakers, so their heirs seemed destined for a life in the wine business, and Joe and his brother Mike, who had married Susie's sister Celia, started making the first Gallo wine in 1906 in Oakland.

Ernest and Julio (born in 1909 and 1910) had quite a different take on Gallo wine's origins. According to them, their parents were merely grape growers, and it was not until after their deaths that the Gallo brothers got a winemaking book from the local library and started making wine. This story may seem like an innocent effort to give themselves folkloric appeal, but their motives were actually quite sinister, as you will see.

Gallo wine was actually first made at Joe and Susie's farm in Antioch, California. Life there was unimaginably hard for the family, and particularly for young Ernest and Julio. They rose well before dawn, toiled in the sunbaked vineyards, went to school, and sweated in the vineyards again until well past dark. If they fell asleep or complained, they were whipped with a belt—buckle end out, to give it more bite.

Thanks in large part to Ernest and Julio's unremitting toil, the family was much better off in 1919, when a third brother, Joe Jr., was born. Because of the family's now comfortable life, or simply because he loved him, Papa Joe treated Junior as his brothers had never been treated. They saw young Joe being given a pony to ride, a shiny new bicycle on his fifth birthday, and a childhood they never had. Like the biblical Joseph's coat of many colors, young Joseph's gifts from his doting father provoked resentment. As Ernest and Julio saw it, Joe was enjoying the fruits of their labor. But their assessment was not altogether true; part of the Gallos' good fortune was due to Prohibition. One would think that it would have been the death knell for grape growers, but such was not the case. Under the Volstead Act, the federal prohibition legislation, people could legally make up to two hundred gallons of wine a year for their own use. This opened up a huge market for grape growers, who were free to sell to people willing to make their own wine. The Gallos shipped grapes by the boxcar-load to the Midwest, where grapes could not be grown and where there were thousands of wine-thirsty Italian immigrants who knew how to make it themselves. The boys made a fortune, even after paying Al Capone up to fifty dollars a car for "protection." Ernest bragged about delivering a case of grapes to Scarface himself.

But they didn't just sell grapes; despite denials, the Gallos also crushed, fermented, and bottled them. And sometimes they paid a price for living outside the law. One frequent visitor to the Gallo ranch was an aggressive prosecutor eager to make a name for himself, Chief-Justice-to-be Earl Warren.

During these years, Ernest and Julio were still boys, and did the things schoolboys do. Julio excelled as an athlete and once saved himself from a whipping by showing his father medals he had won at a track meet. Ernest was the scholar of the family and had an aptitude for math.

In 1931, Ernest married Amelia Franzia, daughter of a winemaker. The following year, Julio married Aileen Lowe, daughter of a mining engineer and insurance salesman. Julio never learned to pronounce her name. He called her A-leen, even though she and everyone else pronounced it I-leen.

With the boys married off and their business successful, Susie and Joe were living well, in a more than comfortable home in Modesto, so no one could understand a baffling event that occurred in early 1932. Without a note of explanation, without any understandable cause, and without any warning, Joe and Susie simply and abruptly disappeared. Months later, they were found near Fresno, in a bleak Wuthering Heights of a place with no phone, lights, or plumbing—and still no explanation. When people came to visit, Joe said hardly a word but held his head in his hands while rocking like a lunatic in a chair on the front porch. Suitcases and boxes were unopened, as if their owners had just arrived—or were ready to leave—and the suitcases sat that way month after month.

No one could understand what was going on, until June 21, 1933, when two hired men came to the ranch and made a gruesome discovery: Susie dead in a pool of blood by the barn, Joe dead in the kitchen, a bullet through his head. It was declared a murder-suicide, provoked by destitution. It was not an uncommon turn of events in rural America in the depths of the Depression, but the forensics didn't add up. First, the Gallos were *not* destitute: they had plenty of money. Plus, they'd secured a $30,000 loan, and the money was missing. Then, too, the pattern of fingerprints on the gun were inconsistent with a suicide, and (inexplicable for a suicide) the family dogs were shot. All signs pointed to a mob-style murder and, judging from their ready-to-flee-at-a-moment's-notice stance, a murder that they had expected might occur.

Ernest and Julio inherited everything and also got custody of Joe Jr., then thirteen. Now wealthy men, the brothers were determined to forget all the unpleasantness by plunging into the business. Over a span of decades, they attained spectacular success, but the more they prospered, the more they seemed to withdraw from the world. At the end, they lived like Howard Hughes, in a fortress, with Doberman pinschers and armed guards at its entrances. They reneged on a promise to the town of Modesto to open a visitors' center for their new winery. Their business ultimately became almost impenetrable except to employees and guards. It was almost a repeat of their parents' retreat to the desert.

Most people thought numerous petty annoyances were taking their toll. The ridicule they suffered as purveyors of cheap, screw-cap wines grated on them. Gallo was mocked as the "wine for the wino," and their "niche" wines like Boone's Farm and Thunderbird were the target of neo-Prohibitionists, who condemned the Gallos for targeting blacks and youngsters in their ads.

Then there were accusations of corruption and of purchases of privilege. During the 1970s and 1980s, the Gallos contributed more heavily to political campaigns than any other family in the country. Much of it went to Alan Cranston, who pushed through the "Gallo Amendment," an act that gave favorable tax treatment to heirs of wealthy families. It assured that the Gallo children would receive the business without inheritance taxes. It was good for Gallo heirs, but the brothers were vilified by the press.

Most seriously, they became targets of labor unrest. Once, in San Francisco, where Ernest was to receive an award, the brothers were raucously and menacingly picketed. The reception was undeserved, for of all growers, they actually were the most sympathetic and cordial in their response to Cesar Chavez and his unionization efforts. Ernest, at least at first, actually liked the guy. Julio, for his part, had developed machinery that eliminated "stooped picking." Unlike other growers, Ernest and Julio knew what working in the vineyards was like and saw Chavez as a brother in toil, until politics and zealotry won out over reason, and the Gallos found themselves singled out to bear the brunt of the grape boycott.

Although national controversies, these issues were mere mosquito bites on the brothers' sun-toughened hides. Their withdrawal from the world followed a great battle with their brother Joe, who started a cheese factory that he called Gallo Cheese which engendered a lawsuit.

Gerber

Baby food has made an immense contribution to the health of the world's infants. Up until its "invention," mothers had to strain vegetables to make them digestible for babies. This was such a messy and time-consuming chore that most mothers just kept their babies on liquid food until about age one. This led to malnourishment and digestive problems in later life. Today, all Mom needs to do is open little jars and spoon the contents into their baby's mouth, promoting healthy digestive system development as well as providing nutritional benefits. It may explain in part the startling reduction in U.S. infant mortality from over thirty per thousand live births in 1930 to about seven today.

The man responsible for this development was Daniel F. Gerber (1898–1974), son of Frank Gerber, who owned a cannery in Fremont, Michigan. Young Dan went to a military school in Delafield, Wisconsin, then served in the army during World War I.

In 1923, he married Dorothy Marion Scott, and the couple had five children. Faced with the chore of straining vegetables for her babies, Dorothy wondered why food couldn't be strained at Frank's cannery and sold as a baby food. Acting on her suggestion, Dan and Frank set up a bench-scale straining process at the plant, and tried the strained peas on the company's first tester, baby Sally Gerber (1927–).

Sally apparently gave the food a thumbs-up as best she could, and the family's pediatrician in Grand Rapids assured them that the idea of commercially produced baby food was nutritionally sound and would be backed by the medical community. Others spoke disparagingly of the venture. They questioned how strained carrots that sold for six times the cost of unstrained carrots could be acceptable to consumers. And think of the risk in marketing such a sensitive product, they cautioned: one bad jar, and the company could be ruined.

The Gerbers ignored the naysayers and went into mass production. By 1929, the company, itself in its infancy, was selling Gerber baby food on store shelves throughout much of country, and they took a giant step in building a large new plant just as the Depression loomed.

During the Depression, they may have wondered if the naysayers were right. Baby food suddenly became unaffordable to most of their customers, and it looked for a while like the company might not survive. But it did, thanks to an expanded product line, advertising and promotions, and, especially, the Gerber baby. Millions fell in love with the infant portrayed in an unfinished charcoal sketch by Dorothy Hope Smith. It became the company's symbol in 1931. Several people (including Humphrey Bogart) have been rumored to be the model, but actually she was Ann Turner, who later married a Mr. Cook and served as a high-school English teacher in Florida until her retirement in 1990.

But Gerber's was more than a baby food company. Even in the company's early days, it received up to twenty thousand inquiries a month from mothers with infant-care questions. Dorothy took it upon herself to answer these letters. Later, the company developed a professional services department and worked with pediatricians and nutritionists to create pamphlets, books, and teaching materials.

The postwar baby boom and prosperous 1950s economy assured the company's good fortune, and they abandoned adult food products altogether. (Until 1941, baby food had been secondary to their lines of conventional foods.) They diversified widely, but always in infant-related products—clothing, toys, and health care. They even set up a chain of day-care centers, and offered baby life insurance.

Gillette

G illette, the razor-blade king, is one of the most colorful figures in American entrepreneurial history. He achieved fame and fortune in business, becoming one of the world's most famous men. But he led a double life, his second one being flamingly inconsistent with his first. Dozens of students of this enigmatic man have tried, but no one has yet been able to convincingly reconcile the two beings that made up this hugely confused and complicated man.

He was King Camp Gillette (1855–1932), born in Fond du Lac, Wisconsin, where his father, George Wolcott Gillette, was a postmaster, newspaper editor, and amateur inventor. His mother, Fanny (incidentally, the first white child born in Ann Arbor, Michigan), achieved some fame as a collector of recipes and household hints. She co-authored a bestselling book, *The White House Cookbook,* parts of which remained in print as recently as 1976.

At age four, King, who was named for a friend of his father's, a Judge King, moved with his family to Chicago, where he and his two brothers and two sisters attended school. He worked in his father's hardware store until 1871, when it was destroyed in the great Chicago fire.

Burned out of his livelihood, King turned to selling, and found he was good at it. He took a succession of sales jobs in Chicago, New York, Kansas City, and even London, before finally being hired by the Crown Cork & Seal Company in New York. (Crown, still in business, is the company that makes all those bottle caps with the cork linings.)

King didn't want to spend the rest of his life selling bottle caps and, taking after his tinkerer father, tried to think of something to invent. He patented a new kind of water valve and an electric cable, but nothing came of them. Then he lost over $19,000 trying without success to market a device he'd invented for carbonating water.

He fell into despair, but one day in 1899, in a hotel room in Brookline, Massachusetts, his fortunes turned, when the idea of a safety razor occurred to him "as lightly as a bird settling down in its nest," as he put it. He designed a prototype that seemed to work, got a patent for it, and in September 1901 formed a partnership with a man named Nickerson, who really did the lion's share of the work in establishing Gillette's company. It was Nickerson who designed the production machinery, a much more challenging task than inventing the razor itself. Had it not been for the unfortunate name for someone in the razor-blade business, the company might have been called Gillette and Nickerson.

They got off to a slow start, selling only fifty-one razors the first year. The second year they did somewhat better, selling over ninety *thousand* of them. Much of the growth was thanks to advertising. In 1910, baseball great Honus Wagner, apparently originating the practice of sports-figure endorsement of consumer products, touted Gillette blades. But it was in World War I, when the blades were issued to soldiers, that the company's success was assured. Gillette got soldiers into the habit of shaving, a habit they carried home. The war blades also introduced the shaving idea into Europe. Soon the company was selling billions of blades, on every continent, all with King's picture on the wrapper, making his face, except for Jesus's, the most recognizable in the world.

By that time, Gillette had withdrawn from active management of the company, although he was still technically its president. He and his wife, Atlanta, traveled the world, sometimes staying abroad for a year or more at a time. Lantie, as he called her, was an Ohio oil executive's daughter, whom he met while living in New York. Atlanta and King (no doubt history's only couple with that combination of names) had only one child, "Kingie," who married but never had children. When he died in 1955, he was running a navel-orange orchard in California.

In his retirement years, Gillette devoted much of his time to economic philosophy, and it is here that our story takes a curious turn. One would think that a man who had developed a product that was used by millions, that had created jobs for thousands, and that had brought wealth and fame to himself would be an ardent advocate of the economic system that brought his success, but such was not the case. Gillette was in fact a utopian socialist who railed against capitalism with stunning ferocity. Of free enterprise, he wrote,

> *It is the most damnable system ever devised by man or devil. It is the cause of every injustice in our atmosphere and is the only cause of all ignorance, poverty, crime, and sickness . . . It is responsible for all fraud, deception, and adulteration . . . It grinds out poverty to some, wealth to others, and crime indiscriminately to all . . . If I believed in a devil, I should be convinced that competition for wealth was his most ingenious invention for filling hell.*

This enigmatic capitalist, seemingly outflanking Marx and Engels on the left, had his own unique take on issues of the day. While virtually everyone else spoke against the power of monopolies and trusts, Gillette actually defended them. "Standard Oil Company practically controls the whole petroleum industry," he wrote approvingly. "What is the use of legislation against syndicates, trusts, and controlling corporations? . . . *Instead of putting obstructions in the way of consolidation, every effort should be made to forward* [conditions favorable to consolidation] *as rapidly as possible*" (emphasis his).

To advance his reforms, he advocated the formation of a political party. One of the chapters in *The Human Drift* begins with the word "REVOLUTION!" in 30-point type. This suggests a discomfiting intensity. Though he never overtly advocated violence, the tone of his writing indicates that he would not have entirely disfavored armed revolt: "Was it not wonderful," he writes, "how the people of the North were roused to enthusiasm which freed the slaves of the South? Was it not wonderful how millions took up arms and risked their lives, when they realized the injustice of human bondage? Now, here around us all is a slavery that is worse in every way and more far-reaching in its effect than was the slavery of the South."

But what did he envision to replace the system he saw as so unjust? His solution was proposed in a later work, *Metropolis*. In it, he put forth his vision of a new economic order entailing centralization of production: *"Under a perfect economical system of production and distribution, and a system of combining the greatest elements of progress, there can be only one city on a continent, and possibly only one in the world"* (italics in original). This mega-city—which, as Gillette envisioned it, would house most of the world's population, except for those on farms or at recreational sites—would be a heaven on earth. All of civilization would be crammed into an area on the south shore of Lake Ontario. All existing structures there would be bulldozed, and factories and housing erected. All the remaining infrastructure in the world (*the world!*) would (presumably) be abandoned, not even excepting sites of historical interest, unless available for recreational use. All the world's commercial goods would be produced in Metropolis. Electric power would come from diverting the Niagara River, drying up the falls and passing the water through hydroelectric generators. Metropolis would become an electric "fairyland." People— possibly almost all the people in the world—would be housed in an air-conditioned complex of mega-structures within Metropolis. Each structure would be twenty-five stories high and would consist of rings of apartments, each of five thousand square feet, built around an atrium. Each structure would be many times larger than the largest hotel or apartment complex then—or even now—in existence, and there would be *tens of thousands* of these structures, all identical except for artistic detail, crowded six hundred feet apart, into the eighteen-hundred-square-mile city. In Metropolis, people would be free from all the annoyances of housekeeping. "These apartment buildings would be conducted on a scale of magnificence such as no civilization has known," he wrote. "The most modern hotel in New York could not compare in beauty of its rooms and liberality of its service with any one of these thousands of buildings of 'Metropolis.' " Connecting the buildings would be gardens, ". . . shrubbery, beds of flowers interspersed with statues, fountains, and beautiful works of art. Can you imagine the endless beauty of a conception like this,—a city with its thirty-six thousand buildings, each a perfectly distinct and complete design, with a continuous and perfectly finished façade from every point of view, each avenue surrounded and bordered by an ever-changing beauty in flowers and foliage?"

To become a resident of Metropolis, everyone would be obligated to serve without pay in one of the World Corporation's factories for five years, but after that, they would be free of all work obligations and could effectively "retire" at thirty to a life of leisure, with all their needs satisfied by products from the factories and farms in perpetuity.

Society would function with perfect efficiency. Since the World Corporation would be the only goods producer, there would be no wasteful duplication of effort and no need for advertising. Since everyone's needs would be met, there would be no crime and no war, so no need for police or a military. Men and women would be equals in Gfilletteworld. No money would be required there either, since there would be absolute trust among people. Even disease (inexplicably) would be eliminated.

He offered to let Teddy Roosevelt be the first leader of the World Corporation, for a salary of $1 million.

Roosevelt declined.

Goodyear
❦

Charles Goodyear (1800–1860) was born in New Haven, Connecticut, two days before the close of the eighteenth century. His father, Amasa, was, like Gillette's father, in the hardware business. He worked for him for a few years but ultimately developed a lifelong interest (obsession, actually) in rubber processing.

Raw India rubber has interesting and unique properties, but becomes a gooey mess when exposed to heat. Goodyear recognized that if that problem could be solved, rubber would have great commercial possibilities. In 1837, he developed a nitric acid process that improved its properties somewhat, and he sold mailbags incorporating his product to the U.S. Post Office, but they melted in the heat.

Charles was devastated by the disappointment, because it came on the heels of a string of tantalizing near successes, and he thought that things might be different with the mailbags. The sting of failure was especially keen because his heavy investment was throwing him and his family into a state of wrenching poverty.

The Goodyear family consisted of his wife, née Clarissa Beecher, whom he had married in New Haven in 1824, and a number of children, some of whom died because Goodyear could not afford medical care. So poor had the family become that Charles could not afford the nickel fare for the Staten Island Ferry, and had to beg for passage from the captain, Cornelius Vanderbilt—who refused.

Meanwhile, another rubber pioneer, Nathaniel Hayward, had discovered (in a dream, he said) that mixing rubber with sulfur improved its properties. Goodyear bought into Hayward's idea, and one day in 1839, after he accidentally dropped some sulfured rubber onto a hot stove, he noticed that the material became, well, rubbery, and the rubber industry was born. He patented his process in 1844, calling it "vulcanization" after Vulcan, the Roman god of fire.

In 1851, he went to the International Exhibition in England (which Gail Borden also attended) and presented, with uncharacteristic flamboyance, a display of articles that even included chairs and inkwells—all made of the curious substance. It attracted public and media interest and won him a Grand Council Medal, but he found it wasn't worth much, for nothing but ill fortune followed. Two years afterward, Clarissa died. Two years after that, he found himself in Paris's Clichy Prison, where he languished as a debtor while pirates infringing on his patent were making millions from his process.

He died penniless.

But what about his tire company? It was never his. The company was named in his honor, but it wasn't founded until 1898, nearly forty years after his death. Just as Betty Crocker never baked a cake and Joseph Campbell never made a can of soup, Charles Goodyear never made a tire.

H&R Block

Henry W. and Richard Bloch are true sons of the West. Their maternal great-grandmother, Betty Wollman, was one of the first white women to settle in Kansas, and their paternal granddad was once a scout for Kit Carson.

H&R's parents, despite their grandparents' frontier origins, led a rather tame existence. Their father was a prominent attorney in Kansas City; their mother, Hortense Wollman Bloch, came from a branch of her family that had become wealthy as stockbrokers. Wollman Skating Rink in New York's Central Park was named for them.

The Bloch boys grew up in Kansas City. Henry (1922–) started college there, but after one year transferred to the University of Michigan, where he majored in math. When he was only a few credits short of graduation, World War II broke out. He was drafted and served in the 8th Air Force and fought thirty-one combat missions. Returning with a richly bemedaled chest, he studied statistics at Harvard and returned to Kansas City, where he was a stockbroker for a year, before starting an advertising and consulting business called United Business Associates with a third brother, Leon. When Leon went away to law school, Richard took his place in the firm.

Richard Bloch (1926–) in his schoolboy days seemed destined for the printing business. In high school, he was making a decent living doing printing jobs. He was also a talented mechanic who worked his way through college fixing cars. He went to college in Iowa, then to the University of Pennsylvania's Wharton School of Finance, where he majored in economics.

The brothers functioned well as a team: "H" had managerial skills; "R" was the aggressive entrepreneur, who had the vision of what the company could become.

In the beginning, their company was a consulting business, but as an incidental service, the brothers offered to do their clients' tax returns. In their first year, 1954, they did three hundred returns, at six dollars apiece. Tax preparation did not become their main focus until the next year, when the IRS announced that it would no longer assist taxpayers with their returns. The Bloch brothers sensed an opportunity, advertised themselves as a tax preparation service, were deluged, and made $25,000. The next year the brothers set up an office in New York, began franchising their business under the name H&R "Block," since people were mispronouncing "Bloch."

In 1973, the firm entered into an arrangement with Sears to provide tax service in Sears stores. This greatly expanded their market share. Today, there is probably no business that is so utterly dominated by a single firm. Not one person in a hundred can identify the number-two firm in the tax preparation field (see answer below). Last year, they did over a billion dollars in business mostly as a tax service, but they also ran training courses. Until recently, the company also owned CompuServe.

The Blochs both had success in raising families as well as building a business. Henry and his wife, Marion (Helzburg) Bloch have two sons and two daughters—all now in their forties. Their second son, Tom, is a retired vice-president and was the only second-generation Bloch in the firm. His interest may have been the result of his early exposure to the income tax preparation field. He was born the night before the income tax deadline. Father Henry could not put off the work, but he could not miss the big event, so what to do? He worked on his clients' tax forms in the maternity ward as Marion was giving birth. A stack of 1040s may have been the first thing Baby Tom ever saw.

Richard and his wife, Annette, have three daughters. In 1978, he was diagnosed with lung cancer, but is in remission. He has written two books on cancer survival and founded a cancer hotline. An early riser, Richard arrives at H&R Block headquarters at 5:30 A.M. during the portion of the year when he is in Kansas City.

The workaholic Henry is still in charge of the business, but he now spends time vacationing in Arizona and Martha's Vineyard. He has a valuable art collection. Henry still does his own personal income tax return. Although he obviously knows how to do it, he is audited by the IRS every year.

Oh, the number-two tax prep firm? Household Finance.

Harley-Davidson

❦

The Harley and the Davidson families were next-door neighbors on Juneau Avenue in Milwaukee when the Harley-Davidson story begins. William S. Harley (1876–1943) was the son of English immigrants, who had come from Manchester in the late 1800s. The Davidson family had come from Aberdeen, Scotland, in 1872. In Milwaukee, Mr. and Mrs. Davidson raised their family of three boys, William (1875–1937), Walter (1877–1942), and Arthur (1879–1950).

Bill Harley and the three Davidson boys came of age at the dawn of the automobile era. Maybe while playing, the four youngsters imagined that someday they could ride around Milwaukee on a self-propelled vehicle of some sort. Harnessing a motor to a bicycle seemed to them no more absurd than using a motor to drive a carriage, and as young men they set themselves to fulfilling their boyhood dream. By the end of 1903, they had produced three handcrafted motorcycles, complete with a primitive form of the distinctive orange logo painted on the gas tanks—a contribution of the Davidson boys' aunt Janet.

Despite the primitive technology (they used tomato cans as carburetor barrels), one of the three 1903 bikes accumulated a hundred thousand miles before being retired from service.

During their second year of production, they painted their motorcycle gray and gave it the nickname "Silent Gray Fellow." The word "silent," says their company literature, implied a desirable characteristic that they were trying to promote in their motorcycles, a muffler to allow operation at a low noise level. (I got a chuckle out of that, too.) Only eight of them were produced in 1904, but they were up to fifty a year by 1906.

Don't let their modest output fool you. These young men may have started out as mere hobbyists, but they were now into their venture in earnest. The founders worked 365 days a year from daybreak to ten at night. One Christmas, however, they quit work early—at eight P.M.—to "enjoy the holiday."

Sensing somehow that their venture was destined for greatness, Bill Harley took a leave from the company to get a degree in engineering at the University of Wisconsin in Madison. When he returned in 1908, he found that he was right: the enterprise had become an honest-to-goodness company, with a registered trademark and something of an assembly line. The Davidsons had gotten financing from their uncle, a beekeeper named James McLay; the boys' father and sister Elisabeth also chipped in. Bill also found out the Davidsons had hired engineers, one of whom was a Norwegian immigrant, Ole Evinrude, who later invented the first commercially successful outboard motor. Company lore has it that Evinrude taught the boys the right way to make carburetors.

Whether by foresight or accident, Harley and the Davidsons were in the right business at the right time. Motorcycles filled an important market niche. Harleys sold for under $300, far less than cars at the time, so demand was huge, and by 1920, H-D was making $30,000 a year and employing thirty-five hundred people in a huge factory that still exists and is only a few blocks from the site of the shed where the first Harley was made.

Engineering improvements, accessory development (sidecars and trucks), and aggressive marketing were the secrets to the H-D story, and each of the partners made his own unique contribution.

Bill Harley, as the only university-trained engineer among the founders, was responsible for many of the technical innovations. Gradually, he made the engines considerably larger and more efficient—powerful enough to

The founders: from left to right, William, Walter, and Arthur Davidson, and William Harley

allow sidecars. By 1915, the company even produced "motorcycle trucks," three-wheel vehicles with the back half of a motorcycle for its rear end and a delivery cart for its front. They were cheap and practical delivery vehicles custom-built for the buyer, and were even painted with the customer's name or logo. The police and the military used another of Harley's designs—"Servi-cars," big, motorized, tricyclelike contraptions often seen driven by "coppers" in gangster movies. When not engaged in engineering innovations, Bill pursued his hobby of wildlife photography and enjoyed hunting, fishing, and golf.

Walter Davidson's contribution was his service as the president of the enterprise. Like Walter Chrysler, he had been a locomotive mechanic in Kansas before being called away to his brothers' motorcycle shed. Although he served as president for forty-five years, he never really enjoyed it, he said. His first love was motorcycle racing, and he was one of that sport's all-time greats. In fact, he may have done more as a race winner than as president to assure the company's success. In his later years, Walter (who looked a bit like Bob Newhart) also served on the boards of Northwest Mutual Insurance and First Wisconsin Bank.

William Davidson was vice-president and works manager. Like his brother Walter, he spent his early years working on the railroad. Bill administered the company's manufacturing operations during its enormous growth from backyard shed to a mega-works. Without formal business training, he had the heavy responsibility of planning expansion and securing and installing production machinery. Affectionately called "Old Bill" by the workers, he was the biggest-hearted of the partners; his office door was always open, and he had a reputation for giving money to workers who were down on their luck, and rarely asking for it back.

Arthur Davidson was secretary and general sales manager. He dispatched a sales staff to major cities throughout the country. He had stringent requirements for his dealers, and even trained them in motorcycle maintenance so they could "speak the language" of their customers. In 1916, he started *The Enthusiast,* a magazine for his dealers and owners. Almost from the beginning, he marketed aggressively overseas, and by 1921, Harleys were sold in sixty-seven countries. Like Bill Harley, Arthur had a love for the outdoors. He bought a farm west of Milwaukee and raised Guernseys. He was a leader in the Boy Scouts and donated land for a Scout camp, and also to a home for the blind. He was instrumental in founding the American Motorcycle Association. In 1950, he and his wife, Emma, died in a car accident.

One of the surprises in the H-D story is their bicycles. In 1917, the company started making them. Perhaps it shouldn't be surprising, since Bill Harley had worked in a bicycle factory before linking up with the Davidsons. The Harley-Davidson variety was made entirely by hand; they are now coveted collector's items, worth more than many of the company's antique motorcycles.

Bicycles, as well as antique H-D motorcycles, including Silent Gray Fellows and a gold-plated replica of the 1903 model, are on display in the H-D museum in York, Pennsylvania. It is the Harley owners' mecca, the place where all must visit sometime before they die. And a new museum, the Harley-Davidson Experience, is planned for the year 2001 in Milwaukee.

Harley-Davidson is indeed a world unto itself. It has a brand loyalty that any other company would die for, and their customers are united by a feeling of kinship virtually unknown for any other product. Unfortunately, they are plagued by an image problem, seeming a bit raucous and intimidating when swarming in large groups. But they are not the lawless misfits they seem to be, and they do not, contrary to rumor, eat their young in Satanic rituals. Members include a surprising number of strait-laced types—doctors, lawyers, morticians, and accountants—and famous people: Larry Hagman and Peter Fonda are among the half-million people with HOG (Harley Owner Group) numbers.

Heinz

The typical diet in much of the United States in 1869, the year H. J. Heinz picked, processed, and sold the first of his fifty-seven varieties (horseradish), was incredibly bland. Vegetables were available only a few weeks of the year. Citrus fruit was so cherished that it was expected only at Christmas. Seafood, except on the coast: forget it. Even the tomato, recently introduced from South America, was considered exotic.

But by the time H. J. Heinz died in 1919, food was actually palatable, thanks largely to him. Heinz's "57" varieties (actually there are about fifty-seven *hundred* now) revolutionized the way America shopped, cooked, and ate. Yet he did more than preserve food. He was a world traveler, social reformer, patron of the arts, and collector of antiques and artifacts. And he was something of an adventurer: he was in the first large party of Westerners to enter the Forbidden City in what was then called Peking and was only the fifth person in history to be a passenger in a seaplane.

He was Henry John Heinz (1844–1919), born in Sharpsburg, Pennsylvania, and the eldest son of German immigrants, John Henry Heinz and his wife, Anna. Henry, or "Harry," as he would always be called by most of his intimates, was the first of the nine children born to this couple. At the age of seven months, he nearly died, and his mother vowed that if God would spare him, she would forever fast on that day. He survived, and until her death fifty-four years later, she refrained from eating, or even drinking water, on the anniversary of her vow.

His father was a brick maker; Harry worked in that trade for a while, and the experience became, if you will, baked into him. To the end of his life, he insisted on testing samples of the bricks used to build his factories, and even on May 9, 1919—five days before he died—he climbed a scaffold and showed the workmen the "right way" to lay bricks.

Heinz began in the food business when he realized he was making more money selling horseradish on the side ($2,400 one year alone) than he was at his regular job. In 1869, the same year Joseph Campbell started his preserves company, Harry converted his old homestead into a horseradish cannery, where he operated under a partnership with two brothers named (some might say misnamed) Noble.

Heinz and Noble became well established over the next four years, with two processing plants, several products (mostly pickles), and more than fifty employees. But then, disaster struck. The food industry is dependent on commodities that fluctuate wildly in price. In 1873, the price of cucumbers whipsawed, and the firm, already heavily in debt, was forced into bankruptcy. The Nobles unjustly blamed Harry for the debacle.

Bankruptcy in those days conferred great shame. Some saw it as a divine judgment, a sign that God did not hold the victim in favor. He was a virtual leper and like Job even broke out in boils from the stress. The bitterest pill was malicious and unjust accusations of fraud.

Owing thousands of creditors whom he thought he could never repay, Heinz finally obtained credit from a sympathetic banker named Jacob Covode and, no doubt to the amazement of everyone, defiantly went into the pickle business again, this time with his brother Fred, as F. & J. Heinz Co.

By this time Harry was a family man. In 1869, he married Sarah Young, a miller's daughter nearly two years older than he. He and Sallie, as she was called, had a daughter, Irene, and three sons, Clarence, Howard, and Clifford, born between 1871 and 1883. In 1877, the family moved to 200 Second Avenue in Pittsburgh, near the pickle plant, but moved back to Sharpsburg two years later to escape the smoke and noise of the city.

The business steadily expanded as the country prospered, and as Americans came to crave the cuisine that depended on preserved foods and condiments. By 1879, he was solvent and, though not obligated to do so, repaid all his creditors, even those who had accused him of fraud.

By the end of the 1880s, he was employing over thirteen hundred workers in a seventeen-building complex he called "The House of the 57 Varieties."* Portions of the factories are still standing, and at one time the complex included the H. J. Heinz birthplace, which you will recall was also the original horseradish factory. It had been transported to Pittsburgh by river barge in 1904, when moving large buildings was rare, risky, and expensive. Later, the building was moved again, to the Ford Museum in Dearborn, Michigan, where it remains.

Photo courtesy H. J. Heinz Co.

"Harry" Heinz. His "57" varieties now number about 5,700.

Heinz conducted tours of his factories, and the visitors must have been impressed. The company's fabled headquarters building looked like a Renaissance palace; its rich and elaborately ornamented forty-foot-high atrium boasted marble columns and spouting fountains. Almost as impressive was the small but beautiful "Time Building," where employees came to use the time clocks. It was a miniature replica of the Library of Congress. But

*The trademark "57 Varieties" originated with Heinz himself about 1892. Actually, there were more than sixty varieties at the time. He simply thought the number fifty-seven had a nice ring to it.

the building that drew the most attention was the horse barn, equipped with a sauna, hospital, and roof garden— all for the horses' comfort. There was even a jail for unruly or disrespectful equines. Mistakenly taking Harry's whimsy at face value, someone seriously reported that "the animals actually exhibited pride in their surroundings."

There were similar provisions for the human employees, notably a roof garden and a swimming pool that the women were free to use after hours.

The last stop in the tour was the auditorium, where visitors could see Tiffany windows that had mottos extolling the virtues of prudence, loyalty, and effort. It was said to be the first auditorium built by a company exclusively for its employees. At the annual Christmas parties, Harry distributed gifts to his workers from the stage. Four times a year, the chairs were removed and dances were held. They were called "promenade concerts," in deference to Harry's misgivings, since dancing was still considered a tad sinful.

Like a number of other industrialists in this book— Hershey, Procter and Gamble, even (arguably) Henry Ford, H. J. Heinz sought to make his plant an industrial utopia, a self-contained microcosm of what he wanted the world to be, and thought it could become. But the range of his idealistic vision was not limited to the site of his plant. Like Gillette, he had a vision that embraced the entire world. He lived at a time when there had not been a protracted conflict in Europe in nearly a century, or a foreign invasion of America for even longer, and permanent peace and prosperity seemed attainable. Two world wars and the rise and fall of Communism were to teach us a hard lesson about the notion of the perfectability of man, but at the time the vision had immense appeal.

Unlike Gillette, who envisioned a secular world order, Heinz saw the world Sunday-school movement as the key to world peace and universal brotherhood. He traveled throughout the world organizing Sunday-school programs.

The idea of Sunday school, which most people assume is long-standing, actually didn't originate until the mid-nineteenth century, and H. J. Heinz was one of its leading figures. His parents had hoped he would be a Lutheran minister, and he may always have felt a tinge of guilt at not becoming one. In any event, his religious impulses came to dominate his corporate behavior.

As fervently as he strove for peace in the world, so he pursued quality and purity in his products. Some in the company believe that the term "quality control" originated at the Heinz factory.

He became active in the pure foods movement. The industry was a haven for unscrupulous purveyors of adulterated food. Unlike shoddy merchandise that causes mere annoyance and economic loss for its victims, bad food has the power to deprive its victims of health and even life, and Congress was considering a Pure Food and Drug Act to eliminate the most serious problems. Much of the industry bitterly opposed it. Heinz supported it, no doubt for business as well as philosophical reasons.

Heinz was also among the first to apply scientific farming methods, creating hybrids to increase yield and disease resistance.

By this time (1904) he was a famous man. He never ran for public office, but he campaigned for Teddy Roosevelt in the 1912 election.

Harry didn't simply run his farms and factories. He was also quite a showman. His Heinz Ocean Pier, built in 1899, was the chief attraction of Atlantic City's Golden Age and was the only pier open in the winter. Until it was destroyed in a hurricane in 1944, it offered free food samples and exhibits of souvenirs from his world travels.

He also had a museum at the family estate. The museum housed his collection of a thousand ivory carvings, the most prominent private collection of such objects in the world. He also had ten greenhouses, mostly for exotic plants. His orchid collection of 250 species was also outstanding.

The Heinzes lived in a thirty-room French Renaissance mansion in the style of the châteaus of the Loire Valley. Known as Greenlawn, it was on Pittsburgh's Penn Avenue, a neighborhood known as Millionaires Row, where Andrew Carnegie and the Mellons lived. The Heinzes' next-door neighbor was George Westinghouse, and across the street lived the family of Thomas Armstrong, founder of Armstrong Cork & Tile.

As gracious as the mansion was, the Heinz family was rarely there. Harry and Sallie were often on their world travels, and Harry was on the road visiting his factories for a good part of the year. Two of Harry's sisters lived in the house and more or less ran it. The children left, one by one. In 1906, his son Howard married Elizabeth Rust. Howard, whose middle name was Covode, after his dad's friendly banker, eventually took over the company after Harry's death in 1919. Howard and Elizabeth's son, Henry J. Heinz II, born in 1908, became president of the company in 1941.

In 1917, Heinz's third son, Clifford, married Sara Young. You may recall that Clifford's mother's maiden name was nearly identical—Sarah Young. Clarence became an invalid in his later life and lived out his days under the care of Harry's brother Peter in Lake Geneva, Wisconsin. Irene married a man named John Given.

Harry became a bit eccentric in his later years.

- He had a curious impulse to measure things and once said that everyone should carry a measuring tape.

- He brought an eight-hundred-pound alligator from Florida and installed it in a glass tank for the amusement of his employees.

- He would go on walks, and would come back without his watch, or cuff links, or money. He simply enjoyed giving things away.

It was this last trait, his generosity, that made him a beloved figure in Pittsburgh. With $500,000, he built the Sarah Heinz Settlement House, which is still in operation. He loved music and was a major patron of the Pittsburgh Symphony and its conductor, Victor Herbert.

He wore muttonchops and always seemed to have a ready smile and twinkling eye. Rare for humans of any station, and extraordinary for those few who become rich and famous, he seems not to have had a single serious character flaw.

Hershey's

"I am going to make chocolate," the dapper, impeccably dressed young man with the well-waxed mustache said to his brother-in-law, Frank Snavely, upon seeing German chocolate-making apparatus on display at the Chicago World's Fair in 1893. Frank must have looked away and rolled his eyes, for Milt Hershey was a perennial loser who had only recently found success in the caramel business after innumerable failures. Now he was going to throw it all away on another wild candy-making venture? People may have loved him, but this man seemed to his family to be as nutty as the nougats he made; they said he couldn't break away from this curious obsession that would end up killing him and would leave him, like his artist father, a nobody. History, of course, would vindicate this dreamer. He would live long, make a fortune, create a new vision of corporate America, and give to the world a rare and exotic confection, up to then known only to a few.

He was Milton Snavely Hershey (1857–1945), born into a Mennonite family in central Pennsylvania. He grew up speaking that quaint German dialect Pennsylvania Dutch. His father, Henry, was a good man, but a visionary, a fruit farmer whose head was too often in a book and whose heart was in his paintings.

The family moved frequently, and little Milt rarely spent more than a full year in any one school. Frequent moving was not a "Mennonite thing." In fact, his home was not at all typical for the culture he lived in. Most notably, his father left when Milt was a boy and forsook his family and "the gray-minded people who cannot rejoice," as he put it.

Leaving one's family and people was a rare and shameful fate for a Mennonite, and Fanny, Milt's mother, may have made him think that his daddy was dead; there is, after all, no shame in that. Milt later learned that his father was alive, and the two became close in later years, but the misinformation about his father's "death" left a strange mark on his personality and sullied his relationship with his mother.

After finishing fourth grade, Milton was apprenticed to a printer for a year, but was inexplicably attracted to the candy business and, at eighteen, gave it a try in Philadelphia. On July 4, 1876, with that city at the heart of the country's centennial celebrations, he peddled his first candies, caramels with paraffin added to give them a chewy texture.

Candy making may sound like fun, but try it sometime; pulling viscous raw caramel is backbreaking work. It must have built up his biceps, but years of working at it past midnight took all his energy, and burns by molten sugar left his hands and arms permanently disfigured. And it was not even profitable. After six years, even with the help of his mother, aunt, and finally even his father, he called it quits, and walked away with nothing.

Soon afterward, his father enticed him to Colorado, in hopes of striking it rich in silver prospecting. They were lucky at first, but not long afterward, Milt barely escaped abduction by a band of kidnappers intent on taking him to a mine, where he would be worked until he died—a common fate for unwary men in the Rockies in the 1880s, when law was weak and life was cheap. He escaped by flashing a gun and probably hoped his mother would never find out about this most un-Mennonite-like way out of his difficulty. But it could have been worse: he had $100 in his pocket, and had his captors known that, he might have killed to protect it.

That was a close call, and he decided that mining, though at times lucrative, was not the life for him, and he reverted to the far tamer pursuit of candy making. It was in Denver that he picked up another valuable lesson: the secret of successful caramels is milk. It was a secret that would ultimately make him rich, but he didn't know that yet. Instead, coming back east, he suffered one failure after another. He would fail in more places than George Washington slept—and some of them were the same places. He went to Morristown, New Jersey, and failed, and then to New York, where he helped his artist father peddle his paintings. In failure number five (or # six, I've lost count), he set up a candy shop in New York and once again, after three years, failed. By this time, even his family had given up hope in their crazy son when he then returned to Lancaster for yet another try. But finally, success! A British candy importer tasted his caramels, liked them, and ordered £500 worth for export to England. It was the break Milt needed. He expanded his little shop into a factory, distributed to new markets, and, almost overnight, became a millionaire.

"Who can make the rain go?" Sammy Davis Jr. asked in song, then answered, "The Candy Man can." Indeed he did. Candy Man now lived in a mansion and was enjoying world travel—visiting the Pyramids, kissing the Blarney stone, gambling in Monte Carlo, where he was no doubt the only Mennonite at the craps table. He even toyed briefly with the idea of retiring and spending the rest of his life traveling.

But he was in the end too close to the soil and his roots to be happy abroad. He remodeled the Lancaster home where he and his mother lived and furnished

Photo courtesy of the Hershey Co.

Milton S. Hershey and his bride, Kitty, a choice that didn't please his mom.

it elaborately. He also refurbished his boyhood home and made it available to his father, at that time still in Colorado, whom he enticed to return.

But now he was willing to risk it all for a new venture. It was 1893, and he was attracted to a new business opportunity. Remember the German chocolate-making equipment he saw at the Chicago World's Fair? He bought it, and then in a corner of the caramel factory experimented for months with different recipes and techniques, trying to find the "perfect" chocolate.

Chocolate was certainly nothing new. Called "Chocolatl" by the Aztecs, it was discovered by the Europeans during Cortez's conquest of Mexico and renamed the "gift of Montezuma." (It was one of his two gifts, actually.) It was slow to catch on, because making something tasty out of mashed cacao beans is not an easy trick, and the Europeans who discovered the secret (principally Swiss chemist Henri Nestlé) guarded it closely. But Milton was convinced that despite his only four years of schooling, he could do as well or better, and with the million dollars he received from the sale of the caramel works, he built a factory without any assurance that he could actually figure out how to make decent chocolate. It was a stunningly brash move, made all the more improbable by his selection of a site for the factory—in the middle of cornfields, far from transportation and markets.

"Build it, they will come," he might have said, reasoning that he would have his two important needs well met: fresh milk and a husky Pennsylvania Dutch workforce that did not shirk hard labor. This hunch paid off, too: the plant would eventually become the world's largest candy factory, producing 114 varieties.

The company's most famous product, the Hershey Bar, was an afterthought. Hershey thought that mass-marketing a single product and distributing it widely in a conspicuous wrapper would bring attention to his company's product line. Once again, he was derided, but proved his doubters wrong. The Hershey Bar, the first product to be marketed this way, became the world's most successful candy bar.

Kisses came soon afterward. Milton named them himself, as he did all his products. "Kisses" may have been suggested by the little sucking sound they make as they come out of the extruders onto the conveyor belts.

Some of his success was due to advertising. Contrary to myth, Hershey *did* advertise, and actually he did it quite aggressively. He referred to chocolate as a "nutritious food"—a bit of a stretch, but this was in the days of almost-anything-goes advertising.

He also promoted his products by painting his logo on the side of his delivery wagon, a Riker Electric, the first motor vehicle ever seen in Lancaster.

During World War I, one of his workers, Harry Reese (1879–1956), branched off on his own. His idea was to coat cups of peanut butter with milk chocolate. Reese's Peanut Butter Cups he called them, and soon after his death his six sons sold the company back to Hershey. It was Hershey's first significant acquisition of another company, and the product, unchanged since Harry's day, is now the nation's largest-selling confection.

For many years, Milton Hershey's private life was uneventful. Obsessed with work, he remained single, even into his forties. But in 1898, to the surprise of everyone, he married. His bride was a young Irish shopgirl from Jamestown, New York, Catherine Sweeney. Kitty, as he called her, came from a working-class background (iron-worker father, nurse mother), but she was refined and cultured and was a talented amateur musician. She was a stunningly beautiful young woman, with glistening auburn tresses and equally flashy clothes that made her a strange contrast to her stern-faced, soberly gray-dressed Mennonite mother-in-law. As you might expect, Mama was not entirely pleased with Milton's choice, and the fact that her daughter-in-law was Catholic didn't help. Not at all. To complicate things further, Milton's father was quite taken with his son's new bride, and their mutual affection created even more ill will on the part of Mrs. Hershey Sr.

After four years of unrecorded but no doubt interesting interactions among the four, Milton built his mother a splendid house in Lancaster. But for Mother Fanny, who was raised to see austerity and simplicity as cardinal virtues, the huge and elaborate mansion must have seemed a strange gift. And what was it for? "To make room for my suddenly-a-millionaire son's papist floozy of a wife," she might have thought. Probably she was larger-hearted than that, but still she must have sulked in her walnut-wainscoted, heavily tapestried surroundings, pondering with some bemusement the many unexpected turns her life had taken.

Kitty was to give her some consolation in her later years by renouncing Catholicism (even though it was to accept the almost-as-heretical faith of Christian Science), but she was to cause Fanny one final disappointment. In 1915, she died, leaving her no grandchildren. Grandchildless Fanny lived five more years, continuing to throw herself into Milton's business, helping wrap candy Kisses till her dying day.

Much is made of Hershey's generosity to his workers. He organized the construction of his own company town, Hershey, Pennsylvania, and the company constructed homes, stores, parks, a zoo (the nation's first private zoo), and a trolley system. It was Gillette world, a very much scaled-back version, but yet a utopian community, and it actually seemed to work. Every employee's family had a home with electricity and indoor plumbing, rare comforts for working-class rural folk in the twenties.

Hershey's beneficence was at its grandest during the Depression, when candy sales plummeted. While other candy makers were laying off their workforce, Hershey put his to work raising community buildings, some of which possess great architectural interest. The community building, for example, boasts the world's second-largest marble dome. During the Depression, Milton S. Hershey did not lay off, or even reduce in pay, one single worker.

The Hershey company is justly proud of their founder's vision and generosity, but like most heroes, he was flawed. He could be pompous and arrogant. His long Cadillac was a familiar sight, as Mr. Hershey—always in full formal business attire: a dark suit with a stiff-collared white shirt and a tie that was never loosened, even on the hottest days—inspected homes and sternly reprimanded the owners of those deemed deficient in neatness and upkeep. When he found out liquor was being sneaked into town, he hired detectives to find out how.

Hershey was a stern taskmaster, making his workers toil fourteen hours a day, seven days a week, at least during construction of the factory. And he had a famous temper: he wanted all the houses to be unique, and when he found out that his construction manager was making them on an identical plan, he blew up, abruptly fired him, and had all the houses torn down.

The workers found that the benefits they enjoyed sometimes came with a heavy price, for everything had to be perfect and to "H.S.'s" specs. But he had a passion for the town, and fondness for its people, even after a disheartening strike in 1937 that turned into a bloody pitched battle between farmers and Hershey workers.

His greatest love was his famous orphanage and industrial training school. It was Kitty's idea, and that may explain its special place in his heart. Originally, it was put in Hershey's birthplace, which his father made available by his death in 1904. The school still turns out boys, all of them needy but no longer necessarily orphans. Before his death, he gave virtually everything he owned to the Hershey Trust, for use by the industrial school. The $60 million gift has now grown to $5 billion.

The school is a curious mix of Philips-Exeter and farm labor camp. Its huge endowment enables it to have an excellent academic program, with a nine-to-one student-teacher ratio and amenities that rival those of Eastern prep schools, yet living quarters remain spartan, and a strict regimen of farm chores—including, until very recently, milking the cows—is still in force.

After Kitty's death, Hershey spent much of his time in Cuba and even built a carbon copy of Hershey, Pennsylvania, there, but when he was back home, he became increasingly withdrawn, ended up as a recluse who confined himself to a two-room suite in his mansion and was visited by only a few close friends.

Hershey, Pennsylvania, remains an interesting place to visit. Much of the important Hershey architectural heritage has survived, although it has been all but buried under subsequent layers of "ordinary" buildings. If you visit the town of Hershey, take a pass on the carnival rides and the Chocolateworld hype and visit the home Milton built for himself and Kitty, just across the lawn (now a golf course) from the factory. Though not especially large for a millionaire's home of its day, the twenty-two-room mansion has to be the most beautiful private home I've ever seen. Now the site of the humble, cluttered offices of the Hershey Trust, it is still well maintained, as is the Hershey boyhood home, which you get to from the mansion by taking "Chocolate Avenue" (with street lamps shaped like Hershey's Kisses) and proceeding south on "Cocoa Road."

Hewlett-Packard
꧁꧂

On a garage behind 367 Addison Avenue in Palo Alto, California, hangs a plaque commemorating a significant event in the nation's history. It was in that garage, in 1938, that the "Silicon Valley" electronics industry was born.

It also was the place where the cliché "garage industry" originated. Some think it's mere legend that electronics entrepreneurs started multibillion-dollar business empires *literally* in garages, but it's true. Steve Jobs and Steve Wozniak of Apple Computer also got their start in one.

The renters of this particular garage were William Hewlett (1913–) and David Packard (1912–1996) and the name of the company they formed—"Will it be Hewlett-Packard or Packard-Hewlett?"—was settled by a coin toss.

Bill Hewlett, the son of a medical-school professor named Albion Walter Hewlett, was born in Ann Arbor, Michigan. His dad died when Bill was twelve, and his mother took him and his sister to Europe. On his return, he enrolled in Lowell High School in San Francisco. He was dyslexic and did poorly in most courses, but he had enough aptitude for math and science to get into Stanford, where he majored in electrical engineering. His penchant for electronics may have stemmed from a childhood exposure to electric trains, he said.

David Packard was born in Pueblo, Colorado, to a lawyer father and teacher mother who lived in a pleasant home in the Rockies. Pike's Peak could be seen through the picture window. He had an interesting combination of musical interests—violin and tuba—but music, which he loved, was a low priority. He would rather be remembered as the center for Colorado's all-state basketball team; he also set the Colorado record for the discus throw. His leadership potential became evident when he was elected class president in all four years at Pueblo's Centennial High School.

One summer, as if to experience life of the century before, he prospected for gold at Cripple Creek. Other summers in the college years were spent as a brick maker, iceman, and short-order cook. After college, he continued his athletic career by playing semipro basketball in New York.

Both boys were athletes, and it was on the athletic field at Stanford—both were on the school's football squad—that they met. They continued their teamwork in 1938 in the Palo Alto garage. The first Hewlett-Packard product was something called an "audio oscillator." Whatever it is, it must have had use for somebody, because they made over $5,000 in sales and a $1,500 profit. They called it "Model 200" to give the impression they'd already been in the business awhile.

The boys started families at about the same time as they started making oscillators. In 1939, Bill married Flora Lamson, a girl he had met when they were children vacationing with their parents in the mountains. Bill and Flora were to produce five little Hewletts over the next several years.

Dave married Lucile Salter, whom he had courted when he was a pot scrubber at her sorority house at Stanford. The Packards had three daughters—Nancy, Susan, and Julie.

During World War II, Bill served as an officer in the army signal corps. (For once the army placed a guy in a job where he belongs.) Dave stayed on managing the company, which prospered during this time from defense-related business. When Bill returned from the war, he found two hundred employees working at long rows of benches in a building the company had built. He also found a plaque on the wall with the army-navy "E" award, an honor bestowed on only 2.5 percent of companies in the country. To this point, the company had doubled in size every year, and HP incorporated shortly afterward.

Rapid growth continued into the fifties, and by the end of that decade, HP was producing 380 products and had annual sales of $30 million.

In 1969, it was Dave's turn to serve his country in the military: Richard Nixon named him deputy secretary of defense. Because the Vietnam War was still going on, Packard's post was one of the hottest seats in Washington. Because of the stress, Lu lost sixteen pounds from hearing her husband vilified in the press. He retired from the Defense Department in 1971 to head Nixon's reelection campaign in California and to serve on the Stanford University board of trustees. Packard figured he lost $20 million by virtue of being divested of HP stock ownership, which was a requirement for his appointment.

HP's most important innovations were developed after Packard's return. They were the handheld calculator, the laser printer, and the light-emitting diodes used in car headlights. The company now has over 650 plants in 120 countries.

HP's employees have shared in their bosses' success. The company has a profit-sharing plan, and many employees who participate retire as millionaires. But more important to many than the pay is the workplace atmosphere, one of openness and trust. Tools are stored in unlocked cabinets, and the headquarters is an open environment, where no one, not even the chairman, sits in an enclosed office. All employees are on a first-name basis, and there is no rigid hierarchy. HP claims it was the first company to institute flex time, where employees could set their own work hours. The company has an unusual fringe benefit—recreational areas that employees are free to use: a ranch in Colorado, a lake in Scotland, a ski area in Germany, and a park called Little Basin in the California redwood country, all exclusively for HP employees and families.

Hilton

Conrad Nicholson Hilton (1887–1979) was born on Christmas day in tiny San Antonio, New Mexico. His father, August Hilton, a Norwegian immigrant, operated the town's general store. What would entice a Norwegian to emigrate to the middle of the New Mexican desert is hard to understand, but that he did. August was exceptionally industrious, and he became successful enough to live in an eight-bedroom house that he built for himself, his wife, Mary, and their eight children. He could even afford to send his children away to school. Young Conrad attended a military academy and went on to St. Michael's University, and to a school now known as the New Mexico Institute of Mining and Technology. He returned from college to work in his father's store, eventually becoming a partner in the venture—A. H. Hilton & Son General Store.

The family's large, sprawling adobe house became, arguably, the first "Hilton Hotel" in 1907, when a recession hit. Business suffered, and Conrad suggested that the family could weather the storm by renting out some of the bedrooms to guests at a dollar a night and providing meals and services. Conrad went to the train station every day to hustle guests, mostly traveling salesmen. His efforts pulled the family though the slump.

The next year, his career as a hotelier was put on hold, and he took a job as cashier in the New Mexico State Bank while still working for his father in the store.

By 1915, the family's finances had recovered, and August bought himself an automobile—a luxury and a curiosity in that tiny place in the middle of nowhere (about halfway between Albuquerque and Truth or Conse-

quences). In 1918, while Conrad was in France as a lieu-
tenant in the First World War, August died in that car, in
what must have been one of the first fatal traffic accidents
in New Mexico's history.

Returning from the war, Hilton moved to Cisco, Texas,
where he tried to buy a bank. He was unsuccessful in
closing the deal, but he noticed in passing that there was
a lack of hotel rooms in Texas. After standing in a long
line to check into the Mobley Hotel in Cisco, he struck
up a conversation with the owner, who, exasperated at the
insatiable demand for his rooms, told Conrad he'd willingly sell his business to anyone who could take it off his
hands. Perhaps remembering how making his childhood
home a boardinghouse had saved his family from ruin,
Hilton smelled an opportunity. With his inheritance,
$5,000 of his own savings, and a little help from his
friends, he relieved the owner of his "problem" and
opened the first true Hilton Hotel.

From this mustard seed grew an enterprise that included the Sir Francis Drake (San Francisco's premier hotel), The Plaza in New York, the Waldorf-Astoria, and the
entire chain of Statler Hotels. He built the thousand-room
Conrad Hilton Hotel in Chicago—the largest hotel in the
world in its day—and it became the flagship of his chain.
By the 1970s, there were over 125 Hilton Hotels.

Conrad Hilton, like many other people profiled in this
book, had political interests, but unlike most, his political
career began early. In 1912, when the United States com-
pleted the Gadsden Purchase, making New Mexico and
Arizona our forty-seventh and forty-eighth states—the
twenty-five-year-old Conrad was elected to the first New
Mexico State Legislature.

His family life also was not without interest. He was
married briefly to Zsa Zsa Gabor, and his son Nickie was
the first husband of Elizabeth Taylor.

Hoover

H oover is generally regarded as the father of the
vacuum-cleaner industry, but he didn't invent the
machine. There had been crude if ingenious attempts to
mechanize the chore of floor cleaning throughout the
nineteenth century, and even earlier. Even in Hoover's
day, some houses were equipped with electrically operated "central vacuum" systems, but their cost, about
$5,000, was more than the total price of the average
house, so there wasn't a big demand for them. What the
world needed was a portable vacuum cleaner that could
be mass-produced commercially, and that was Hoover's
contribution.

He was William Henry Hoover (1849–1932), the oldest
of the three sons of Daniel Hoover, a tanner from Stark
County, Ohio. Will's mother, born Mary Kryder, was
called Aunt Polly by most everyone. She had a clever and
inventive mind, and Will must have gotten his talent for
getting things done by observing how ingeniously she ran
the household. The Hoover story is a lesson he may have
learned from her, a lesson in adaptation—in the ability to
take hopeless situations and turn them into opportunities.

In 1875, Will took over Dad's tanning business and
operated it successfully for a while, until crisis number
one loomed: a glut of leather. Finding himself stocked
with cowhide he could not tan at a profit, he decided to
use the hides to make leather products—horse collars,
buggy whips, and such. Tanning to saddlery may seem an
easy transition, but it's really like going from making steel
to making cars. It required learning a whole new set of
skills.

He became as insistent on perfection at making saddles

Photo courtesy Hoover Co.

William "Boss" Hoover was well into his fifties before he made his first vacuum cleaner.

as he had been at tanning. When someone suggested stitching at ten per inch instead of twelve to cut costs, he would have none of it. He called his saddle "the Perfection," a name that indicates how seriously he took his obligation to make a quality product. It also indicated something of his character. In a gesture that would please today's animal rights activists, he patented a horse collar that didn't chafe the necks of horses.

Crisis number two occurred with the rise of the automobile. With horse collars and buggy whips of little use in horseless carriages, Hoover pursued contracts with the auto industry for straps, belts, and other leather parts. If you have visited an antique-auto museum, you have seen, probably without knowing it, many Hoover-made leather products on early Fords, Buicks, Cadillacs, and dozens of now forgotten makes. He also diversified into sporting goods—leather coats, leggings, and wading boots.

Although modestly called a "leather shop," the Hoover Company actually had become quite a substantial enterprise by 1904, when it had more than two hundred employees and a capitalization of $312,000.

The employees affectionately called Hoover "Boss." The nickname stuck throughout his life.

His family was growing along with his company. In 1871, he married Susan Troxel, a farmer's daughter, and over the years they had six children. All three boys and the husband of one of the daughters were eventually to join him in his business. As kids, the boys played around the tannery, tempting fate by jumping from rim to rim across the soaking vats; once one of them fell, and was saved from certain death by frantic rescuers who saw him dangling by a nail and caught him before he descended into the lye.

Boss was a devout Christian and was active in the Disciples of Christ Church. In 1882, he was ordained as a minister. In opposition to the Baptists, the Disciples did not insist on baptism by total immersion. The Baptists did so, even in winter. Pneumonia cut short the lives of many who were immersed through ice holes on the Ohio River and whose clothes froze stiff before they could reach shelter.

Hoover was also active in outside business ventures. In 1902, he became president of the Canton-Akron Railroad. And as if he needed something more to do, this tanner, saddler, minister, railroad president, and father of a good-sized family assumed the duties of mayor of North Canton upon its incorporation as a town in 1905.

At this time he was well into his fifties, retirement age for many today, and he was yet to make his first vacuum cleaner, or even imagine himself in such a business. That part of the story began in 1907, when James Murray Spangler, a family friend, made himself a "dust collector" consisting of a fan, a soapbox, a pipe, and a pillowcase. Murray (as he was called) had asthma, which was aggravated by the dust that was raised when he swept floors. He made this crude device to reduce his exposure to dust.

Soon he saw the potential of the unwieldy device for carpet cleaning and then, in what may have been history's first vacuum-cleaner home demonstration, showed it to Susan, who in turn showed it to Will. He grunted in perfunctory interest, but the strange machine remained stored in a closet, as Murray, with his children Jennie and Clarence, began producing the things and trying to sell them. The Spanglers obtained a financial backer, who unfortunately lost interest, and the venture would have died had it not been for an abrupt reversal in Will's fortunes. It was crisis number three. The bottom fell out of the leather-auto-products business when leather car parts went out of fashion. Looking for something to do, Hoover struck out in a most unlikely direction. Will Hoover, who for fifty-seven years had known nothing but leather, set out to make a forty-pound machine whose only leather part was a half-ounce drive belt. He bought the patent from Murray and formed the Electric Suction Sweeper Company. He put Murray in charge of the shop, located in a corner of the leather works, and he and six employees produced 372 vacuum cleaners in the last five months of his first year (1908) and sold them for sixty dollars apiece. The cleaners even came equipped with attachments, for an extra fifteen dollars.

The 1908 machine (called the Model O) was heavier than most women would care to lift, was ugly as sin, and must have roared like a jet plane, so selling over 350 of them in the five months after its introduction was really quite astounding, especially considering that only one household in ten even had electricity.

At first, the vacuum cleaners were a curious sideline that may have caused the leathermen to look at the little band of Spangler's workers in the corner and wonder, "What *are* they *doing*?" The company, after all, remained primarily a leather business, and, in fact, enjoyed a resurgence during World War I, with military contracts. After the war, however, it was vacuum cleaners or nothing, for there was no longer any demand for leather: military contracts were terminated, and the automobile's triumph over the horse was virtually complete.

Over the years, as the company came out with technical improvements and progressively more pleasing designs, the once strange machine became attractive to an ever-wider range of consumers. Hoover patented many innovations, including the vacuum-cleaner "headlight" so people could see what they were vacuuming, and the disposable bag. Innovative marketing approaches also helped his sales. Herbert, the middle son and company marketing genius (the one who, incidentally, nearly fell to his death in the lye vat), offered a David-Oreck-style free trial and gave stores a commission for handling the sales of his cleaners. Rather than selling the cleaners to department stores for them to resell, Herbert hired his own salesmen to work in the store. He trained his salesmen to service the machines.

By the 1920s, the company was so successful that it was marketing worldwide, with operations in Canada and England, but the company's headquarters and main factory have remained near the site of Hoover's original factory in North Canton to this day.

As you might imagine, "Boss" could not have had much of a hobby life, but he was an avid baseball fan, and he fielded a semipro team consisting of Hoover employees who once won the championship of their league. He also spent a lot of time walking. It is then that he did his thinking. Today, there is a Hoover Walk held annually in North Canton to raise money for the physically challenged.

The Hoover home and tannery in North Canton are now a museum, with an extensive vacuum-cleaner collection, including a 1908 Model O and one of Murray Spangler's dust collectors.

Jack Daniel's

Jasper Newton Daniel (1846–1911) was the tenth and last child of Lucy and Cal Daniel, of Lincoln County, Tennessee. Lucy died when Jasper ("Jack") was a baby. Cal remarried, but his new wife and Jack didn't get along. At age six, he thought it might be better living with their next-door neighbor, so he moved. That didn't work out either, so the next year he was more or less adopted by a local couple, Dan and Mary Jane Call, who raised him.

His stepfather, Dan, was an unusual combination of things—a minister and a distiller. He always struggled to reconcile the two sides of his life, until 1859, when he fell under the spell of an evangelist who went by the name "Lady Love." She preached on the evils of strong drink, and that apparently was what it took to get Dan to abandon the business. That left Jack Daniel, age thirteen, the proprietor of a whiskey distillery.

Despite his youth, Jack had learned how to make good whiskey. Years later, at the St. Louis World's Fair, it was proclaimed the finest in the world. His whiskey gets its distinctive flavor from filtration through ten feet of charcoal. The process was discovered by Dan's slave, named "Uncle Nearest" Green, who stayed on at the still, working for Jack, after Dan left for more respectable pursuits.

A turning point in Jack's fortunes occurred during the Civil War, when he made a mint smuggling whiskey to the Confederate troops in Huntsville, Alabama. That made him enough money to build a bigger plant, this time near Lynchburg, Tennessee, where the water was better and there was railroad access. He hired Uncle Nearest's two sons, Eli and George, to manage the distillery. In 1862, the federal government raised money for the war effort by registering distilleries and taxing them. Jack's was the first in the country to be registered.

In 1895, he started using square bottles, suggestive of honest, square dealing. He was indeed fair and honest, and was kind and generous in his private life. It was a remarkable and unexpected turnout for a man who had such an unconventional childhood, and who was involved in a business that many held in contempt.

At age twenty-one, when he recognized that he was a success, it suddenly occurred to him that he should look the part. One day, the casually dressed ragamuffin went into town and came back in elegant, formal business attire. For the rest of his life, he was never seen in public dressed any other way.

JCPenney
❦

James Cash Penney (1875–1971) was born and raised near Hamilton, Missouri, where his father, also named James Cash Penney, was a farmer and Baptist preacher. His mother, Mary Frances Penney, had come from Kentucky. Jim was one of twelve children.

He began his life as a farm boy, and his heart never really left the farm. In his later years, he returned to Hamilton and bought up parcels of land around his birthplace. He named the assembled property "Homeplace Farms," and there he gained an international reputation as a raiser of Guernseys and Herefords, and his Black Anguses were probably the best-known herd in the country in its day.

Penney was also the founder of Foremost Dairy and was a major benefactor to 4-H Clubs.

Of course, before all this happened, JCPenney had achieved fame and fortune as a merchant. His career in merchandising started with a watermelon stand when he was eight years old. He set up outside the county fairgrounds to avoid paying a fee, and his father gave him a good dressing-down for competing unfairly with the folks selling melons inside. The experience set him out in the right direction, and he never forgot his lesson: always conduct business by fair and honest dealing.

At sixteen, he left the farm to go out west for health reasons. He took a job in a butcher shop in Longmont, Colorado, but quit after his boss ordered him to bribe his customers with liquor. He went into a partnership with two other presumably more compatible individuals, and on April 14, 1902, opened a dry-goods business that they called the Golden Rule Store because of their belief in the importance of fair dealing. The one-room wood-frame

144

building between a laundry and a boardinghouse in Kemmerer, Wyoming, would later become the first JCPenney store, and would be followed by more than sixteen hundred others. Jim and his new bride, Berta Hess, whom he had met in Longmont, lived in an attic above the store, and the couple had two sons before her tragic death from pneumonia in 1913.

It was also in 1913 that Penney renamed the stores (there were thirty-four by this time) JCPenney and established the company headquarters in Salt Lake City. The chain continued to grow. Only two years later there were eighty-six stores in thirteen states, and the headquarters of the chain moved once again, this time to New York City. In 1929, the peak year of the expansion, the chain was opening one new store every three days. Store number five hundred, incidentally, was in Hamilton, Missouri, Jim's birthplace.

On October 23, 1929, the company's stock was listed on the New York Stock Exchange, initially at $120 a share. Not the best time for this to happen: six days later was the Great Crash, and the stock plummeted to $13. To meet his debts, Penney, who had most of the company's stock, had to sell out, and his $40 million fortune was wiped out. He went to the Kellogg Sanitorium to be treated for depression.

Although Penney was involved with the company until his death in 1971, he was not always its president. In 1917, only fifteen years after he founded his first store, he abruptly resigned, although he continued to serve for forty-one more years on its board of directors.

Working behind a desk, he perhaps missed the routine of retailing. Even in his eighties his favorite thing was traveling around the country to visit his stores and wait on his customers. He created a sensation among shoppers, who could brag to their friends that they had been waited on by J. C. Penney himself. He gave advice to shopgirls on how to wrap packages. He even swept floors. He never wanted to forget where he'd come from and to teach his "associates" (he never called them employees) that there is no shame in even the most menial work.

Though a kindly man, his stern Baptist upbringing left an imprint on his store's policies. In the chain's early days, he would not hire anyone who smoked or drank. He was frugal, even as a millionaire. For years, his clerks did not have typewriters and did correspondence in longhand. He used the backs of empty envelopes as memo paper.

He had a near-photographic memory. Of the thousands of people he met in his life, it is thought by some that he never forgot a name or a face.

After Berta's death, he met his second wife, Mary Hortense Kimball, a talented musician and a reporter for the *Christian Herald*. The couple met on a trip to the Holy Land and were married in 1916, but she also died after only a few years. In 1926, he married his third wife, Catherine Autenreith, with whom he had three daughters.

Johnson & Johnson

❦

The company that makes Band-Aids, baby powder, and hundreds of other health-care products originated through the efforts of three sons of a prosperous cattle farmer, Sylvester Johnson, who lived near Carbondale, Pennsylvania.

Robert Wood Johnson (1845–1910) was the eldest of the three. At sixteen, he went to work in a drugstore—Wood and Tittamer's it was called—at 66 Market Street (now the site of a social service agency) in Poughkeepsie, New York, where his uncle James taught him to make gooey poultices called "plasters" that contained herbs, barks, and other "healants," such as mustard. Later, he moved to New York City, where he applied his natural gift as a salesman and his newly acquired expertise in the healing arts to enter the medical products business. In 1873, he went into a partnership with George Seabury. The two didn't get along, and things turned even worse when Robert brought his two brothers, James and Edward Mead Johnson, into the business.

The 1876 Centennial celebration in Philadelphia was a turning point for R. W. He went to a lecture on antiseptic techniques given by English surgeon Joseph Lister. Dr. Lister, after whom Listerine was named, was the first to recognize the importance of disinfection during surgery.

In those days, surgeons operated with bare hands and unsterilized instruments and used sweepings from cotton-mill floors as surgical dressings. Medical science did not yet appreciate the power of germs, and postoperative mortality was as high as 90 percent. Though well meaning, Dr. Lister's solution—surrounding the patient with a disinfectant vapor—was clumsy and impractical. It may have protected the patient, but it choked the surgeons. "There has to be a better way," Johnson figured. His idea was to make sterile dressings, individually wrapped to protect them from contamination.

Photo courtesy Johnson & Johnson.

Robert Wood Johnson, the company's founder, was not one of the "Johnsons" in the firm's name.

He had the right idea, and in March 1886, with fourteen employees, he enticed his brothers James and Mead to set up shop on the fourth floor of an old wallpaper factory—probably at the site of the parking garage of their current world headquarters—and began manufacturing the world's first sterile surgical dressings.

Each of the brothers had unique strengths: James, an engineer, designed much of the production machinery; Mead (as Edward preferred to be called) had a degree in law as well as talents in sales and promotion; Robert was the "idea man" and entrepreneur and also the one who provided much of the start-up money.

The brothers hired as their principal scientist Fred Kilmer, who was then operating New Brunswick's local drugstore. Kilmer, whose son Joyce was to become the poet of "Trees," had come from the same part of the country as the Johnsons and had even gone to the same school, Wyoming Seminary, in Pennsylvania. One of the Kilmer's customers was Thomas Edison, from nearby Menlo Park. Edison bought carbon for his experiments on incandescent lights from him.

Kilmer was a major force in the company's future. In addition to product development, he wrote manuals promoting sterile techniques. His book *Modern Methods of Antiseptic Wound Surgery* became the definitive work on the subject. Later, his first-aid manual became the standard text on emergency medical response. No doubt it saved the lives of thousands of people whose Good Samaritan lifesavers had received their instruction from it.

Over the years, the company prospered, and by the end of the century, its operations had expanded to fill sixteen buildings, with over four hundred employees. Incidentally, more than two-thirds of them were Hungarian immigrants. New Brunswick could have been called New Hungary, since it had the highest percentage of that ethnic group of any city in the country.

Serving as president from 1887 until his death in 1910, Robert Wood Johnson kept his company under close control, and operated it under a regime as pure as the products it made. He was a large man with immense personal charm, commanding brown eyes, and a thick mustache; he looked rather like a stocky Keenan Wynn. R.W., as he was referred to by his employees, though certainly never to his face, enlisted unswerving loyalty from his workforce.

He expected a lot from his workers and was particularly annoyed by clock watchers. Even today it is hard to find a clock at the company's headquarters. He opened much of the company's mail personally and often wrote letters in his own hand. He had a contagious enthusiasm for product development, and "It's a go!" became a trademark phrase of his when a new product was approved. The phrase resounded through the office frequently, for the company came out with hundreds of new products over the years, including kangaroo tendons used as ligatures for blood vessels, toothache plaster, papoid tablets (for indigestion), and an array of now forgotten cola drinks, which were thought at the time to have medicinal value. There was even a J&J dog soap.

While building his company, Robert also built a family. In 1892, he married Evangeline Armstrong in Mary-ville, Tennessee. It was his second marriage, the first one, which ended in divorce, having been brief. Robert and his new bride had three children, Robert, Evangeline, and Seward. Together with Roberta, R. W.'s daughter by his first wife, they lived in a Victorian mansion called Grey Terrace, close to the factory. A graceful stone wall that once surrounded the mansion is all that remains.

R. W. was a successful investor in the stock market and enjoyed raising orchids as a hobby. The family vacationed in Colorado, where Robert was part owner of a ranch.

Upon his death in 1910, his brother James (affectionately called "Uncle Jimmy" by the employees) took over as president. R. W.'s widow moved to New York City with Seward and Evangeline and enrolled them in private schools, while the eldest son, R. W. Jr., attended a prep school run by Rutgers University, right across the street from company headquarters.

Robert Jr. always had an interest in the company and even as a small child would accompany his father to business meetings. In 1932, he assumed the presidency and stayed in the office except during World War II, when he served as chairman of the Smaller War Plants Board, with the honorary rank of brigadier general. Though he served as chairman only a matter of days, the experience stuck with him, and after his return, he was always referred to as "the General," and he played the role with relish. A fanatic for neatness, he would not let a car onto his driveway because of the risk of oil drips. Anyone whose desk was cluttered or even dusty could be fired on the spot.

Under his leadership, the company developed into an international business and diversified into pharmaceuticals. A complicated individual, he was a family man, but he also established a reputation as a "man about town." Sometimes he flaunted his wealth; other times he was ashamed of it, and asked his chauffeur to let him off down the street from the plant, so his workers wouldn't see him in his Rolls. He spent lavishly on himself, but he gave abundantly to charity and with a billion dollars established the Robert Wood Johnson Foundation, one of the nation's largest, and was a major donor to countless charities. He donated his family home, Morven, to the state, and until recently it served as the New Jersey governor's residence.

When "the General" walked into board meetings with his erect West Point posture, in his briskly starched shirt and never-varying dark blue suit, all the other "suits" in the room reacted with a deference one accords a military commander. All except one, a man in farmer jeans, dusty from that morning's plow, slouching in a chair at the far end of the room. It was his brother Seward.

Officially the company's treasurer, Seward Johnson had little interest in his work and let his employees do pretty much what they wanted. He divided his considerable spare time between philandering, yacht racing, and farming. In his later years, his interest turned to undersea exploration, and he even took on the appearance of an old sea captain. He was married three times, the first time to Kirk Douglas's sister-in-law. His third wife was a beautiful, seductive Polish girl forty-two years his junior, with whom he lived in a home whose splendor rivaled that of William Randolph Hearst's San Simeon. His divorce from wife number two to marry her became a major scandal in its day.

Evangeline, R. W.'s third child, was a politically active art collector and licensed pilot. She was the wife of Leopold Stokowski, the conductor of the New York Philharmonic.

PERHAPS a question has occurred to you: the name "Johnson & Johnson" implies a twosome, but there were *three* Johnson brothers. R. W., as the company's first president, must certainly be one "Johnson," but who was the odd man out? Did James and Mead go to their graves wondering, "That second Johnson: was it *me*—or *him?*" "It is not a mystery why the company was named Johnson &

Johnson," explains Elisabeth S. King, manager of the company's corporate library. Though its product line was R. W.'s idea, the incorporation papers mention only James and Mead. Robert didn't join the brothers until shortly after the company was formed.

Kellogg's

It was on the seventh day of the week and the seventh day of the month when Willie Keith Kellogg (1860–1951) was born. He was the seventh son of a man who had himself been the seventh child in his family. Understandably, W. K. Kellogg (whose family name has seven letters) had a lifelong fetish for the number "7" and always insisted on it for such things as license plates and hotel-room floors.

His church denomination was—you guessed it—Seventh Day Adventist. In fact, it was because of the SDA Church that Willie's parents, John Preston and Ann Janette Kellogg, came to Battle Creek. Its founding prophet, Ellen H. White, and her husband, James, had made Battle Creek its headquarters in 1855. The strict discipline and healthful, vegetarian lifestyle appealed to the elder Kelloggs and had an important influence on W. K. and particularly on his older brother, John.

Willie started his working life in the broom business, first as a delivery boy for his father, later for his brother Albert, and finally in Dallas, where SDA Church cofounder James White had set up a broom factory. In 1879, at age nineteen, already toothless from overwork and malnutrition, Willie returned to Battle Creek to work for his brother John as a self-described flunky.

By that time, John was already a famous man. A skilled surgeon, nutrition expert, charismatic orator, and author of ultimately over fifty books, he had founded a health spa that he called a "sanitarium"—he coined the term—a hugely successful venture that attracted the most prominent of the world's ailing, including dozens of movie stars and European royals, and at least three subjects from this book: Henry Ford, J. C. Penney, and Dr. Scholl.

Not all patients were rich and famous. Some were charity cases, like one who arrived in 1891. Brought in by a lovely and devoted wife, he was a nearly penniless suspender salesman and unsuccessful inventor cursed by recurring nightmares and nearly dead from nervous exhaustion. In exchange for a donation of a few blankets, he was treated for weeks before being discharged as incurable, though actually his life was probably saved by the Kelloggs. More about him later, for excepting members of the family, he was to become the most significant person in the rest of the brothers' lives.

Despite its failure with this mysterious stranger, "the San," as it was called, had an impressive record of cures. Dr. Kellogg's regime included fresh air, vigorous exercise, and a balanced, low-fat diet containing fruits, yogurt, and grains. Decades ahead of his time, he was among the first to note the connection between smoking and cancer.

His phenomenal energy and endurance made John Harvey Kellogg the Richard Simmons of his day, a charismatic figure despite his small stature, which he sought to enhance by mounting his desk on a platform so he could look down on his patients and underlings. In his later years, this most colorful little man ironically took to clothing himself entirely in white—all five feet four inches of him, from shoes and socks up to the starched collar that matched his snow-white hair, goatee, and pet cockatiel. He never dressed in any other kind of clothing, except at home, where he often dashed about in only a loincloth, even in the presence of female help.

W. K.'s appearance and role in this grand enterprise were as humble as his brother's were exalted. His duties were clerical and even janitorial, and for twenty-five years, the workaholic doctor-who-never-slept kept him as a virtual slave. W. K. always called him "doctor," even though John was his *own brother* and only eight years older. W. K. claimed that he even shaved him and shined his shoes and got spanked like a child if his performance was found wanting.

He nevertheless had something of a life of his own, for in 1880, Will, as he called himself now—he'd always hated "Willie"—married Ella Davis, the daughter of a watch repairer. He and "Puss," as he called her, had five children, two of whom, Irvin and W. K. Jr., died in childhood. Will rarely saw his family, since he was "always" at work.

Ella worked also, and in fact was head cook at the San. It was quite a challenge, for in those days health foods were bland, and Will and John were constantly trying to develop a grain-based cereal product that patients would actually eat. One night in 1893, after seventeen fruitless attempts that are curiously reminiscent of Mr. Goodyear's travails with rubber, the brothers accidentally left some grain mash in a tray overnight, and it dried out. They discovered the next morning that they had happened upon the missing step they needed to make a palatable flaked cereal. Over the next few years, the brothers went on to invent over a hundred other food products, including granola and peanut butter.

To Dr. John Kellogg, breakfast cereals were simply a means of delivering health care to his patients. W. K. Kellogg, however, saw cereals as a business opportunity. Others saw it that way, too, and breakfast food soon became a rage among both consumers and entrepreneurs. No fewer than forty-two companies—some imitators, others outright thieves—were making cereal in Battle Creek in the early years of the century. The most prominent of them was the "mysterious stranger" we met earlier, the man whose life the Kelloggs had saved back in '91. He was C. W. Post, who by the early 1900s had already become a millionaire from his Postum and Grape-Nuts.

Charles William Post (1854–1914) came from the Land of Lincoln, and was born just a few blocks from where Honest Abe was then practicing law. His father was in the farm products business, and Charlie was something of an inventor, mainly of agricultural implements, but of other things, too. In 1873, he "invented" the bicycle as we know it—i.e., the kind having two equal-size wheels— only to find later that it had been invented and patented by somebody else two years before.

It was while he was a patient at the San that he first tried breakfast cereals, and he liked them so much that (according to the Kelloggs) he stole their secrets and set himself up in business shortly after his release. Within a few years, Post had built a huge factory, a "company town" for his workers, and even a sanitarium, to compete with the Kelloggs in health care as well as cereals. He believed in the power of advertising and at one time was the nation's largest purchaser of newspaper advertising space.

He called his factory "White City" for its invariably immaculate condition. Its owner was equally immaculate, always nattily attired in starched collars and elegantly tailored suits. There was never a hair out of place on the head of C. W. Post.

He became a Christian Scientist after his release from the San, so now his religion prevented him from seeking the psychiatric treatment that might have helped him deal with the persistent nightmares that deprived him of sleep. His health continued to deteriorate.

One result of his bad health was an urge for ruthless competition. In 1907, when fire destroyed Kellogg's new plant, C. W. tried to buy up all the cereal rollers in existence to corner the market on the equipment Kellogg needed. It was only because Will luckily found some old used rollers that he was able to rebuild.

The victim of such ruthlessness was not inclined even to pretend to like his competitor. The two corporate neighbors, whose properties were contiguous, hardly ever spoke, and so diligent were they in keeping their distance that of the hundreds of photographs taken of them only one includes the images of both men.

C. W.'s private life disgusted Will as much as his over-

Photo courtesy Kellogg Co.

Will Kellogg, about 1930.

the-edge business style. In 1905, the now wealthy Post dumped his wife—the one who had so lovingly carted him on a stretcher to the San to save him—to run off with his cute secretary, Leila Young. Post and his new honey toured Europe, staying in the most luxurious resorts and hotels. But soon Leila tired of her aging husband and found a lover, a hotel manager by the name of Lawrence J. Montgomery, whom she would marry after the despondent Mr. Post finally ended his recurring nightmares by blowing his brains out with a 30-30 Winchester rifle.

Meanwhile, back at the appropriately named Battle Creek, Will and John continued their squabbles. Will had quit the San to start his cornflake company against the near-violent protests of his brother. Out of spite, John established his own company to compete with him. The brothers then fought incessantly over the rights to the Kellogg name. Finally, at a cost of over $200,000 to John, the courts decided in favor of W. K., and Kellogg's cereals display his signature to this day.

W. K. continued to prosper, and the company developed operations overseas. Even the Depression barely affected it, since cereal was still the cheapest breakfast to be had. He built a mansion, modest for his means, next door to the looming San, in whose shadow it sat, much as W. K. had always lived under the shadow of Doctor John.

The Depression was not so kind to the good doctor. He had just built a fourteen-story tower in the ominous year of 1928—an addition of nearly empty rooms, as it turned out, for the San's occupancy fell from 1,500 at its peak to 157 at its closing in 1942. It then became an army hospital, where Bob Dole and the other war-wounded were treated, and is now a federal office building. With much of its original splendid decor still in place, it has to be the poshest setting for federal desks anywhere.

W. K.'s dealings with his children fared little better than those with his brother. He disowned his son John L., called "Len," whom he had made acting president while he toured the Orient. Sales declined during his absence, and he blamed the luckless son. Len also disappointed him by divorcing his wife and running off with Helen, winsome hostess of the company lunchroom.

Disgusted with Len, W. K. turned to his grandson, John L. Jr., whom he meticulously groomed to take over the company after his death. He had great hopes for the competent but intense young man, but John was to disappoint him even more than his father had. One day in 1938, horrified workers found his lifeless body, revolver in hand, slumped over his desk at the Kellogg office in Chicago.

So each in his own way, son and grandson, had followed the example of the hated Mr. Post. After this, the tired old man became more and more withdrawn. Maybe it was for the best, he thought, that his senses were going. During his final ten years, he was totally blind, and he spent most of his time listening to the chamber music of Schumann and Brahms and railing against the decadence of jazz. He socialized little, didn't walk with his children anymore, never laughed, rarely smiled.

Mercifully, in his final days, he was too senile to realize where he was: he died at a hospital endowed by Leila Montgomery, the widow of C. W. Post.

Kimberly-Clark

The story of Kleenex, Kotex, and countless other consumer products made by the Kimberly-Clark company begins with John Alfred Kimberly (1836–1928), who was born in Troy, New York. When Alfred (as he was called) was eleven, the family moved to Wisconsin, where he attended St. Lawrence College in Appleton. With a partner, Alfred bought his father's general store and became prosperous.

Charles Benjamin Clark (1844–1891) was born in the place where he died, Theresa, New York. His father, Luther, died when Charley was nine, and his mother, Theda, moved to Neenah, Wisconsin, where Charley found work in a furniture factory. During the Civil War, he enlisted with the Union Army and accompanied Sherman on his infamous "March to the Sea."

In 1872, Clark and Kimberly, together with two other partners, founded Kimberly, Clark, & Company, initially for the manufacture of paper from rags. From those rags they made riches, and by Kimberly's death in 1928, the company was one of the world's major paper producers.

For their first mill, the boys bought out the furniture factory where Clark had worked. It was there that they developed the two major innovations that accounted for their success: rotogravure paper and creped cellulose wadding.

The rotogravure process made it possible to print photographs onto newsprint. For decades, the pictorial sections of newspapers were printed exclusively on Kimberly-Clark's paper.

Creped cellulose wadding was the material Kimberly & Clark used to make Kotex (packaged at first discreetly in plain brown wrappers). The material also became available in sheets and was marketed as a makeup remover and facial cleaner (hence the name Kleenex). It was only by accident that the company learned that people were using the product as a disposable handkerchief.

In 1878, the partners built their second mill, where they continued developing new products—some minor, such as photo-album paper and "poison flypaper," and some major, such as toilet paper. By this time, they were employing 140 people, but the most substantial growth was yet to come as they bought one building after another in order to make a paper mill.

In the 1880s, Charley Clark, like so many other industrialists of his time, became politically active and served as mayor of Neenah and a representative to Congress. He was defeated for the Senate by a mudslinging opponent by the name of Tom Wall. When Wall later became ill, Clark graciously took his archenemy into his home to recuperate. Clark himself died not long afterward, in 1891, at age forty-seven.

Kroger

Bernard H. Kroger (1860–1938), founder of the largest
grocery-store chain in the United States, was the son
of John Henry Kroger, who emigrated from Hanover,
Germany, in 1827. John Henry literally walked from the
wharf in Baltimore to his eventual home in Covington,
Kentucky, a town which, you may recall, had been laid
out by Gail Borden some twelve years before. In Covington, Mr. Kroger opened a store.

His mother, a stern disciplinarian, didn't allow toys in
the household. To amuse himself, Barney (as young Bernard was called) made a miniature grocery store out of a
cigar box. Store building must have been in the genes of
that family.

Life in Covington wasn't too bad, at least for a frontier
family in those days—until 1873, when the store went
bankrupt and John Henry died. Barney went to Cincinnati
to work in a drugstore, but Mom didn't like him working
on Sundays, so she made him take a job on a farm. He
hated farm labor, partly because he contracted malaria;
just moving about in his room took all the energy he had.
He came crawling home and asked for a job with a coffee
and tea company. He was hired, and did much better than
he'd expected. Then he took a better job with another tea
company, and then another, the Imperial Tea Company.

Imperial wasn't doing well, and the owners offered to
let him run the company for a 10 percent commission;
Barney would have full authority to buy, price, and sell
merchandise.

The store prospered, mostly because of his insistence
on quality merchandise. Housewives learned they could
buy goods from him with confidence. The store made

$3,100 during its first year. Unsatisfied with his 10 percent share for doing all the work, Barney left Imperial and joined with a guy named Branagan to open their own store, at 66 Pearl Street.

The first year, their inventory was wiped out by flood, and their delivery wagon was hit by a train. Other than that, it went well, and the guys came out ahead by $2,600. Barney bought out his partner and became sole owner, but his workload doubled. Day after day, he worked from six A.M. to midnight, and slept in his clothes.

He plowed 90 percent of his profits into the store, and he brought his family into the business. By June 1885, he had four stores, one managed by his mother, another by his brother William.

The family, now prosperous by their own standards, thought it was high time that Barney got married. He did just that (actually more for his own reasons than theirs), to Mary Emily Jansen, from nearby Newport. They eventually had seven children.

The Panic of 1893 came close to wiping him out, but luckily the bank where he had deposited his money weathered the storm, though barely. As many of his competitors went under, his chain expanded to seventeen stores. He was one of Cincinnati's richest men. He and Mary planned a trip to Europe, but she died on the eve of the voyage. A few months later, Ray, his eldest son, died of diphtheria. B. H. (he was B. H. now—nobody called him Barney anymore) became sullen and difficult to live with and work for. He once fired a manager for having dirty windows in his store.

But he kept at his business. Around 1900, he started manufacturing his own products (perhaps the first "store brands"). It started with his mother's pickles and sauerkraut. In 1902, he built a factory to can his products. Kroger was the first grocery chain to bake its own bread and the first to have a meat department.

By World War I, Kroger was a millionaire, and famous. At President Woodrow Wilson's request, he served on the National Food Board and raised money for Liberty Bonds and the Red Cross. B. H. also became noted for small and large acts of charity to employees and acquaintances.

His last great act of charity occurred in 1933, when there was a run on a bank, of which he was chairman of the board. He took his money from the vault, left it on display, and made people file past it as they were withdrawing their accounts. Seeing the money, people were convinced that the bank was still solvent, and they quietly went home.

Barney, too, quietly went home, fortunately sold all his stock shortly prior to the Depression, and spent his final five years occupied mostly with golf, bridge, and generally enjoying life.

Lear

❦

L ear is famous for his LearJet, which few of us have ever flown in, but gained little fame for inventing at least three products that almost all of use every day.

William P. Lear (1902–1978) was born in Hannibal, Missouri, and was perhaps the last of the true "frontier dreamer" entrepreneurs, the kind that in yesteryear used to peddle liver tonic or speculate on railroad land and had to work in absolute freedom. He made notch after notch in his belt, not by shooting buckaroos, but by making one invention, selling it for a fortune, then moving on to the next, throughout his life. And it wasn't until age sixty that he made what he is famous for, his LearJet.

Billy Lear started in business when he figured out how to start people's stalled cars. He made such a good living at it that a garage owner enticed him to quit school and work for him as a mechanic for a full six dollars a week.

His boss didn't have to twist Billy's arm very hard to get him to quit school. Schoolrooms have walls. They have order and discipline. They have rows of desks with paper on them that you're supposed to write on. None of that would do for young Lear. In fact, he quickly outgrew the garage, too, and became an airplane mechanic, at no pay. This boy liked wide-open spaces and took a lifelong interest in radio and airplanes—things that aren't fenced in.

In his first noteworthy venture, he worked in a factory on Long Island that made radios. This may seem ordinary enough, but it happened in the early 1920s, only a few years after Marconi had invented the radio, and Lear's radio, the "Majestic," which he developed, was the world's first mass-produced model for home use.

His next coup was modifying the radio so it could run off a car battery. When you turn on your car radio next time, you may thank Mr. Lear. He invented it and sold it to the company that became Motorola. You also have a tape deck? Thank him for that, too. Eight-track stereo? Yep—also that.

These inventions and 150 others came from a man with a grade-school education, whose natural ability and lifetime accumulation of hands-on experience sometimes overwhelmed the engineers he hired from the finest technical schools. What he lacked in book learning he made up for with sheer determination and effort. He worked seven days a week, and even on Christmas.

He rarely wrote memos or letters, but made decisions on impulse. "Normal" manufacturers submit a design change to a series of reviews; Lear would make a rough sketch of a change he wanted made to, say, a connecting rod, and tell his people, "Make it like this," and the next day all the connecting rods would come out looking that way.

There was a negative side to his one-man-show business style. If somebody took any initiative, Lear quickly put the kibosh on whatever they did, not because there was anything wrong, but because it wasn't his idea. Example: the LTRA-7 combination radio and navigation device. Never heard of it? Of course not. Neither has anyone else. It was invented by his staff, so it never saw the light of day.

Lear had a mean temper. He and his black poodle "Jet" struck terror in the hearts of workers as they wandered through their factory and barked out expletives at people who weren't quite measuring up. Hiring and (especially) keeping competent people became harder and harder. The only ones who stayed long were those who learned to say "Yes, Mr. Lear" in their sleep.

He drove himself as hard as he drove his staff, and he never gave much thought to retirement. "If someone offered me $160 million for my company [its book value at the time] with the provision that I would have to retire, I'd spit in his eye," he told one interviewer. At an age when most men think of retiring, Bill started a new business—making airplanes.

That idea occurred to him when he was in Switzerland. He saw that military aircraft had commercial potential, if they could be made more stylish and comfortable. In 1963, the claustrophobic Lear sold his electronics company in Switzerland, where he felt confined by red tape and mountains and went to the wide-open spaces of Wichita, Kansas. He had invested his entire personal fortune ($11 million at the time) to compete in a crowded field with sophisticated, well-established, multibillion-dollar companies. His version of the story contains the typical Learian can-do rhetoric: "People told me I couldn't build it, and if I built it, it wouldn't fly, and if it flew, I'd never sell it. Well, I could, it did, and I did." The result was the LearJet (one word), the world's first independently financed mass-produced plane. He later designed a larger jet, the twelve-seat LearStar.

In his personal life even more than in his career, Bill Lear didn't like boundaries. After days at the Long Island factory where the Majestic radio was made, he spent evenings womanizing in New York's Stork Club, where he was a regular for years. As headstrong and gruff as he was, he could be a charmer, and all his life, he took pride in his sexual prowess. No doubt this annoyed his wives (there were four of them, the last being Moya Olsen, whose father was Olsen of Olsen & Johnson, the vaudeville team). He and Moya had four children, and there were three others by the previous wives.

He lived in a rather modest home for a man worth $100 million and kept only one servant, though he could afford many. Mrs. Lear did the cooking, and when she was entertaining, the order of service was Mr. Lear first, any other men that might be present second, and women last.

He would never be a passenger in a car. He always had to drive, no matter whose car he was riding in.

He learned to play the organ and bought one for his home. In the closest thing to a hobby he ever had, he became quite good at it, without ever taking a lesson.

Levi's
❧❧❧

L evi's jeans, one of the most familiar and popular consumer products in the world, were named for, and
first manufactured by, Levi Strauss (1829–1902).

Levi (born Loeb) Strauss was born in Buttenheim, Ba-
varia, and was one of two children of Hirsch and Rebecca
Strauss. The other child, a sister named Fanny, was the
most important other person in Levi's life.

By a previous marriage, Hirsch had five other children.
Two of Levi's half brothers (he never called them "half"
brothers), Jonas and Louis, came to America about 1840
and established a dry-goods business in New York. After
Hirsch's death in 1847, Rebecca brought the rest of the
family to join them.

After a while Levi left to pursue his own fortune, peddling his brothers' dry goods in the hills of Kentucky. No
mean feat for a diminutive (five feet six inches) Jew who
knew no one and spoke little English. The Jewish Yankee
peddler, a stranger in a strange land, was an oddity that
few would have seen as ever amounting to anything, but
some of these hoboesque loners—Adam Gimbel, Meyer
Guggenheim, Henry Lehman—and Levi Strauss—became major players in late-nineteenth-century mercantil-
ing.

In 1849, Levi heard that gold had been discovered in
California and went there, not on the fool's errand of prospecting, but on a venture much more likely to succeed—
selling to those who actually found gold. San Francisco
was booming, and dry goods that Louis and Jonas could
produce for dimes in staid old New York could be sold
for dollars in the bustling gold-rich West.

The problem was getting it there. Many ships didn't

make it through the perilous Strait of Magellan, and many a covered wagon or Wells Fargo stage fell prey to Indians, bandits, or nature.

In 1852, Levi and his sister Fanny's husband, David Stern, opened a dry-goods shop on the San Francisco waterfront, and in 1856 moved to larger quarters. Levi continued to peddle goods from his wagon and spent much of his time on the road, leaving David to run the store. Levi and Stern were unusually close business partners. They even lived in the same house and later on added a third partner, David Sahlen. With such a full house, Levi's home life could not have been a quiet one.

A turning point in Levi's life occurred in 1872, when he received a letter from Jacob Youpres, a tailor in Reno, who had come from Latvia and had Americanized his name to Davis, of all things. "Davis" had something of a success making and selling denim pants with reinforcing copper rivets. Far more durable than run-of-the-mill pants, they were selling as fast as he could make them. He was ambitious and thought he could make a fortune if he could just get a patent to protect his innovation, but he couldn't afford one. He approached his fabric suppliers (Strauss and Stern) with an offer: they would secure a patent and manufacture the pants; he would receive a portion of the profits. In 1873, the patent was secured, and the world's first four Levi's "overalls" (as Levi called them) were sold to a shopkeeper named Ferguson in Wadsworth, Nevada, for twelve dollars.

Levi did not build a factory, but paid women to make pants at their homes at a piece rate that allowed them to earn as much as three dollars a day, a generous wage then.

Levi retired, but even in his old age, he never lost touch with his business. Frequently, he came to his store or his factory on Fremont Street, where he schmoozed with his customers and employees. At his request, they called him Levi, in an age when such familiarity seemed unnatural. In a 1977 newspaper interview, 101-year-old Mary Rossi, who had worked for him at age sixteen, described Levi as a fair and kindly man who supported orphanages, old-age homes, and other charities—Catholic, Protestant, and Jewish.

In 1874, Stern died. Fanny, the mother of Stern's seven children, was intent on keeping Levi single so that his business would be left to her sons. She arranged for Levi (perhaps the most eligible bachelor in the Golden West, in spite of his age, girth, and dark, heavy features) a succession of liaisons with married women to keep him amused. The arrangement was fine with Levi, and in his golden years, he enjoyed the life of a bon vivant.

Levi was indeed a lucky man. He had been at the right place at the right time, gotten into the right business, and had the right kind of sister. He also had the good fortune to barely avoid disaster—twice. The first time was in the period of economic depression that began in 1873, with consequent labor unrest that ended up in riots in July 1877. The rioters could have focused their anger on the capitalist barons, or the Jews (either of which would have meant certain death for Levi), but instead they targeted Chinese laborers. Over a period of three days, the rioters slaughtered the Chinese and burned their homes, all the time moving closer and closer to Levi's mansion. But finally, the riot spent itself, very near his doorstep.

The second "near miss" was the San Francisco earthquake. He had the good sense to die shortly before that disaster leveled the huge factory he had built.

Incidentally, Fanny's scheme worked as planned. Levi never married, and upon his death in 1902, the Strauss fortune was inherited by the four Stern sons.

Lionel

❧❧❧

Whereas Levi Strauss gave his first name to his product, Joshua Lionel Cowen (1877–1965) gave his middle name to the company he founded. Asked why, he explained, "Well, I had to name it *something*." That was typical Josh Cowen. He didn't do things the way anyone else did.

Josh was the eighth of nine children born to prosperous Jewish immigrants from New York's Lower East Side. His parents, Hyman and Rebecca, had come from Poland originally but spent several years in London, where they both learned to speak English Cockney style, and Hyman learned the cap maker's trade. They arrived in New York shortly after the Civil War.

The household was "a proper home, a quiet home, a kosher home," as the song from *Fiddler* goes, with "the Papa" a scholar, spending his days making caps and his evenings debating fine points of the Talmud with his friends, and "the Mama" managing the affairs of the home. Rebecca, it is said, spoke Yiddish with a Cockney accent; interesting to imagine how that might have sounded.

When Josh was twelve, the family moved to 104th Street and sent him to the Peter Cooper Institute, but he preferred to play hooky and tinker, especially with electrical things. In his teens, he made his first invention: the electric doorbell—at least he *claimed* that he invented it. Actually, the doorbell was "invented" independently by a number of people. Joshua made quite a few questionable claims in his life, as we shall see.

Despite his less-than-perfect school record, he got into college, but he was a fitful student there as well, staying only briefly at Columbia and at what is now the City University of New York. He preferred tinkering and went to work for the Acme Lamp Company, where they let him do just that. It was there, he claims, that he invented the dry-cell battery, the kind we use in flashlights. It was a ridiculous claim, but he himself may have believed it. Perhaps he did "invent" it, though independently, not knowing it had existed for years.

He also claimed that he invented the flashlight—and actually that claim may be half-true.

He invented what he called a "flash lamp," but it was a device used to ignite the flash powder that photographers used as a light source. It consisted of a cylinder with two of his dry cells in it and a wire that went through a switch to a heating element embedded in the flash powder. Later, a man named Hubert placed an incandescent light at the end of the cylinder and capped it with a glass lens. Instead of flashing, the device now threw out a steady beam, but it was called a "flashlight" in reference to its origins. Hubert began producing them, and the company he founded later became Eveready.

The navy became interested in Cowen's flash-lamp idea as a means of setting off mines. He sold it to them— he says, but who knows?—for $12,000.

On September 5, 1900, he entered into a partnership with a coworker from Acme and rented manufacturing space on the third floor of 24 Murray Street, a building that now houses a rifle range in its basement but is otherwise vacant.

They both liked to tinker and "invent" but really hadn't any idea what they were going to make in the new space they'd rented. They started off making electric fans (another Josh Cowen "invention") but abandoned that venture, when, after two cool summers, nobody bought any.

What to invent next? Cowen somehow hit upon the idea of making active shop-window displays. He devised his first display in 1900 and sold it to a Mr. Ingersoll for four dollars. It consisted of a little open-top box mounted on wheels that were driven by an electric motor that he had salvaged from one of his unsold fans. The cart rode around a track that was wired to two batteries. When Ingersoll saw that it attracted crowds, he bought six more. When a company from Providence ordered twenty-five, Cowen knew he was onto something, and in March 1902, he incorporated his business and went into mass production.

Noticing that some people were buying his displays to use as toys, he decided they might have more appeal if he used the bodies of windup toy trolleys instead of box-like carts. He bought a few of the trolleys and sold the sets—trolley, batteries, and thirty feet of track—for seven dollars apiece. In 1903, inspired by the trains that the Baltimore & Ohio Railroad was using, he made his first true model train. After that, in the words of his biographer Ron Hollander, "boyhood and Christmas would never be the same."

Through the years, Cowen added many locomotives and dozens of kinds of cars, as well as accessories like bridges, tunnels, and signals. And there were technical improvements—transformers with rheostats that allowed variable speed, track that came in sections to allow assembly into many different layouts; there were stations with trainmen moving like figures in a Bavarian town clock; there came smoke pellets, headlights, and literally, bells and whistles. Business boomed as interest in model railroads paralleled the public's fascination with real trains. Even the modest fortune that Cowen made seemed to be an authentic miniature of the Vanderbilt billions. By 1920, Lionel was employing seven hundred workers and turning out hundreds of thousands of train sets a year.

And millions of catalogs. Every day in late fall, thousands of boys rushed home from school hoping the Lionel catalog had arrived. At one time, they were exceeded in volume only by those of Montgomery Ward and Sears & Roebuck. Like Richard Sears, Cowen knew how to write "ad copy" to appeal to his audience. He cleverly perceived that fathers bought trains as much for themselves as for their sons, so he aimed his spiels at dads—without being too obvious about it. He used the smiling face of the "Lionel boy" on the train boxes to convey the joy the buyer's son could feel when he played with his trains.

The boy pictured was never identified to the consumer, but it was Cowen's son, Lawrence. Larry was one of the two children (the other, Isabel) born to Josh and his wife, Cecelia Liberman, an office clerk, whom he married after a two-year courtship. They met, appropriately, on a train— the Manhattan Trolley.

Larry actually had little interest in playing with trains. In fact, he felt little closeness to his father; only one picture from the family's hundreds shows the two together in Larry's teen years. His fascination was with Wall Street, where he became an orders clerk on the exchange floor. He married a wealthy woman named Clarisse Bernard and moved into the posh Marguery Hotel on Park Avenue. Finally, resigned to Lawrence's interest in the stock market, Joshua bought him a seat on the stock exchange, for $585,000, the most ever paid up to that time. It couldn't have been at a worse moment. The year was 1929.

The Great Depression not only devastated his son's career; it nearly ruined his own. Developed in the late-twenties euphoria that nearly everybody thought would never end, the 1929 Lionel catalog showed the most elaborate train sets ever (costing up to $110), and most of the trains had already been made and sent to stores. The Depression also really did a job on Joshua's personal fortune, since he was heavily invested in stocks. As if that weren't enough, he became involved in a banking scandal, in which he lost hundreds of thousands and almost went to jail, even though he was clearly a victim of manipulation and deceit at the hands of his nephew.

This may have been a time when he thought he could never recover, but as quickly as he had fallen, he rose again. During World War II, the company did a lot of defense-related business; then, after the war, with the baby boom, sales of the toy trains soared. Happy days were here again, and Joshua lived the high life, with his chauffeur-driven Rolls, extended European vacations, and leisurely winters in Palm Springs. Cowen celebrated his company's golden anniversary in the fall of 1950 at the peak of this prosperity.

At this stage in his life, J. Lionel Cowen was a distinguished-looking man, in spite of his diminutive (five foot five inch) stature. He was an object of adulation. The halolike ring of gray hair that framed his cherubic face made him look like the angel that he for the most part was. He was indeed loved and admired by his employees as few corporate leaders of his day were, for his personal generosity and for the interest he took in their lives. He gave abundantly to charities, and was a major endower of Beth Israel Hospital. At the golden anniversary ceremonies, he was feted with plaques, toasts and speeches, and applause. Fortunately, he had no inkling of how suddenly and overwhelmingly fate would turn on him once again. His fortunes in his final fifteen years would descend more steeply than they had risen the previous ten.

During the fifties, toy trains simply went out of fashion. Train layouts sat idle in the rec room while their owners sat idle in front of the TV. Kids now went to airports to watch the planes take off instead of to the depot to watch the trains come in. Sputnik, hot rods, soccer— the whole culture had changed, and model trains were no longer "cool." The world turns, and not even Joshua, at least this Joshua, could make the sun stand still.

Maybe he should take some of the blame. For one thing, he never made a serious attempt to appeal to girls— half the children's market—in his advertising, and during both wars, Lionel made some toys that were shockingly violent for the times. He made desperate, even crazy moves to stay afloat—ventures like fishing reels and outboard motors, product lines about which he knew nothing.

But the company's most pathetic attempt was making pastel-pink-and-lavender trains that they thought would appeal to girls. What were they *thinking*?

Son Lawrence attempted a rescue but to no avail. In desperation, Cowen finally sold out to his grandnephew, Roy Cohn—the same Roy Cohn who had served as Senator Joe McCarthy's counsel during the Army-McCarthy hearings. Cohn became CEO, and the shocked and disheartened Lawrence quickly resigned and became president of Schick razor company. His daughter, Isabel, stayed with Lionel as treasurer for a while, but not long.

Cowen continued to live seven more years in comfort but disgrace, and was buried in a lonely grave in Brooklyn beside his first wife, Cecelia. The tombstone reads JOSHUA L. COWEN, BELOVED HUSBAND AND FATHER, DEPARTED SEPT. 8, 1965. No mention of Lionel trains, or of what the man had done to enrich the lives of America's youth. The minutes of the next meeting of Lionel's board of directors does not even mention the founder's death.

Mary Kay

ᴹary Kay Ash (1918–), the current grande dame of cosmetics, was the daughter of innkeepers in Hot Wells, Texas, near Houston. Born Mary Kathlyn Wagner, Hot Wells's most famous daughter showed superior talents and drive early on. She earned straight A's throughout school and graduated from high school in three years.

Texas during the Depression was a tough place to scrape out a living, which she had to do to support her father, who was suffering from tuberculosis. College was out of the question, and there were no jobs, even for someone with her abilities. She needed a man, and in 1930, she married one—a musician named Ben Rogers. Within three years, there were three little Rogerses: Ben Jr., Marylyn, and Richard.

Then life turned sour. Returning from the war, husband Ben promptly divorced her. And it got worse. She took a second husband, George Hallenbeck, a businessman from Dallas. He died of a heart attack at their breakfast table. Then she married another businessman, Mel Ash. He also died. Mary Kay has not had an easy life.

But it has been a phenomenally successful one. She knew she had a knack for sales, and took sales positions with Stanley Home Products and the World Gift Company. Passed over for promotion at World Gift because she was "thinking female" too much, she got the idea—judged absurd at the time—of forming her own company. She discovered a potential market in skin creams, but her most important innovation was her sales approach. She used the house-party sales method pioneered by Tupperware to reach customers on a person-to-person level.

Skeptics laughed, but from 1963 to 1978, Mary Kay's

company grew at an average *annual* rate of a phenomenal 28 percent. Fleets of trucks, painted with the flaming Mary Kay pink that must have embarrassed their drivers to a similar shade, rolled first throughout the South, later throughout the country.

In 1976, Mary Kay Cosmetics became the first company headed by a woman to be listed on the New York Stock Exchange. It was a proud moment for female American entrepreneurdom, but guys, there's room for us. Of Mary Kay's 145,000 salespeople, 2,000 are male.

Maytag

Frederick Louis Maytag (1857–1937), the oldest of ten children of German immigrants, was born near Elgin, Illinois, but the family moved to Iowa when he was ten. In 1893, with two brothers-in-law, he invented and began to manufacture a mechanical feeding device for threshing machines. These feeders made the machines safer and improved their efficiency, and sales were robust. However, the equipment was breaking down, and Maytag recruited a mechanical genius named Howard Snyder (the first "Maytag repairman"?) to service the machines. By 1902, Frederick, his in-laws, and repairman Snyder were doing a roaring business.

But farm machinery is a seasonal affair. To keep their workers occupied in the winter, Maytag had to diversify. Like three thousand others in the period between 1900 and 1910, he tried the car business. His attempt was the Maytag-Mason car, capable of climbing an unheard-of 50 percent grade with eight passengers in it. As successful as it was, it was produced for only two years. The car is now forgotten, although the name of two of the engineers Maytag hired—Fred and Al Duesenberg—became famous in automobile lore.

A more lasting off-season sideline was the washing machine. The first model, a hand-cranked device that looked like a barrel mounted on table legs, was seen as a real labor-saving device by the housewife accustomed to using a washboard. Called the "Pastime," it was the first of a number of curiously named products. The "Hired Girl" (a name that marketing types of the 2000s would probably not consider) was the Pastime's successor. It could be operated from any source of mechanical power,

Frederick Maytag made cars with the Deusenbergs before trying his hand at washing machines.

and was truly "laborsaving," even in the modern sense of the term. This was followed by an electric-powered and a gasoline-powered model, the "Multi-Motor." The housewife of 1915, seeing her clothes mechanically agitated in a machine, must have felt almost (but not quite) guilty for having such a laborsaving device in her house.

By 1920, the washing machine was so successful that the firm abandoned farm machinery altogether. The next year, Louis, one of Frederick's two sons, assumed control, and produced the next curiously named model—the "Gray Ghost."

The Depression, which decimated almost everyone else, left Maytag's company nearly unscathed. In the early thirties, Maytag introduced appliances made with porcelain enamel, and the term "white goods" (now applied to all appliances) originated from this first use of porcelain.

Frederick's two sons, Elmer and Lewis, succeeded him in the business, but barely succeeded him in life. Both died in 1940, outliving their father by only three years. Elmer's son Fred took control of the company in 1940, and guided it through the war years and the Korean conflict, producing applications his grandfather would never have dreamed of: Maytag was a major supplier of aluminum castings for bombers and "track pins" (whatever they are) for tanks.

Fred Maytag, grandson of Frederick the Iowa farm boy/inventor, died in 1962, and sadly control of the company then passed out of Maytag family hands.

McCormick

Willoughby Madden McCormick (1864–1932), the giant name in spices, was born in Dover, Virginia. At age fourteen, he moved in with relatives in Texas. They put him to work in a general store, and somehow he emerged from that experience with a lifelong interest in manufacturing foods and drugs. When he was twenty-four, he went to Baltimore, because it was a major distribution hub for food and other products. In a facility consisting of a basement, a single upstairs room, and a storage shed, he set up shop as a wholesaler. Working with two women as office help, he hit the pavement each day to sell merchants his various wares—fruit juices, root beer, insecticides, and medicines such as "Uncle Sam's Nerve and Bone Liniment" ("for man or beast").

He got into the spice game when he bought out the F. G. Emmett Spice Company in 1896, moved its machinery to Baltimore, and began grinding spices that he imported from all over the world.

The business expanded so rapidly that he moved to progressively larger quarters seven times in twelve years. But in 1894, the great Baltimore fire decimated much of the city, including McCormick's plant and his records. But it was even worse than it seemed. McCormick could not pick up the pieces and start over, because there *were* no "pieces." He had supplied his merchandise to his customers, who then repackaged it under their own labels. After ten years of accumulating "brand recognition," he could have started again from the place where he left off, but his company had no such recognition. He had learned his lesson. Now he would market his wares under his own brand, Bee Brands. (He was always impressed with the bee as a symbol of energy and industry.)

He rebuilt, this time in his own five-story building. Soon the company was again prospering.

In 1912, Willoughby began grooming two of his nephews to succeed him. Hugh was an expert in spices, but it was Charles who took over after his uncle's death in 1932, even though he had been fired seven times over the years by the company's irascible founder.

Charles introduced a new management style to the company, "multiple management," which it has retained ever since. McCormick's thinks employee morale is important, and it was twice featured in *The Best 100 Firms to Work for in America*.

Charles retired in 1962 and was succeeded by his son, Charles Jr., who remains as CEO.

McDonald's
❦

Richard and Maurice McDonald were born in New Hampshire in the early 1910s. Their father, a shoe factory foreman, lost his job in the Depression. Optimistic or desperate, or both, Dick and Mac (as they were called) went to Hollywood in the early thirties to seek their fortune in showbiz, the only business other than funeral parlors and breweries that seemed to be doing well in those days. They ended up moving scenery on stage sets of Ben Turpin movies.

Their next showbiz venture was a movie theater they opened in Glenview, but it closed after a few years.

Destitute, their hopes for fame dashed, feeling their name would be forever forgotten, they opened a tiny drive-in just east of Pasadena in 1937, which they called "McDonald's." It was actually a hotdog stand, but it was successful enough to give the brothers the capital they needed to set up a larger fast-food restaurant in 1940: "McDonald's Hamburgers." It was a queer-looking, octagonal-shaped thing at the corner of Fourteenth and E streets in San Bernardino, but this, the first "true" McDonald's, drew hour-long lines, making the term "fast food" seem absurd, and making the brothers wealthy beyond what they had ever imagined.

The success of the McDonald's venture attracted the attention of shrewder minds. Among them was Ray Kroc, then a lowly vendor of malted-milkshake machines. He wondered what possible use the McDonald brothers could have for *ten* of his machines. It wasn't until he visited the McDonald's stand with its hour-long lines that he realized that the place was a gold mine.

It was like a factory—an assembly line, with ham-

Dick McDonald (pen in hand) and his brother, Mac, (seated) show off a restaurant design to friend Ira Rowe.

burgers and "fixin's" assembled as if they were miniature engine blocks mounted onto a chassis, then wheels attached. McDonald's had become the Ford of food, except they were selling billions instead of millions.

The McDonald brothers never knew the potential of their venture—or maybe they did and just didn't care. Children of the Depression, they were glad to be surviving, let alone prospering, so they willingly sold for as little as $1,000 their processes and the rights to the McDonald's trademark to a number of people who wanted to capitalize on their idea.

It is a myth that the McBrothers were simple hicks who didn't know what they were doing. They were true innovators: preparing burgers for immediate consumption so that people wouldn't have to wait for their meals was a truly new concept, and it was theirs. McDonald's focus on its youngest customers was important to its success, and this also originated with the brothers, although Ronald

McDonald and his Happy Meals came later. Even the "golden arches" was their idea—an embellishment they insisted on over the objections of their architect.

It is also a myth that the McDonald brothers never lived to reap the fruits of their labors. True, they did not become *filthy* rich, as Ray Kroc did, but they amassed wealth beyond what they had ever imagined. They shared a twenty-room mansion that they bought for $90,000 (not too shabby for the 1950s) and drove Cadillacs—new ones every year. Their greatest problem, according to Dick: "We just became bored. The money was coming in, and there wasn't much for us to do." When they sold out in 1961, they spent most of their time watching boxing on TV and dining out at California's most expensive restaurants—presumably not being served by a waiter who asked, "Do you want fries with that?"

Merrill, Lynch, Pierce, Fenner & Smith
❦

U ntil recently, the brokerage firm Merrill Lynch, sometimes even shortened to "Merrill," went by a name that honored five of its onetime principals. The first, the real founder of the firm, was Charles Merrill (1885–1956). He was one of three children, and the only son, of Charles and Olivia Merrill. His dad was a doctor who also ran a pharmacy near Jacksonville, Florida. Charlie went away to Amherst, Massachusetts, to attend college but had to drop out because of money problems. He returned to Florida, where he became a reporter for the *West Palm Beach Tropical Sun*. An athletic young man, he later played semipro baseball in Mississippi.

In 1907 he moved to New York, where he became engaged, and took a job as office boy in his fiancée's father's textile company. In his free time, he liked to play basketball at the Twenty-third Street YMCA. The ball court, unaltered since Merrill's time, is still in routine use by Y members, some of whom are stockbrokers, who have no idea they are treading on hallowed ground: it was on that court in 1907 that Charlie Merrill met a drugstore-equipment salesman named Eddie Lynch.

Edmund Calvert Lynch (1885–1938) was raised in Baltimore and graduated from Johns Hopkins University in 1907. He went to Chicago, where he took a job with Liquid Carbonic, and soon moved to New York to peddle his wares—gases for soda fountains.

Merrill and Lynch, who lived together briefly, opened a stockbrokerage office at 7 Wall Street in 1914, and the nature of the business would never be the same. Stocks in those days were almost exclusively a rich man's game. Merrill was the first to see the potential of attracting small, middle-class investors. From his experience in financing grocery- and department-store chains came the idea of a "chain," so to speak, of brokerage offices, at which small investors would be welcome to set up accounts. It's the standard way of all brokerages now, but at the time it was revolutionary.

Merrill Lynch became prosperous, but it was during the Depression that the firm was set apart from the competition. Merrill was the only major broker who saw the crash of 1929 coming. He converted the company's stocks to safe investments and encouraged his clients to do the same. This move greatly enhanced Merrill's stature and kept his firm's head above water, but the public was soured on stocks, and the 1930s saw a horrendous decline in business. The only solution seemed to be to combine with some other brokerage that had survived. The logical choice was Merrill Lynch's chief rival—E. A. Pierce & Company, headed by Eddie Pierce.

Edward Allen Pierce was born August 31, 1874, and was to live for the next hundred years and 107 days. He was from Maine and, perhaps in mockery of his accent, was referred to by his initials, pronounced ee-AP. This young Bowdoin graduate and onetime lumberman started out in the brokerage business in the firm of A. A. Houseman, where he worked with Bernard Baruch and Bernard's brother, who had the intriguing name Sailing Baruch. E. A. eventually took over the firm, which he named E. A. Pierce, and by 1940 it had become the largest brokerage house in the country when it merged with Merrill Lynch. Ee-Ap came to work daily even into his mid-nineties, despite being a heavy cigarette smoker. He never sat down at his desk, preferring to stand while he worked.

Despite the volume of business they were doing, the firm was losing money. In 1941, only a year after taking on Pierce, they merged again, this time with the largest commodities trader in the country. One principal in the firm was Charlie Fenner.

Charles Erasmus Fenner (1876–1963) was born in Guatemala City, where his father, Dr. Darwin Fenner, had retired to nurse Civil War injuries. Charles went to Tulane and became a lawyer, but the law failed to hold his interest for long, and he moved to Florida to grow pineapples. Failing in that venture, he got into cotton futures trading with one Alpheus C. Beane.

The twice-merged firm became known as Merrill, Lynch, Pierce, Fenner & Beane, until 1951, when Smith replaced Beane in the lineup to honor the man who was most responsible for effecting all these mergers—Win Smith.

Winthrop Hiram Smith (1893–1961) from South Hadley Falls, Massachusetts, followed Charlie Merrill to Amherst, where he was an English major. He came to Merrill Lynch after a brief flirtation with investment banking in Boston.

These five men, and other partners whose now forgotten names were once etched on the firm's shingle, continued the revolution that Charlie Merrill started—to make stocks available and attractive to the masses. They published a biweekly newsletter. They were the first brokerage to release an annual report, displaying the company's finances. This was an especially nervy thing to do when the firm had to bare a negative earnings sheet.

They also changed the way brokerages did business. In 1945, they recruited and trained young brokers, army vets fresh back from the war, who were likely to be more innovative and aggressive than the stodgy *Bleak House* types (average age, fifty-two) who sat behind the firm's desks at that time.

They streamlined the stock sale process. It cost fourteen dollars in 1940 to process a trade, and the company charged only ten dollars in commission. That had to change. They also moved to cheaper offices, at 70 Pine Street.

To make it seem easy and fun to invest, the company bought and equipped a fleet of buses that served as mobile offices. The buses parked in shopping centers and train-station lots, and sold stocks from the bus the way Good Humor bars are sold from a truck.

But the partners, the "Ben & Jerry" of securities, also wished to project an image of steadiness and responsibility and became earnest promoters of securities reform. They advocated the creation of what became the Securities and Exchange Commission and successfully pushed for reform of the New York Stock Exchange structure.

Also, they succeeded in winning brokerage houses the right to incorporate, and thus sell shares of stock in themselves. Today every brokerage, even Goldman Sachs, the last holdout, is publicly traded.

Much has been made of "Good Time Charlie" Merrill's unbrokerlike private life. Say what you will about the flamboyant, thrice-married, ever-philandering, good-time Charlie; he was also a generous and charitable man. By 1981, the Merrill Trust had distributed over $113 million to a wide variety of needy causes. Fenner also was a major benefactor, favoring medical research and blindness prevention.

Incidentally, Merrill was a founder of *Family Circle* magazine.

Milton Bradley

M ilton Bradley (1836–1911), founder of the game company that bears his name, left much more than games as a legacy. He was a founding father of the kindergarten movement in America, an important contributor to modern pedagogy, a manufacturer of school supplies, an inventor of some things that may surprise you, and a player in the development of animation.

He was the son of Lewis and Fannie Bradley of Vienna, Maine. Lewis ran a mill that produced potato flour. The mill, the first of its kind in the state, laid the foundation for Maine's potato industry.

Milton graduated from high school in Lowell, Massachusetts, in 1854. He had a talent for drafting, and went to work for a patent solicitor in Lowell. His job was to prepare drawings for inventors who were applying for patents. This ambitious young man also printed stationery on the side and attended school evenings at Lawrence Scientific School in Cambridge. At age twenty, he came to Springfield, Massachusetts, where he worked as a draftsman for a company called Wason that made railroad cars. He was laid off in the financial panic of 1857, but the company's financial health returned two years later, when, in an event that stunned Springfield, the khedive of Egypt placed an order with Wason for $300,000 worth of rolling stock, including a $10,000 private railroad car for his own use. Mohammed Sa'îd—that was the khedive's name— was as cruel and rapacious a leader to his people as he was physically loathsome, but he was an important figure in modern Egyptian history. It was he who granted Ferdinand de Lesseps the license to construct the Suez Canal, and he also founded the Bank of Egypt and was instrumental in giving his country a sound financial system. Nevertheless, his name lives in infamy for the corruption of his regime and the transformation of his people into virtual slaves in order to support his sumptuous and polygamous lifestyle.

How the repugnant Sa'îd came to choose—or even learn of the existence of—the obscure New England company is a mystery, but Milton, called back from the unemployment rolls by the unexpected news, designed what the khedive wanted, the world's most extravagant railroad car, built entirely of mahogany and rosewood, with an observation deck and opulent, ornately appointed sitting rooms for the enjoyment of himself and his numerous wives and concubines.

From this project, Milton earned more money than he'd ever dreamed he would have; and he spent every cent wisely. Much of it he used to pursue his interest in lithography, a process by which images are etched into a stone surface, inked, and printed onto paper. He went to Providence, Rhode Island, where he became one of the few to master the craft, and bought a printing press, which he brought back to Springfield the following year. In May 1860, with an almost unique talent in this challenging and unforgiving trade, he hung a shingle at 247 Main Street:

MILTON BRADLEY COMPANY
Publishers
Lithographers

That event signaled the birthplace and birth date of the Milton Bradley Company.

He spent the rest of the money from the railroad-car job equally wisely: to buy an engagement ring for his sweetheart, Vilona Eaton, his landlady's sister, whom he married on his twenty-fourth birthday, November 8 of the same year.

With the outbreak of the Civil War, business declined, and Milton took a job with the Springfield Armory, where his drafting talents were badly needed for the gun trade. The Armory dissuaded him from volunteering for Civil War service, and wanting to do something, he came up with a card game to relieve the soldiers' boredom. It was during the war that he saw a potential for saving his lithography business by creating games. The first of these he called "The Checkered Game of Life." Game pieces were moved around a board, paced by the roll of dice. This idea was the seed of "Monopoly," "Sorry," "Chutes & Ladders," and hundreds of other lesser-known parlor games.

His second important invention he called the "Wheel of Life." It was a wheel that had a series of slits through which the viewer could see pictures. When it was spun, the succession of pictures through the slits gave the views an illusion of movement. This invention, later called a Zeotrope, arguably laid the foundation for animated films. While Bradley's status as the "father of animation" may be questioned, he was certainly a figure in its development.

Bradley also popularized croquet. Though in existence in Europe for centuries, he made some charges to it, established standard rules (little changed since), promoted the game in the U.S., and sold sets for as much as twenty-seven dollars apiece.

As he entered his thirties, Bradley grew increasingly interested in education, and he became a major force in the kindergarten movement. Robert Owen, Friedrich Froebel, and Maria Montessori founded the first ones in Europe and called them "kindergartens" because they would be places where, in an atmosphere of "sunshine," the children would grow freely, like plants in a garden. In 1860, the missionary-to-America of the movement, Elizabeth Peabody, founded the first U.S. kindergarten in Boston. Peabody, who, incidentally, was sister-in-law to both Nathaniel Hawthorne and Horace Mann, was a mesmerizing speaker, and a leader in the Transcendental movement. She held Milton in thrall, for she had just the message he

Milton Bradley.
His role in public education was
even more important than his
career in parlor.

wanted to hear: learning should be fun. Hardly anyone disputes that nowadays, but it was a radical notion to educators in the fun-hating 1860s, when schools were more likely to resemble those found in *David Copperfield* and *Jane Eyre*.

It wasn't just the educational establishment that held Bradley up to ridicule. Even—and maybe especially—his cohorts in his own company started wondering about him, since he was driving the company to become principally a maker of school supplies, a far less profitable product line than toys. He became interested in color, that potent stimulant of childhood curiosity, and spent hours in a tiny room, pausing only for baked-bean sandwiches (his favorite lunch), mixing paint pigments to develop standard, reproducible hues. The watercolors we used as kids in art class were based on these standardized colors. He pioneered in crayons, too. Though he did not "invent" them, the manufacture of MB crayons started in 1898, five years before the eventual leader in the product, Binney and Smith, started making its Crayola crayons.

By the time Bradley retired in 1907, the company was already making hundreds of school supplies, including furniture—desks, chairs, even cafeteria tables.

Bradley also had his own ideas about how children should be taught. He promoted reading by phonics. And among the educational ideas that he may have originated were flash cards.

In 1869, he published *Paradise of Childhood,* the first

book in English that prescribed a program for kindergartens; later, he wrote guidance books for teachers in one-room schools and, with Daniel Beard Wesson (whom we will meet later—he was the Wesson of Smith & Wesson) tried to found an industrial school for boys in Springfield.

But his first love remained kindergarten. He saw the movement grow from fewer than two hundred programs in 1878 to over three thousand by the turn of the century, partly as a result of his promotion of the idea.

Two beneficiaries of the kindergarten experience were Milton's daughters, Florence (born 1874), and Lillian Alice (born 1881). Their mother, Ellen "Nellie" Thayer, was a woman he'd met through a mutual friend, George Tapley, after Vilona's tragic early death in 1867. Milton retired in 1907, to be succeeded by this same George Tapley, and he divided his time between Springfield, where he enjoyed puttering about in his Stanley Steamer, and Casco Bay, Maine, where he had a summer cottage and took to sailing. And painting: one day he picked up a watercolor set, one of the thousands that he had made for schoolkids over the years, tried his hand at it, and actually became a watercolorist, producing some pictures not at all bad for an amateur.

A final bit of trivia you may want to share with your friends at the office: he invented the paper cutter.

Monsanto

❦

Olga Mendez Monsanto (ca. 1870–1938) must have had difficulty fitting into the social life of Hoboken, New Jersey, in the 1890s. She was decidedly not your typical Hobokenite. Her father, Maurice, was the son of Don Emmanual Mendez de Monsanto, who was not only a Spanish nobleman but also a "prince of Denmark," having been knighted by King Frederick VII of that country. Olga's mother was Emma Cleaves, whose father had been a secretary to England's King George IV.

The Monsanto family had left their native Spain to pursue Maurice's interests in the Caribbean—first on the sugar plantations of Vieques, then on St. Thomas. In 1878, the family came to America and settled in New York, then moved to Hoboken. The behavior of these Monsantos, with their royal lineages and courtly upbringing, must have been interesting to observe as they mingled and moved among the folk of Hoboken.

One of these folk was a young Irish lad named John F. Queeny (1859–1933). Queeny was the eldest of five children, whose parents (John and Sarah) were children of Irish-potato-famine émigrés who came here by the thousands in the 1840s and 1850s. Young John, with only a sixth-grade education, could not hope for better than menial work, so he took a job as a delivery boy for a local drugstore. He started wooing Olga, and in 1897 the two were married. What her parents thought of the match is lost to history, but any misgivings they may have had were belied by a subsequent history of continuing success. Soon he became a sales manager for Merck & Company in New York.

The following year, the couple moved to St. Louis,

where John worked for a company called Meyer Brothers to raise capital for his own business venture, because he knew this was the only way he could "make it" in America. In 1901, with $1,500 of his own savings and a loan for $3,500 more, he founded a chemical company, of sorts. Its principal product was saccharin, up to then obtainable only by import from Germany.

Perhaps thinking the name "Queeny" sounded a bit prissy for a chemical company, he chose instead the rugged, broad-shouldered name "Monsanto," with its suggestions of mountains and holiness, to give the firm an appropriate gravitas. Unfortunately, the name alone was not enough to overcome the great hardship and risk that characterized its early years. Soon, though, they prospered, and the economics of sugar were favorable to saccharin, so prospects looked good. In only two years, he had built up enough capital to erect a plant in East St. Louis for making his own sulfur. But on the first day of its operation—with no insurance—the plant burned to the ground. Olga had planned to entertain guests that evening, and in an episode that says much about Queeny's character, he didn't even mention the disaster to her until the next morning.

The company continued to grow despite setbacks such as these. They diversified into caffeine, vanilla extract, and aspirin, but their major success came during World War I, when Monsanto scientists discovered the way to make basic chemical feedstocks, such as phenols and coal-tar products.

Although Olga was never directly involved in the Monsanto Company, she was supportive of her husband's work, had a leavening influence on him, and bore him a son, Edgar, who really made the company a household name.

Olga died in 1938, while visiting her daughter Olguita in England. A company historian declared that her life "was so closely interwoven with the lives of her husband and family that some future commentator or historian is in danger of giving credit to those around her when rightfully, the rewards should be shared."

Mrs. Fields
❦

Debra J. Fields (1957–), the cookie baker, was the youngest of the four daughters in the Sivyer family in Oakland, California. Her dad was a welder.

Debbi started her work life as an elf for a department store Santa. Later, she became a "ball girl" for the Oakland A's and got to go with her team to the World Series in 1972 and 1973. She later worked with dolphins at California Sea World.

It wasn't until 1976 that the nineteen-year-old Debbi Sivyer became Mrs. Fields, when she married Randy, whom she describes as a "mop-headed intellectual from Stanford." They met while waiting for flights at the Denver Airport.

The working-class Sivyers and the more comfortably positioned Fields family were a bit uneasy with each other at first, but the relationship warmed. The marriage has been happy, though sometimes strained by the stresses of two quite different careers. But Randy's talents and temperament have complemented Debbi's nicely. Both business and family have flourished: they have three girls—Jessica, Janessa, and Jennifer, now in their late teens.

Randy was a "futurist economist"—not a *glamorous* thing to be, certainly, but at least intriguing and respectable. He carried with him articles that had been written about him in *Time* and *Newsweek*. Debbi felt ashamed and apologetic when his friends asked her what *she* did, and she had to "admit" to being a housewife. Homemaking, the world's most important occupation, should certainly not have been a source of shame, but it is to many women, even those who are good at it. Debbi felt she needed a career that would make her Randy's social equal.

She addressed her self-esteem "problem" in a curious and ironic way: by going into the cookie business. Baking cookies—that most housewifely of pursuits—was the activity that would elevate Mrs. Fields from her humdrum life and make her a star of American commerce.

In pursuing her dream, she received financing from Ed Sullivan—no, not *the* Ed Sullivan, but a Bank of America loan officer with the same name—and against the advice of everyone, opened a shop to bake and peddle her wares. It was on August 18, 1977 (coincidentally, the day of Elvis Presley's funeral) that Mrs. Fields opened the first of her five hundred retail outlets, in what she termed "a rather dark and forbidding corner, between a deli and a sort of Tibetan store" in Palo Alto.

Photo courtesy Mrs. Fields.

Mrs. Fields at the oven. She has proved to be "one smart cookie."

An immediate success it was not: as of noon on her opening day, she had sold not one cookie. Our desperate and dispirited entrepreneur took her bakings out to the street and tried giving them away. Not even that worked. Some people were actually refusing free cookies.

But those who did take the samples came back, and her product soon caught on. So much so that at store number two (in San Francisco) other merchants were complaining that her long lines were disrupting their business. Free samples had done the trick. They became a hallmark and even today are an important part of her marketing plan.

As of 1987, Mrs. Fields had over five hundred retail outlets, including one in Tokyo. No one would have predicted her success. She broke every rule: she went into business with no training or experience; she never advertised; she gave away her product; she ignored market studies and expert advice. When she went public, she chose to go on the *London* stock exchange. Everything she did she did differently.

How does one account for her success? Reason number one probably was sheer determination and energy. She is as energetic as her name implies. The name "Debra" means "bee," and, appropriately, the Fields family now lives in Utah, the Beehive State.

Reason number two was simple decency—to her employees, customers, and suppliers. For twenty years, she has stuck with one chocolate supplier, eschewing the business of his rival, who dismissively called her "Sweetheart" and hung up on her, taking her account for chump change. I hope this loser is reading this and finding out that the Fields account he could have had is now worth $7 million a year.

A charitable soul, she gives away unsold cookies to the Red Cross as a treat for blood donors. Her charity of choice for money donations is cystic fibrosis research.

I had always pictured Mrs. Fields as the portly, grandmotherly type, but pictures of her reveal that she is amazingly thin for a cookie baker and has movie-star good looks, quite resembling Stefanie Powers.

Newman's Own

M y next subject doesn't just resemble a movie star; he is one. He is Paul Newman (1925–) born in Shaker Heights, Ohio, where his father, Arthur, co-owned a sporting-goods store. His mother, Theresa (Feutzer) Newman, was of Hungarian parentage and was a Catholic turned Christian Scientist. She and her Jewish husband and religiously unaffiliated son must have had some interesting theological discussions at home.

Paul graduated from Shaker Heights High in 1943 and went into the navy, where he fought in the Pacific as a gunner on torpedo planes. After the war, he attended Kenyon College in Ohio.

In December 1949, in Woodstock, Illinois, he married a vivacious young actress-model named Jackie Witte. They had three children—Scott, Susan, and Stephanie. The sometimes-stormy marriage ended in divorce in 1956, but Jackie and Paul are on good terms now. Tragically, Scott died of a drug overdose.

In 1958, he married another actress, Joanne Cignilliat Woodward, daughter of a vice-president of the publishers Charles Scribner's Sons. With her, Paul fathered three more daughters—Eleanor, Melissa, and Claire. Paul and Joanne have been together forty-two years now.

Paul is known for his practical jokes. He once sawed a friend's brand-new sports car in half. Why (or especially, *how*) I don't know, nor do I know how the joke was in any way "practical."

Paul began his Newman's Own products with a salad dressing in 1982. The product and its successors are excellent and became almost instant successes.

The company is run Ben & Jerry style. The board of

directors meets on patio furniture grouped around a Ping-Pong table in the Newmans' rec room, with the part-time office help playing darts when they aren't busy. Paul regards the whole operation as something of a joke, but he does take quality control seriously. It shows in his sales, and in the fact that Beatrice Foods offered to buy him out for "countless millions," according to Newman's partner in the venture. A. E. Hotchner.

Newman's Own is unique among the companies described in this book in two respects: it is the only one that is not-for-profit, and it is the only one that is run as a sideline for its owner. Paul's principal claims to fame are, of course, acting and car racing. Many of his films, *Exodus, Cool Hand Luke,* and *The Sting,* for example, are regarded as classics, and over his racing career he has won fifty races, including three national titles.

The profits from Newman's Own, which have totaled over $100 million from its inception, go to dozens of charities. Some, but by no means all, goes to liberal causes, in which Mr. Newman has always been active. He marched in the South for civil rights in the sixties, campaigned for Eugene McCarthy, and was a delegate to the Democratic National Convention in 1968. He later served as a delegate to the U.N. Conference on Disarmament.

Otis

By inventing the safety elevator, Elisha Graves Otis (1811–1861) transformed the central city from a sprawling landscape of low-slung buildings to a compact core of skyscrapers. He changed the urban landscape in its vertical dimension as certainly and as dramatically as Henry Ford changed it in the horizontal.

Elisha was born to Stephen and Phoebe Otis of Halifax, Vermont. Stephen, a farmer, served as a state legislator and was the local justice of the peace during Elisha's childhood.

Elisha was one of those rare individuals who combine mechanical aptitude with the showmanship needed to sell a hard-to-market product.

He did not invent the elevator—not by a long shot. Hoisting devices go back to ancient times; even Archimedes wrote of them. The oldest one still extant is at the Abbey of St. Michel of the Normandy coast, and dates back to 1204. The donkey-powered device is no longer operating, though the treadmill/wheel in which the poor beast "walked" to hoist the monks up the cliff still exists.

St. Michel's hoist never made it to the marketplace. Maybe the church viewed it as enticing the monks to sloth, or bringing them into danger of death—either way a proof that the hoist was the devil's work. But Otis freed it from its nine-hundred-year curse and made it commercially viable as a passenger vehicle—and made it mechanically powered, too, which was certainly a plus.

The invention of the mechanical passenger elevator was an accident of history. Otis, unlike many of the subjects in this book, whose destiny seemed fixed from early on, floated aimlessly from career to career, never finding anything suitable, and even at his death, he had only the faintest idea that he'd accomplished anything special. He began as a builder in Troy, New York; he then became a wagon driver between Troy and Brattleboro, Vermont. He next moved to Greenville, Vermont, and tried his luck at a succession of other jobs—miller, sawyer, machinist, and carriage builder. He finally took a job in a factory in Yonkers that made bed frames.

It was in the Yonkers factory that he was told to make a platform hoist for lifting bed frames. Many factories had such hoists, but Elisah's innovation was a system of ratchets that would "catch" a falling elevator if its cable broke. The safety feature pleased his boss and also attracted the attention of a prominent New York City merchant, A. T. Stewart, who asked him to make two similar elevators for his store at 275 Hudson Street in New York.

The order came just in time, because Elisha had already packed his bags and was set to leave for California on his eighth career venture, panning for gold. At the time, it must have seemed as good a bet as any.

Making the two elevators kept him in town. Meanwhile, the bed factory went out of business, and Otis, hoping he might sell more of these elevators, moved into the abandoned building and set up a shop. To his dismay, no further orders came in, but he heard about an upcoming exhibit at the Crystal Palace in New York City, so he hurriedly assembled a demonstration elevator. Before the assembled crowd, the strange device lifted him high in the air, as a trapeze artist is lifted to his perch. After a brief speech and gestural flourish that brought all eyes up to him, he dramatically cut the rope that supported the elevator. To the gasp of onlookers who thought he would plunge to his death, he was saved from falling by the ratchets in the safety system.

The crowd was amazed, but orders were slow in coming, and those that did come were for freight lifting. That was probably all Otis ever envisioned, but one day in 1857, he received an unexpected order from a New York merchant named E. V. Haughwout, who wanted an elevator for carrying passengers.

The Haughwout store was a five-story china and glassware emporium at 488 Broadway in what is now the Little Italy section of lower Manhattan. The business is long gone, but the building remains. Its ground floor houses a Staples store, and a textile-company office occupies the fourth floor. Amazingly, the elevator still exists and remains in routine service and carries employees to its offices every day, as it has for 142 years, apparently without mishap. It operates probably in its original shaft, although the cab has been replaced, and it is now electrically operated and has been updated to meet safety codes.

Haughwout's store elevator was not only the world's first passenger safety elevator. It was probably the first elevator as we normally think of one—an enclosed cab moving up and down in a shaft, with its door opening in tandem with shaft doors at each floor. It was a hit with the customers, and the era of the passenger elevator was born.

Little is known of Otis's private life. He married twice: first to Susan Houghton, when he was in Halifax, and later to one Elizabeth Boyd. He died at age fifty in a diphtheria epidemic. He died no doubt feeling he had led an ordinary workman's life, but his two sons, Charles and Norton, were to reap the fruits of his labor. They were the ones who made Otis a household name. Mr. Otis died only four years after the sale to Haughwout's—never even imagining the gleaming alabaster cities of multistoried buildings that his invention would make possible.

The site of the old bed frame factory, where Otis did his first work, later became the company's main production facility. It now houses a factory that produces the horizontal equivalent of his invention: subways cars. A final irony: 275 Hudson Street, the site of the A. T. Stewart store where Otis sold his first elevator, is now occupied by a one-story building. Nestled among skyscrapers, it is almost unique: it has no elevator.

Pillsbury
※➤◆➤

The world's largest milling business was founded through the efforts of Charles Alfred Pillsbury (1842–1899). He and his wife, Mary, were enticed by his uncle John Sargent Pillsbury (1828–1901) to come to St. Anthony Falls in the Minnesota Territory from their native New Hampshire. Charles had graduated from Dartmouth and gone into business in Montreal. He was the son of John's brother, also named Charles. John, Charles Jr., and Charles Sr. had discussed the possibility of going into the milling business, and in 1869 they pooled $10,000 to buy a one-third interest in a run-down flour mill. The company became known as C. A. Pillsbury & Co., with the slogan "Pillsbury's Best" and the trademark of 4 *X*'s. (The *X*'s were derived from a medieval milling tradition. The best flour was reserved for baking communion bread, which was so marked by crosses.)

Charles went to Europe to study milling innovations, and bought roller presses to replace the cumbersome millstones for grinding grain. In 1874, Charles's brother Fred joined the company. So successful had the company become that in 1883, it boldly proposed building the world's largest flour mill, despite recent crop failures, the worst of which had been in 1877, when a grasshopper plague wiped out many farms.

Pillsbury had their own plague to worry about: fire. Between 1887 and 1891, four of their seven mills burned down, yet the three remaining mills produced ten thousand barrels of flour a day, making them still the region's dominant miller. Being located in the nation's breadbasket and having mills on major railroads with favorable rates were factors in their success, but luck and/or skill in grain-futures trading played a part also. In addition to being financially successful, Charles Jr. was an industry leader. He was a principal organizer of the Minneapolis Millers' Association and the chamber of commerce.

Charles and his wife, Mary, had twin boys, John and Charles, born in 1878, both of whom assumed the second generation of leadership.

In 1889, in a move that disappointed and upset many, the company merged with Washburn Mills to become Pillsbury-Washburn, under British ownership. The firm prospered, and started packaging and selling its flour in labeled paper bags (up to that time, it was sold only in bulk). Charles stayed with the firm but wasn't happy with his diminished status. He also suffered devastating losses in grain speculation. Nevertheless, at his death he had made a considerable fortune, due partly to successful side ventures in railroads and timber. He was a devout Baptist and donated much of his fortune to his church, including the establishment of the Pillsbury Settlement House.

In 1923, long after the founders had died, Pillsbury once again became independent of British ownership.

Procter & Gamble

W illiam Procter and James Gamble led remarkably
parallel lives. Both were born in the British Isles
and emigrated to America at about the same time; both
were in the candle business; both were devout Protestants;
both took flatboats down the Ohio River, intending to settle further downstream, but ended up unexpectedly in
Cincinnati as a result of illness—all this before they had
even heard of each other. In Cincinnati, both married
women with the surname of Norris, and both had exactly
ten children; the firstborn son of each had his father's
name and took a prominent position in the second generation of the company management.

Procter (1801–1884), one of eleven children, was born
in Hertfordshire, England. At fifteen, he took a job in what
we would call a general store. He saved up enough money
to open a woolens shop in London, but was robbed of his
entire inventory on his second day of business.

Determined to get a new start, the disheartened William and his wife, Martha, came to America and settled
in Cincinnati. Their destination had been Louisville, Kentucky, but Martha came down with cholera and died while
on the journey down the Ohio River. Heavily in debt from
his losses in London, and grieving for his wife, the despondent William, at the nadir of his life, took a job as a
bank teller in Cincinnati.

To augment his income, he started making candles, a
skill he had learned in the "general store" in Hertfordshire.
Soon he met another candlemaker, Alexander Norris, who
was already well established in the business, and the two
became friends. While not making candles, William

Photos courtesy of Procter & Gamble.

William Procter (left) and James Gamble. In an age when men were often given names like Eliphalet and Caleb, P&G's founders were just plain Bill and Jim.

kept himself occupied by courting his patron's daughter Olivia. The two were married in 1833.

The husband of Olivia's sister Elizabeth was also in the candle business. Alexander suggested that the two merge. The brother-in-law and prospective partner was, of course, James Gamble.

James Gamble (1803–1891) was born in Ireland, but came to America with his parents in 1819, intending to farm in Illinois. Like the Procters would do a few years later, the Gambles floated down the Ohio by flatboat. It was a slow and horrible way to travel, with several families and their pets and livestock crammed into small quarters for weeks in all kinds of weather. James became very ill, and the family mercifully debarked at Cincinnati. Cincinnati was a prosperous and attractive city by frontier standards, and the Gambles decided to stay there, and James's father, George, opened a greenhouse. Recovered from his illness, James worked for his father for a while, but later became apprenticed to Norris and met and married Elizabeth.

On October 31, 1837, Procter and Gamble founded their little company, which they immediately called Procter & Gamble. Though the economy was not good, P&G prospered, and by 1848 was clearing $26,000 a year in profits.

In the ensuing years, the company achieved even greater success, partly because of its favorable location on the Miami-Erie Canal, and partly because of the discovery of a process for making glycerin out of candlemaking waste.

P&G prospered during the Civil War. In the late 1850s, as war seemed imminent, the founders' sons, also named William Procter and James Gamble, had the foresight to buy a boatload of rosin, an ingredient in soap. It was available only in the South, and without it, their business would be ruined. Without intending to, they cornered the rosin market, and the price shot up from one dollar to fifteen dollars a barrel, driving out many of their competitors. Using this rosin and other ingredients, they made soap for the Union Army during the war. While the soap was much appreciated, the soapboxes were almost as valuable, since they were practically the only items of "furniture" available in the camps.

Procter and Gamble chose not to exploit their advantage for economic gain. They criticized others for profiteering by selling shoddy merchandise, and saw their idealism rewarded by vandalism to their homes.

The end of the war relieved anxieties for their safety and allowed them to restore their rosin supply, which had been depleted almost to the last barrel. It also brought a new set of opportunities: exposure of the P&G name throughout the South, and later the West, created new markets for their products, and the three hundred workers they had taken on to supply the war effort were available for whatever new products the brothers-in-law could think to produce. James's son, James Norris Gamble (who included his middle name to avoid confusion with his father), developed a floating soap in 1879 that William

Procter's son Harley named Ivory. Floating soap was an appealing gimmick, and the white color suggested purity. A chemical analysis revealed that it contained 0.11 percent uncombined alkali, 0.28 percent carbonates, and 0.17 percent mineral matter, making it 99.44 percent pure. An impressive statistic to use for an ad campaign.

In 1884, the factory was in need of expansion, and the founders, now in their eighties, had their first serious disagreement: whether to add on to their existing plant on Central Avenue or to build a whole new facility. The issue was settled by a disastrous fire that destroyed most of the plant. Later that year, perhaps partly from the shock of the loss, Procter died.

The next year, James Gamble broke ground for the new factory in a town he created and named Ivorydale. It was a showplace, with manicured grounds; attractive, ornate buildings; and a laboratory for research and development. P&G recognized the importance of employee morale. The new facility was extravagantly made for that reason, and Harley suggested giving employees a half day off on Saturdays. Although there was some strife with labor, everybody regarded P&G as a good company to work for. Their first employee, Bernard Kreiger, was with the company for forty-seven years.

The firm first issued stock in 1890. James Gamble was offered a position on the board but declined, because of his age. He died the following year.

R. J. Reynolds

In 1874, Richard Joshua Reynolds (1850–1918) was referred to in the Winston, North Carolina, press as "RJR," and somehow it stuck. He is one of a handful of people in history, and probably the only private individual, readily identifiable by his initials alone.

He was one of the sixteen children of Hardin W. and Nancy Cox Reynolds of Patrick County, North Carolina. Only half the couple's children survived childhood. Four of them—two sets of twin boys—died in infancy. Three of those who lived into their childhood died within a single week in 1862 as a result of smallpox vaccinations that "went bad." Dick, as R. J. was called, received the vaccine at the same time, but somehow survived.

The Reynolds family lived in the poorest part of the then poorest state in the union, during the Civil War and its terrible aftermath, Reconstruction. But Hardin, well noted for his industriousness and savvy, actually prospered in that extraordinarily barren place and time—so much so that he was able to send his children to the public school and could even afford a private tutor. In 1868, young Dick could even afford college, and he enrolled in Emery and Henry College, where he stayed two years; he later went to a college in Baltimore.

Beginning in 1873, he followed his father into the tobacco business; eventually all four of his brothers were to do the same, though with far less success. R. J. started out working at his father's plant, which was located at a place curiously named Nobusiness Mountain. He left late the next year for Winston-Salem, where he would have railroad access and proximity to the main area where "Virginia bright" tobacco was grown. In Winston, he built what in company lore is called the "Old Red Factory," setting up operations on the first floor and living upstairs. This humbly begotten enterprise was the fourth of twenty-three tobacco factories that had set up shop in Winston by 1883.

Despite the intense competition, R. J. was successful and was soon employing 110 people, ten of them children, in a factory that produced no fewer than eighty-six different brands of chewing tobacco—some with names that sound like racehorses—Daisy Girl, Sunny South, and Dixie's Delight—and others that must have been people in his life—Lucy Reynolds, Lula Hurst, and My Pet.

In 1890, the company went public, although there were only a handful of shareholders. Through this incorporation, R. J. raised enough capital by 1892 to build the "mammoth" plant, the largest in the state for flat plug tobacco. Indicative of R. J.'s seemingly reckless optimism, the factory was five times as large as business then warranted. It was equipped with automatic sprinklers—an unusual but eminently sensible innovation, since these kinds of places frequently burned down.

This factory, and all the others in Winston, were devoted primarily to manufacturing chewing tobacco. This was partly the result of a trust developed by Benjamin Duke that gave the American Tobacco Company exclusive rights to smoking tobacco. R. J. wanted to make smoking tobacco, too, but mostly as a way to make use of "scrap" tobacco, then considered a useless by-product of chewing tobacco.

Meanwhile, he had heard about a new product, small cigars wrapped in paper, that started to appear on the American scene in the 1880s, or 1890s. The first ones were imported from Turkey. When American companies started making "cigarettes," as they came to be called, they were inclined to adopt names that evoked the mystique of the Land of the Sultans. The first American-made cigarette enclosed in a wrapped package was called "Fatima" and was made by Liggett & Myers.

In 1913, with the breakup of the Duke trust, R. J. announced his intention to make cigarettes and produced his first one, a blend of Turkish and domestic tobaccos. He wanted a name that was short and catchy, suggestive of Turkey, and a logo that was yellow and striking, to catch the eye of the still largely illiterate population. He decided on "Camel."

At that time, no one in the company knew exactly what the animal looked like, so to design his package, R. J. went to a Barnum & Bailey Circus and took pictures of a camel the circus workers affectionately called "Old Joe." Old Joe's image has been imprinted on billions of packs of Camel cigarettes, and has not significantly changed since its introduction in 1913.

From 1914 (the first full year of production) to 1918 (the year of RJR's death), annual sales grew from 425 million to 15 billion cigarettes.

RJR popularized the cigarette in America, but lest we be too quick to condemn him as the angel of death, let me mention that nothing was known in his day about the adverse health effects of smoking. In fact, it is said that he was reluctant to introduce his cigarettes until he was assured that the *paper* was not injurious to health.

Richard Joshua Reynolds was a commanding presence in his business. He was tall for his time (six feet two) and possessed an extraordinarily thick mustache and a goatee that grew to a full beard in his later years. Physically intimidating, robust and energetic, he had the autocratic manner of most company owners of his day, and then some.

He could be a Simon Legree: he made sure that white workers had better jobs, higher pay, and more rights than black workers, and separate (and better) bathrooms. His employees worked near dangerous machines in stifling heat for long hours. Even as late as his death in 1918, children were employed in his factories.

But he was not without humanity. Seeing terrible working conditions, he directed that workers be given ten-minute breaks. Like Henry Ford, he would give a raise on the spot to workers who implored him with a sufficiently convincing story. Partly through the influence of his wife, Katharine Smith Reynolds, he provided free ice water and at-cost lunches to his employees, day care for employees' children, and safe communal lodgings for unmarried female workers.

In spite of his college education, aptitude for math, and obvious intelligence, many assumed he was illiterate, because of a rare reading disability—not dyslexia, but something akin to it: he could read only character by character and could not make out words. His handwriting is virtually illegible.

He spoke with a stammer, but nevertheless was sociable and popular as a young man. He did not marry until he was fifty-five, but had four children, including Zachary S. "Z. Smith" Reynolds, who succeeded him in the company. RJR Jr., his namesake, forsook the business to become a marine biologist.

R. J.'s other interests included real estate development, local politics, quail hunting, and breeding horses.

He died in 1918 at age sixty-eight of pancreatic cancer.

R. J.'s influence on his company lived on well after his death. As his successors charted his company's course, an eerie portrait of their founder's pasty-complected, almost ghostlike visage hung alone on the company's boardroom wall, looming over their deliberations. So completely did he rule his company that it was not until more than forty years after his death that anyone dared hang a picture of anyone else in the same room.

R. S. Reynolds

A among the portraits so reluctantly placed in the RJR
boardroom is that of his nephew Richard Samuel
Reynolds (1881–1955). He is not nearly so famous as his
uncle R. J., yet his name, too, lives on in America's
households. But, who *was* he?

He was born in Bristol, a city that straddles the Tennessee–Virginia line, and was the son of Abram and
Senah Hoge Reynolds. R. S.'s father, Abram, was the oldest of R. J.'s siblings. Soon after Abram returned from the
Civil War to farm a tobacco plantation, he "got religion"
and saw that farming the nicotine weed was sinful.

Young Richard continued in the business, however.
After graduating from the University of Virginia in 1902,
he went to work for Uncle R. J. in Winston, where he
helped develop Prince Albert tobacco and "Kaiser Wil-
helm" cigarettes, which R. J. wisely renamed "Camel."

After working for R. J. for about ten years, he left to
found his own company, making soaps and other cleaners.
He was married by this time and had four children, to
whom he wanted to leave a business. His hopes were
dashed twice—first when his plant burned down, and a
second time when a plant he built in Louisville was closed
during the World War I emergency, because it was considered "nonessential." After trying his hand at two completely unrelated businesses, asphalt and coated paper, he
began to produce materials for product packaging. He had
gotten some experience with that during his days with
RJR.

The product was successful, and Reynolds became
wealthy enough to diversify into railroads and mines; he

owned a part of the company that makes Eskimo Pies as well.

The packaging material, thinly rolled tin, he later deemed to be inferior to rolled aluminum, and he soon switched into that business. In 1926, he established the Reynolds Metals Company, which prospered even during the Depression with its principal product, Reynolds Wrap.

So now you know that Reynolds of Reynolds Wrap was a nephew of R. J. Reynolds, the tobacconist. Interesting, eh? But R. S. Reynolds is more than a curiosity: he may have made a difference in the course of history. During the thirties, when he was in Europe buying aluminum ingots, he discovered that the Nazis were stockpiling the metal. He surmised, rightly it turned out, that they were preparing to use it in their war effort. Quickly he mobilized to obtain half a million tons of aluminum to keep it out of Nazi hands. This may have made an important difference in the outcome of the war.

Scott

Thomas Seymour Scott was a New York lawyer when in 1865 he suddenly decided, for unclear reasons, to move to Philadelphia and go into the paper wholesaling business. Two years later, he brought his younger brother, Edward (called Irvin, his middle name), into the business, after having had a falling-out with Otis Ballou, his original partner. Irvin was a schoolteacher, fond of fishing and duck hunting, who also aspired to the bar, before being lured away into the paper business. A third brother, Clarence, who posed for the camera with an almost unique (for the mid-nineteenth century) bright smile and twinkling eye, came on board in 1872.

Thomas, Irvin, and Clarence Scott were to become immortalized in a way most of us wouldn't want to be: their family's name emblazoned on countless millions of toilet-tissue rolls.

The brothers, and four other siblings, were born to devout Quakers, Sophronia and Alexander Hamilton Scott, in Saratoga County, New York, not far from where arch competitors, later partners, Kimberly and Clark were born, and nearly at the same time.

Business was touch and go, but the brothers survived—even through the Panic of 1873. That event, plus losing $30,000 (a fortune in those days) embezzled from them, was a bitter pill, but the boys lived through it. The three brothers, and two other partners, formed a limited partnership in 1874, not formalized until September 1, 1879, the "official beginning" of the Scott Paper Company.

Shortly afterward, Thomas, who was the founder, but who seemed always to be the most ready to call it quits, finally tendered his resignation, to become treasurer of the

Curtis Publishing Company, the publishers of *The Saturday Evening Post*.

The Scott Company's primary product was toilet tissue, an item first commercially produced by someone named Joseph Gayetty, but never successfully marketed because of Victorian taboos. Their product posed an interesting problem for the Scotts: how does one market something nobody is supposed to talk about? Their solution was "ghost marketing," i.e., distributing the toilet paper (in their case) to drugstores and letting them worry about how to sell it. Most of the stores chose to market it as a medical product until it finally attained "respectability."

Briefly, the Scotts toyed with diversification—into the bicycle business, of all things—and produced a bike they called the "Great Scott." Soon they decided that the bicycle business wasn't for them, and toilet tissue, lowly and humble as the product is, would be their claim to fortune and fame.

Sears Roebuck
%%%

O ne day in March 1887, the following classified ad
appeared in the Chicago *Daily News:*

> WANTED: Watchmaker with reference who can fur-
> nish tools. State age, experience, and salary required.
> ADDRESS T39, Daily News.

The ad was run by a young salesman of watches and
mail-order goods, Richard Warren Sears (1863–1914),
who had been born in Stewartsville, Minnesota, and raised
in Spring Valley and Mankato. His father, James Warren
Sears, had achieved some success as a blacksmith and
cartwright, but had lost his modest fortune in an unsuccessful farming venture. The family's financial loss, along
with his father's ill health, forced Dick to leave school
and look for work. He sold coal and lumber for a while,
dressed venison for the Indians, and trained himself to
operate a telegraph. At twenty-two, his telegraphing skills
won him a job as agent for the Minneapolis and St. Louis
railway station in North Redwood, Minnesota.

One day in 1886 a shipment of watches was delivered
to a store in town. The jeweler refused to accept it, but
Sears offered to buy the watches and resell them. This he
did, and encouraged by his success, he bought more. The
North Redwood train station had become Sears's first
"store," so to speak. In North Redwood, Dick made $500
in his first six months and moved to Minneapolis to expand his customer base. He set up shop as R. W. Sears
Watch Company.

The next year, he moved to Chicago, the nation's rail
center, hoping to facilitate distribution and expand his

*Richard Sears and Alvah Roebuck both got their start in the watch
business.*

markets even further. He diversified into jewelry, and (in
1887) started issuing a catalog.

Meanwhile, the watches he sold back in North Redwood were being returned for repair. He needed a watch
repairman. Hence the ad in the *Daily News*.

Among the respondents was Alvah Curtis Roebuck
(1864–1948), son of English immigrants who were living
in Lafayette, Indiana, when Alvah was born. He was mechanically inclined and taught himself how to repair
watches. In 1886, he got a job in a jewelry shop in Ham-
mond, Indiana, and in April 1887 he moved to Chicago
to work for Sears.

Alvah had no idea that they would soon become two
of the world's richest and most famous men, though I
suspect Dick had at least an inkling. To understand the
success of their venture, consider what the life of the consumer was like in their day. Nearly three people in four
lived on farms or in small towns and had little access to
stores. Such stores as there were, operated in isolation;
there was no competition to keep a lid on prices, and

stores often sold their merchandise for twice what they paid for it. Meanwhile, the growth of railroads and the expansion of the post office made mail-order shopping feasible and attractive. Sears did not originate catalog shopping (Aaron Montgomery Ward was first to do that, in 1873), but he did much to make it accepted.

The first Sears catalog, which appeared in 1888, featured only jewelry and watches. Within seven years, it had grown to 532 pages displaying a full range of merchandise, including clothing, furniture, stoves, guns, dishware, and even buggies. Eventually, entire houses could be obtained by catalog. Except for the Bible, the Sears catalog was the nation's most-produced publication. Every year, enough were printed to fill the boxcars of a railroad train thirty miles long.

The catalogs featured dresses modeled by lovely young women. Susan Hayward, Lauren Bacall, Ginger Rogers, and Gloria Swanson all got their starts as Sears models.

To make his merchandise even more attractive, Sears offered a money-back-if-not-satisfied guarantee. But the real secret of his success was his salesmanship. He described his offerings in a way that appealed to rural folks; he had a knack for knowing just how to pitch his products.

Though basically honest, the catalogs did feature some dubious merchandise—blood purifiers and "pink pills for pale people," for example. The most infamous was the "Heidelberg Belt," an electric belt that was purported to cure impotence and every other male health problem. Though the belts were completely worthless, hundreds of people paid twelve to eighteen dollars for them. Sears had developed such a reputation for square dealing that only three people returned the belts for a refund.

In 1895, Sears gained a bride and lost a partner. He married Anna Lydia Mechstroth, and with her raised a family of two sons and two daughters. In that same year, Roebuck sold out his interest in the company. This was only seven years after meeting Sears and only two years after the company incorporated under the name Sears,

Roebuck & Company. Roebuck had worked honestly and hard, but is thought to have contributed little in the way of ideas or talent. He idolized Sears, and may have felt resentment over the addition of a third partner, Julius Rosenwald. Rosenwald streamlined Sears's order-handling process through an innovative system of belts and chutes through which orders and merchandise flowed. It greatly increased the number of orders that could be processed. Henry Ford is thought to have used it as a model in designing his assembly line. In a fairer world, the company would have been called Sears and Rosenwald, in recognition of the latter's contribution.

Roebuck's role after the rise of Rosenwald was to be shoved off into a corner of the operation, mostly out of sight, doing what he knew best, managing repairs of watches and jewelry. Soon afterward, he quit Sears altogether and got into the motion-picture-projector business. He also served as president of a typewriter company. In the early twenties, he became a real estate developer in Florida and retired to St. Petersburg.

Thirty-five years later, long after Sears had died and been forgotten, Roebuck returned to Chicago to work on the company's archives. There he found himself treated as a kind of Ulysses, a grand graybeard returning after decades of aimless wanderings to his homeland, now a merchandising giant headquartered in what was then the largest commercial building in the world. He found to his delight that he was an object of curiosity and respect, and came to enjoy visiting the S&R stores as the company's grand old man, though he had served as a partner in the venture for only a scant two years.

Singer

Isaac Merritt Singer (1811–1875) did not invent the sewing machine—Elias Howe gets the credit for that—but he developed the first practical model that could be mass-produced. It was a business he fell into by accident. While in Boston, he saw one being developed by an Orson Phelps. It didn't work well, and Isaac suggested changes in its design. In just eleven days, I. M. Singer, who had never seen a sewing machine before, or probably even thought about such a thing, made one that really worked, and the era of laborsaving machinery for the American housewife was born.

Isaac was the son of a millwright from a village near Troy, New York, and spent his childhood in Oswego, on the Lake Ontario shore. Though obviously a mechanical genius, as the episode with Phelps shows, his first love was the theater, and he spent the first thirteen years of his adulthood as an itinerant Shakespearean actor.

In 1830, even more than now, acting—even classical acting—was a disreputable and precarious way to make a living, but Isaac somehow obtained the grudging consent of a Mr. and Mrs. Haley to take their fifteen-year-old daughter, Catharine, as his wife. Isaac—tall (six feet two inches), dashing, and handsome—had utterly captivated Catharine, and he was so taken by her that he was willing to accept lowly jobs as a lathe operator and a store clerk to earn her hand. He kept his marital vows for six years, but finally the siren song of the stage was irresistible, and following the example of the Bard, who left his wife and young family to go to London and theatrical fame, Isaac left Catharine. Perhaps declaiming, "Is love a tender thing? It is too rough, too rude, too boisterous. It pricks like thorn," he left his despondent bride; a son, William; and a daughter-to-be, Lillian, to join a roving troupe of players.

But soon our Romeo found himself again "sore impierced with [Cupid's] shaft" upon meeting Mary Ann Sponsler, a Baltimore oyster shucker's daughter with whom he cohabited without the trouble of getting married—a scandalous act in those days, even if he'd been single. When Mary Ann by chance found out about Isaac's wife, he explained that Catharine was deluded and only claimed to be married to him. Meanwhile, Catharine retreated in shame to live with her parents in Palmyra.

Mary Ann and Isaac were a bizarre pairing of souls. Although he was only seven years her senior, she addressed him as "Father" and seemed utterly enthralled by him. But the feeling was not mutual, at least not for long, for Isaac was soon on the road again, leaving yet another luckless, abandoned "wife," with a son, Isaac Augustus ("Gus"), born in 1837.

Fate was to be a bit kinder to Mary Ann than to Catharine. On the road, Isaac somehow found time to tinker between productions, and came up with an invention, a rock-drilling machine, which he sold for $2,000, a lot of money in 1839, and with it he enticed Mary Ann to come to Chicago, where he was at the time, and be reconciled.

He trained Mary Ann in the acting art, and for years after the windfall had been spent, she and Isaac and his troupe roved about in a covered wagon, gleaning a pittance here and there staging productions. During this penurious period, three more little Singers were born.

Desperate for money, he finally quit the stage and settled in Fredericksburg, Ohio, where he found work as a typesetter. There, Isaac invented a machine for carving letters into wood. The family moved to Pittsburgh, where Isaac further developed his carver, and Mary Ann bore two more children. Then it was on to New York City to get financial backing, but in a boiler explosion that killed sixty-three people, the worst such accident in history, his just-perfected model was destroyed. Fortunately, someone came along who had seen the invention and was willing to finance it. Hoping to make these type-carving machines, he and his patron, a man named Ziebert, moved to Boston and rented space in a factory owned by Orson Phelps. It was then and there that the sewing machine incident related above took place.

Isaac and Ziebert were so intrigued that they dropped all plans for a carver and went into partnership with Phelps to make sewing machines. Off to an ominous start, they quarreled over patent rights. Under cover of darkness, Isaac spirited away the machine to New York to tinker with it and solved one of the major problems in its design. This firmed up his patent claim, but the sneaky way he went about it didn't bode well for his future relations with his partner. Nor with his wife, for this tinkering was done in the same room where Mary Ann had just given birth to their seventh child.

But they went into business, and in 1850, I. M. Singer & Company made its first sewing machines—heavy-duty ones, designed for tailors and shirt makers. It was not until 1856 that the first machines designed for home use were made.

Meanwhile, Elias Howe had heard of the Singer machine and was demanding money—lots of it—under threat of a patent infringement suit. Singer finally agreed to give Howe a hefty twenty-five-dollar royalty per machine, a big chunk of the sixty-four-dollar retail price.

Despite the costly deal with Howe, I. M. Singer & Company prospered. Its success was due partly to interchangeable-parts production, but mostly to two unique marketing innovations.

• "Rent-to-buy." Singer is thought to have originated this idea. The housewife would rent the sixty-dollar machine for five dollars a month and after a year she would own it. Sales quadrupled the year this idea was introduced, and by 1860, Singer was making thirteen thousand machines a year.

• International production. I. M. Singer & Company was the first American multinational corporation, with factories in Scotland, Brazil, and France as early as the 1860s. Singer's machines were marketed even in Madagascar in the late nineteenth century.

One of the early Singer sales agents was William, son by his long-ago wife Catharine. Other agents were two former members of his theater troupe, who were amazed that the now famous Singer was the same guy they'd trod the boards with a few years before.

While the company prospered, the partnership did not. Phelps sold out, fed up with what Ziebert called Isaac's "most brutal and insulting manner." A fourth partner, who would sometimes "sob like a child" after Singer's ravings, also quit in disgust. Indeed, Singer was not the easiest guy to work with. Nor the most selfless: he enticed the seriously bedridden Ziebert to sign over his interest for $6,000, a fraction of the company's ultimate value.

This left Isaac the sole owner, and it made the Singers rich beyond their wildest imaginings. They lived in resplendent quarters at 14 Fifth Avenue in New York City, with ornate furniture, priceless paintings, and a staff that included a resident physician who stayed in the home like a servant.

Singer's fleet of carriages included an elaborately carved 3,800-pound, canary-yellow, Russian-style imperial coach, equipped with a water closet, nursery, beds, and chairs with a capacity for thirty-one people in its interior rooms and outside deck. Drawn by a team of nine horses, it must have attracted quite a crowd of amused and amazed onlookers on its first outing along the roads in Washington Square Park, in 1860.

But all was not well in the Singer household. For twenty-four years Isaac and Mary Ann had been living together, and she had borne him ten children, yet they had never married, and he had never even gotten a divorce from Catharine. Mary Ann was profoundly unhappy, and not just because of the quarter-century delay in marriage vows. She was unhappy because the tyrannical Singer had abused her. Her lawyer cataloged the horrors: "He has repeatedly beaten and choked her to insensibility, frequently forcing the blood to flow in streams from her nose, face, head, mouth, and neck, and [bragged to the family about] savage barbarity toward herself and her children . . ." Anything could set him off. One incident was provoked by Mary Ann's failure to close the lid on a book of matches in the couple's bedroom.

But it would become yet worse for the hapless Mary Ann. On August 7, 1860, "a difficulty occurred," she almost comically understates in her diary. On that day began a series of revelations that would destroy her world and rock the nation with the steamiest society sections *The New York Times* ever thought fit to print. She learned that she and Catharine were not the only women in Isaac's life. She heard first of one, and then of yet another rival. Worse, they were not mistresses: they were "wives"— women he was supporting, women with whom he was living and who had borne him children.

Incredibly, for the nine years from 1851 to 1860, Isaac had successfully juggled three whole families, without any of the women (who incidentally were all named Mary) knowing about the other two. It is particularly astounding for a man who led such a large and flamboyant life. How did he keep them apart? Where did he find the energy to head three households and conduct a major business enterprise? How did he explain all his absences, all the rumors, all the inevitable signals and signs? He must have been the fastest-talking guy ever.

But it had to happen: on that fateful August day in 1860, Mary Ann saw Isaac with one of the other Marys and sued for "divorce." The desperate and beleaguered

Isaac—one pictures him running down the street with lamps and rolling pins flying after him—fled in disgrace to London. But the fifty-year-old polygamist was not alone; he was accompanied by yet another companion, the nineteen-year-old sister of Mary number two.

Settled in Europe, Singer married another woman, Isabella Summerville, with whom he was to beget yet a fifth family, consisting of six children. One of them, Paris Singer, married the famous dancer Isadora Duncan; she bore him two children whom he accidentally drowned in the Seine. The incident was the Chappaquiddick of its day.

Isaac Singer, about 1870.

Years of scandal were taking their toll. With his long, full beard, a sad and tired countenance, and a curious penchant for dressing in robelike garments, he looked like an Old Testament patriarch in a Rembrandt painting. Indeed, he may have resembled the biblical Isaac in form, but he didn't in spirit; Isaac—the name means "one who laughs"—was not laughing much now. In 1863, when he and Isabelle returned to America, it was in disgrace. In Yonkers, they built a magnificent home, at which they threw a lavish party to which no one came. They returned to England, not very far from Stratford, where the ghost of the Bard may have drawn them, and where they built a castle and contented themselves entertaining tradesmen, since they were shunned by the aristocracy.

The pitiful man finally died in July 1875, but at least his funeral was in the grand manner to which he had become accustomed in his golden years. His hearse required the service of twelve horses to pull the massive weight of the three-layer casket. He was buried in Torquay Cemetery, near his English castle.

Smith & Wesson

Horace Smith (1808–1893), son of a carpenter named Silas, was born in Chelsea, Massachusetts, and moved a few miles west to Springfield at age four. Silas worked in the armory at Springfield, and young Horace at age sixteen became an apprentice to a bayonet maker. He demonstrated a talent for metalworking, and during his eighteen years with the armory invented several machines for the gunsmith trade.

In 1834, Horace moved to New Haven, Connecticut, where he worked briefly for Eli Whitney, in what was by some accounts the world's first factory to employ interchangeable parts. Horace then moved on to Norwich, Connecticut, where he became one of a number of people credited with inventing the explosive-fired harpoon, which eliminated the treacherous practice of hand-flinging harpoons from longboats.

In 1850 or 1851, Horace moved to Windsor, Vermont, to work for the Robbins & Lawrence Company, probably as a production supervisor. Robbins & Lawrence manufactured rifles based on a design patented by Lewis Jennings three years earlier. Smith made a number of improvements on the Jennings rifle, most notably making the breech pin and lifter move in response to the movement of the trigger. This is the standard operation of rifles today.

It was probably in Windsor that he first met D. B. Wesson.

Daniel Baird Wesson (1825–1906) was born in Worcester, Massachusetts. He was the son of a farmer named Rufus and his wife, Betsey (Baird). By the time Daniel was a young man, his older brother, Edwin, had

Horace Smith and Daniel Wesson developed the rifle as we know it.

already achieved some fame as a marksman and gunsmith. In fact, Edwin's target rifles were reputed to be among the finest in the world. In 1842, Edwin took Daniel on as an apprentice in his shop in Northboro. Within two years, Daniel was left in charge of operations for extended periods while Edwin was away negotiating business and fighting against patent infringement, a major plague in that fast-developing industry.

In 1848, the Wesson brothers moved to Connecticut, which could have called itself the "Gun State": Eli Whitney, Oliver Winchester, Eliphalet Remington, William Sturm, Alexander Ruger, Samuel Colt—all spent part of their lives and careers there.

In Hartford, Edwin Wesson formed a partnership with a Thomas Smith (no relation to Horace) to produce a thousand military rifles. The company was called Wesson & Smith. If that's not confusing enough, Horace Smith was at one time in partnership with an Asa Smith, apparently no relation to either Thomas or Horace.

In January 1849, Edwin suddenly died, and his interest in the company devolved onto a group of sixteen stockholders, who could not sustain operations. By November, the company's assets had been auctioned off, and Daniel was left with nothing, not even his tools.

With two other brothers, Franklin and Martin, Daniel tried the rifle business again, but failed. In 1851, he took a job as superintendent at the Leonard Pistol Company. Leonard pistols were being produced under contract with Robbins & Lawrence, which, you will recall, is the company that Horace Smith was working for at the time.

Smith teamed up with Wesson in 1852, when Smith was "let go" at the expiration of the Jennings contract. The partners recognized that the Jennings rifle, though flawed, was promising and set about to develop it further. Their principal innovation was the development of the metallic cartridge (what we recognize today as a "bullet") based on French design patented in 1846.

Smith and Wesson moved to Norwich, Connecticut, where they manufactured pistols designed for cartridges. The guns didn't sell well, and the partnership dissolved after a total run of only fifteen hundred to two thousand units. Wesson went to work for an outfit called Volcanic Arms, where he developed a pistol that fired .22-caliber rim-fired cartridges. Smith left the gun business entirely to run a livery stable with his brother-in-law in Springfield.

In 1857, the two teamed up again, this time successfully. They got off to a slow start: the first year, they made only four handguns. But during the 1860s, their Model One sold by the thousands, and business boomed, especially during the Civil War. They started making their own cartridges, and that part of the business became nearly as lucrative as the guns. "The boys" became rich, and even more so after the war, when the company aggressively marketed military arms overseas. They supplied much of the firepower used in the Crimean War—to both the Russian and the Turkish sides.

Meanwhile, Wesson found himself involved as an investor in more business ventures: a barbed-wire company in Iowa, a bank in Springfield, and a railroad.

In 1873, Horace retired to live his final twenty years pursuing his hobbies of astronomy, travel (mostly in the Western U.S.), and politics. He served as a Springfield "alderman," a quaint Massachusetts term that means, roughly, councilman. In his will, he established a scholarship fund and generously endowed his church.

Meanwhile, Wesson plodded on at the gunnery until his death in 1906. Although he was never able to retire, he did enjoy a rich recreational life. He and his wife, Olivia, traveled extensively, had fine horses and expensive carriages, and bred Irish setters. But his principal avocation, as you might expect from a gunmaker, was hunting.

In his will, he endowed his hometown generously, supplying the money for two hospitals. He also left to the company three sons and a grandson, who became its second- and third-generation leaders. During their tenure, the company prospered and diversified into such things and handcuffs and even flush valves for toilets.

Smith Brothers

❧

There is a remarkably persistent myth that the names of the Smith Brothers were "Trade" and "Mark." On the coughdrop box, the word "Trade" appears below the picture of one brother and "Mark" below the other. When the box first appeared, people assumed that those were their names, because they had never heard the term "trademark." (The legislation authorizing them had been passed only the year before the boxes came out.) So widespread did the story of the names become that even the brothers eventually called themselves "Trade" and "Mark."

Actually, "Trade" was William (1830–1913), and "Mark" was his brother Andrew (1836–1894). Their story began in 1847, when their father, a carpenter named James Smith, came from Quebec to Poughkeepsie, New York, to open a restaurant on Market Street, incidentally only three blocks away from where Robert Wood Johnson was also working at the time. Certainly, at one time or another, Johnson must have come into the restaurant to be waited on by the Smith brothers.

According to legend, James started making coughdrops after an itinerant peddler by the name of Sly Hawkins sold him the formula (sugar, corn, charcoal, anise, licorice, wintergreen, horehound, and peppermint) for five dollars. In 1866, James died, and his sons took over the business and expanded it. They began packaging the drops in the familiar little boxes with their portraits on them in 1872.

Packaging was done by thirty poor families in a nineteenth-century version of a "make money at home" deal; the brothers delivered the day's supply of drops and empty boxes to the families. The families filled them (sixteen to a box), and the brothers collected them the next morning.

Business grew, and in 1880 the brothers bought an ice-house on Church Street in Poughkeepsie and converted it into a twenty-six-kettle factory. As growth continued, the company built a three-story factory from scratch, and came to regard the restaurant as a sideline, with the coughdrops as their primary enterprise.

Smith Brothers is the oldest coughdrop brand and was at one time the largest company making that product exclusively. They were hounded by an army of imitators: "Smyth Brothers," "Schmidt Brothers," even "Smith Sisters," all marketing their drops in nearly identical packages. The trademark helped preserve the brothers' market share, and at their peak, they were employing 221 workers and turning out two billion coughdrops a year. Their brief foray into diversification—a gum called Smithereens—never made it in the marketplace.

The Smith Brothers plant had the happy-family ambience of a typical small-scale enterprise. Smith Brothers was among the first companies to offer health benefits and vacation pay and had a unique bonus system for "perfect attendance." In 1918, they became perhaps the first factory in the world to provide air-conditioning. It was a primitive arrangement, electric fans blowing over ice, but it was better than nothing. It was not for employee comfort, though; it was to keep the coughdrops from sticking together.

But who were the Smith brothers, really? They were a study in contrast. "Trade" was hard driving and puritanical. He believed in keeping wages low on the theory that too much money would tempt his workers into sin. Young women could work for him only with a minister's recommendation and had to live in a dormitory over the restaurant under the eagle eye of a stern, hatchet-faced matron. In his restaurant, he forbade the consumption of alcoholic beverages; he even refused to serve ginger ale, because of the connotation of the word "ale." He ran for governor of New York on the Prohibition ticket, and was a founder of New York's Women's Christian Temperance Union.

Trade was generous to the community. He gave a building to the WCTU, endowed two churches and the local YMCA, where a plaque thanking him still hangs in the entrance. He donated a park (locals call it "Cough Drop Park") on the condition that liquor never be allowed in it.

"Mark" was as casual and live-and-let-live as his brother was stiff and unyielding. He is the one with the untrimmed beard, as if he were too lazy to get out the scissors, which may have been the case. And he was not above having an occasional nip. His amiable, easygoing nature made him a soft touch. He was called "Easy Mark."

Mark died a bachelor, but Trade married and had a son and daughter. The son, Arthur, had little interest in the business, or apparently anything else. The wealthy heir spent most of his time traveling around in his chauffeur-driven Rolls-Royce or listening to the radio in his mansion, "The Smithy." Fortunately for cough sufferers, he had two sons, Bill and Brud, who took over the business upon his death in 1936.

So, beginning in 1936, the company was being run by a second set of Smith brothers. Unlike their dad, they had an interest in the business. They even grew beards to resemble their forebears and introduced themselves as "Trade" and "Mark." It was as if the original brothers had risen from their graves, for the new brothers' personalities were in some ways carbon copies of old Grampas Trade and Mark. Like Trade, Bill was a straitlaced teetotaler. Like Mark, Brud was a free spirit. His casual attitude showed up in his academic record: five prep schools in four years, and a college dropout at the end of his freshman year.

The boys are gone now. Bill died in 1955 and Brud seven years later. Both died sonless, but not for want of trying: they had five daughters between them.

So there were no new Smith brothers to take over. The factory in Poughkeepsie is gone, too. And the company itself is gone really, swallowed by Warner-Lambert the year after Brud's death. Sadly, the package that had sold so many billions of coughdrops over the years is also gone. It didn't suit the new owners, I guess, but at least the new design retains the familiar pictures of the world's most famous bearded brothers, with their names, "Trade" and "Mark," still under them, where they were first placed 127 years ago.

Spalding

The name "Spalding" appears on countless articles of sports paraphernalia, but the establishment of A. G. Spalding's flourishing business was actually only one of his achievements. His most important was turning sporting events, particularly baseball, from roughhouse amusements for beer-sotted ruffians into respectable outlets for youthful energy. Equally important, it was Spalding who gave American sports the institutional foundation they needed to prosper as commercial enterprises. More than anyone else, he determined the shape and character of American sport.

Albert Goodwill Spalding (1850–1915) was born in Byron, Illinois. His father, James, a prosperous farmer, died when Albert was eight. His mother, Harriet, who thus became heir to a second sizable estate (her first husband had died and left her independently wealthy), raised Albert, his brother, Walter, and sister, Mary, in nearby Rockford. Albert owed much to his mother in childhood and later life as well, and she was still living when he died in his sixty-sixth year.

In his teens, Albert, a shy grocery clerk, spent most of his free time playing baseball. It was a game that, as played in 1867, would be scarcely recognizable to today's baseball fan. Typically, the batter stood almost midway between the pitcher and the catcher. The pitcher lobbed nine balls underhand, low or high—the batter's preference. There were no "balls" or "strikes"; the batter simply swung at the ball. If he hit a fly, the fielder would catch it in his hands (no gloves were used) or by removing his cap and using it like a cesta in jai alai. For a grounder, the fielder would scoop up the ball and throw it at the

Photograph of A. G. Spalding courtesy of Spalding Sports Worldwide, Inc.

Albert G. Spalding was baseball's first 200-game winner.

runner. The only way to get him out was to hit him with the ball. This was hard to do, so games were high scoring, with sometimes over a hundred runs by a single team.

Harriet and Mary were concerned over his preoccupation with this strange, frivolous activity and urged him to find a steady occupation, like bookkeeping, in which he could make a success of himself. Dutiful son that he was, he went to what we would call a community college to study accounting, but the temptation to play baseball was strong, for he was exceptionally good at it. He was the pitcher for his hometown team when it upset what was reputed to be the best amateur team in the country. He even attracted the attention of the pros, who offered him as much as $2,500 a year—a lot of money for a seventeen-year-old, five-dollar-a-week grocery bagger.

But he said no. Heeding his mother's wishes, he went to Chicago to take a succession of jobs, mostly in bookkeeping, but he had a string of bad luck. In every job he took, his employer failed shortly after hiring him. This happened seven times. Fearing he was some kind of jinx, he quit the accounting field and joined the Boston Red Sox (or Red Stockings, as they were quaintly called then). If he was a curse, he certainly didn't carry it to baseball. In his first four years, he won 241 of the 301 games he pitched. He was baseball's first two-hundred-game winner.

Four years later, he changed the color of his "stockings" from red to white and moved back to Chicago, where he compiled an even better record. In 1880, the White Stockings won nearly 80 percent of their games, a feat never approached, even by the vaunted New York Yankees in 1927—their best year—with Ruth and Gehrig. Two famous White Stockings were John Montgomery Ward and Billy Sunday, the evangelist, who said he first learned to pray while leaping into the bleachers to make a game-winning catch.

Spalding was interested in baseball as a business as well as a game. Those who bemoan the way modern sport has become obsessed with the dollar, and point to early baseball as pure sport, haven't read about A. G. Spalding. To him, the purpose of "Base Ball," as he spelled it, was to make money, and he engaged in practices not unlike those of steel and oil barons. He was sometimes ruthless in suppressing competition and abusing his players, but his organizational efforts put baseball on the firm financial footing it needed to prosper.

In 1876, he formed the National League and developed coordinated schedules, uniform rules, and consistent policies on ticket prices, and he excluded teams not meeting league standards. Six years later, a rival league began in St. Louis. Called officially the American Association, it was derisively labeled the "beer and whiskey" league for its tolerance of "strong spirits" at games, a sensible policy in the eyes of its financial backers, who were distillers and brewers. The two leagues had a love-hate relationship and learned to mutteringly coexist. While not happy with American's base standards, Spalding negotiated an agreement with them that even included postseason games between the champions of the two leagues, beginning in 1884—a ritual that developed into the World Series.

In 1889, a Players' League was formed by disaffected players from the two established leagues. It was so successful that it nearly ruined the majors, but later it, too, fell on hard times. Through shrewd, aggressive bargaining, and not a little luck, A. G. effectively carved it up, presided over its demise, and then saw himself accused of trying to make baseball an antilabor trust, in the image of Standard Oil.

In 1876, Spalding capitalized on his fame by opening a sporting-goods business called A. G. Spalding and Brothers, though only one, Walter, was really a brother. The third partner was actually a brother-in-law, sister Mary's husband. Although Albert must have been well off by this time, his mother provided the entire capital for the venture. It was a family enterprise, with Mary as book-keeper and Harriet as seamstress, sewing team names onto uniforms. They operated at 118 Randolph Street in Chicago, where the company's first product was baseballs. Three years later, they were making bats and croquet equipment in Michigan, and soon they had a catalog with dozens of items, like a catcher's mask "filled with goat hair and faced with the finest imported dogskin, which, being impervious to perspiration, always remains soft and pleasant to the face."

The company moved to Chicopee, Massachusetts, where it still is, and further diversified. Spalding invented the volleyball. He made the first tennis balls, golf balls, and footballs in the U.S., and the country's first golf clubs. In 1891, he worked with a Springfield YMCA coach, James Naismith, who asked him to design a ball for a new game he'd invented, basketball. Spalding made bicycles at one time and even toyed with the idea of making rickshaws, which caught his fancy on a trip to the Orient. He established retail outlets and by 1909 had thirty-six stores, six of them in a foreign countries.

By now, Spalding utterly dominated the sports equipment field. Both major baseball leagues had chosen Spalding as the official ball.

In addition to being an all-time great player and equipment manufacturer, Spalding was the first to take an American team on a foreign tour. He was also the first to publish an authoritative guide, *Spalding's Official Baseball Guide,* in 1878, followed by other guidebooks and record books for baseball and other sports. Perhaps most important, he lent his prestige to an effort to reform the game and cleanse baseball of its seedy image. Games were often scenes of brawls and drunkenness. Gambling was rampant, and players made small fortunes throwing games for bribes. Sometimes ruthlessly, he established and enforced strict behavioral standards. He paid premiums to players who agreed to abstain from drink. "A professional ball player . . . who weakens his play by indulgence in strong liquor," he said, "is a fool unfit for a position on a first-class team." He must have been called a "real bastard" by some—he even sent Pinkerton detectives to spy on his men—but he cleaned up the sport.

But his rigorous standards were more than an effort to keep his men sober and fit. They grew out of his view that the purpose of sport is more than amusement: its discipline and order foster "all those essentials of manliness, courage, nerve, pluck, and endurance characteristic of the Anglo-Saxon race," the muscular virtues the nation needs in its leaders and workers. It was a Kiplingesque worldview, one that conspicuously excluded women (whom he apparently didn't feel belonged in sports) and implied that W.A.S.P.s were the only true exemplars of all that is good in humankind.

But Spalding was a product of his age, and he was a tireless worker with the strength to make American sport wholesome. In recognition of his accomplishments, twenty-five years after his death, he was elected to the Baseball Hall of Fame, one of its first five inductees. He also was appointed commissioner of the 1900 Olympic Games, in Paris.

Spalding married twice, first to Sarah Keith, whom he called "Josie," in 1875. Two years after her death in 1899, he married his mistress, Elizabeth Church Mayer, with whom he had had a long-standing affair, during which he fathered an illegitimate son, whom he named Spalding. Yes, Spalding Spalding was the kid's name, and Albert sent him off to live with his sister, Mary. Upon marrying Elizabeth, he adopted Spalding Spalding and renamed him

A. G Spalding, Jr. (It has been frequently, but erroneously, claimed that young Albert went on to become a novelist and a famous concert violinist, the first American virtuoso to tour abroad. Actually, it was his nephew, also named Albert, who had those distinctions.)

Soon after his marriage to Elizabeth, the couple retired to Point Loma, near San Diego. There, in a development that must have left friends and associates seriously wondering about him, Spalding became enamored of theosophy, an occult belief system that has ancient roots but had been recently revived by Madame Helena Blavatsky, a Ukrainian mystic, who claimed to have achieved mastery from seven years of study at the feet of lamas in Tibet. Not everyone thought highly of the cult, described as a fusion of Christianity, Hinduism, and Egyptian serpent worship, and Madame Blavatsky was arrested for fraud.

In 1902, Spalding became involved in a much-publicized controversy over the admission of eleven Cuban children into the theosophical Raja Yoga School. He fought in court against the government, who sought to prevent their emigration, declaring the school and its principal, Katherine "Purple Mother" Tingley, unfit guardians. He won.

Elizabeth was active in the movement as well, in fact more so than Albert. She supervised the cult's Sunday schools and later became musical director at Point Loma.

Despite Albert's new spiritual life, he continued to maintain interest in his company and baseball, and soon became involved in local politics. He ran for the U.S. Senate, receiving a majority of the popular vote, but the victory was overturned by the California House of Representatives.

Standard & Poor

❦

"**W**hat a name for a company!" exclaimed Brenton Harries, S&P's CEO in a speech at Hartford, Connecticut, in 1977. "If you were founding a company, would you call it '*Standard . . . and Poor*'? Why not '*Excellent and Rich*'?"

It is indeed a strange name for a company. It sounds like the names of two people, but in fact, only one, Mr. Poor, was an actual person. The "Standard" comes from Standard Statistics, a company that merged with the Poor Company in 1941.

Mr. Poor was Henry Varnum Poor (1812–1905). He was the fifth of the six children of Mary and Silvanus Poor, of Andover, Maine. Contrary to their family name, the Poors were actually among the more prosperous citizens of Andover. Silvanus was the town Pooh-Bah—first selectman, treasurer, postmaster, legislative representative, and librarian. His importance was even greater than his titles indicated: he virtually ran the place. It was he who appointed the minister of the local church and paid much of his salary. When the town doctor left, it was Silvanus who went to Philadelphia to learn medicine, returning one year later to become the town doctor. Also a politician, he was among the writers of Maine's first constitution. Prominent politicos of the day, including Daniel Webster, routinely visited the Poor home.

Silvanus's life of frenetic and unremitting activity was a tough act to follow, and much of Henry's development can be traced to the trouble he had living up to expectations. Henry rarely mentioned his father in his later years.

In contrast, his relationship with his mother, née Mary Merrill, was unusually close. He confessed to his wife that his mother was "almost the only friend and companion of my boyhood and youth." Though a lonely youngster, he had the cold but loyal companionship of books: the village's "public library" was in the Poor home, and he made full use of it.

In 1841, Henry was the first person from the village to attend college; he went to Bowdoin, at whose library he pursued his love of books, particularly on political and economic philosophy—books dutifully checked out by the school's librarian, Henry Wadsworth Longfellow. Though he did well, earning both a bachelor's and a master's degree, he was not happy with the stone-gray Calvinist conservatism of Bowdoin, a school that held his religious liberalism as anathema. It might be surprising based on what I've said about Silvanus, but the Poors were flaming "freethinking" liberals who believed in the essential unity of Creation and the innate goodness of man. They—particularly Henry—had fallen under the influence of a boarder in the Poor home, Thomas Treadwell Stone, an early leader of the Transcendental movement, which soon would include Emerson, the Alcotts, Thoreau, and Margaret Fuller, and that would influence a great flowering of mid-nineteenth-century American literature, including the essays of Emerson and Thoreau and the novels of Hawthorne, Louisa May Alcott, and Poor's daughter Alice.

After graduating from Bowdoin in 1835, he moved to Bangor, Maine, where he established a law practice and became a partner in a lumber business. Once again, he brushed up against Transcendentalism: his best friend in Bangor was Reverend Frederic Henry Hedge, a man so influential in the movement that for a time the Transcendental Club was referred to as the Hedge Club. Hedge was a leading Harvard intellectual who helped introduce Kant's transcendental idealism into America. It was also through Hedge that Henry met his future bride, Mary Pierce, youngest of the ten children of a Congregational minister who once served as secretary to Harvard's board of trustees.

Henry and Mary were by all accounts a devoted couple, yet they were often isolated from each other—sometimes by circumstances, but frequently by Henry's choice. He worked until late at night, returning home exhausted; he chose to undertake business dealings that forced him to travel far from home for long periods.

It may come as a surprise that Poor, a champion of business, was a devotee of Transcendentalism, since the movement spawned a succession of capitalism's most vociferous critics—Theodore Parker, who called entrepreneurs "Ahabs" and "Herods," Henry Demarest Lloyd, who called them "the kind of men the devil wants," and Thorstein Veblen, who watched with "bleak amusement" the public's admiration of men whose success he attributed to "cupidity and chicane." Even Emerson had little good to say about the merchant class. Poor was not oblivious to the nature of the system, but he believed that it could be made to work for the public's benefit, and he became an entrepreneur himself, investing in the lumber business as a sideline to his law practice. At the time, the industry was undergoing rapid growth, and speculation on timberlands was rampant. His business suffered a severe financial reversal as a result, and perhaps the experience told him that entrepreneurs can be victims as well as predators, and also planted the idea that some sound investment advice might have prevented the disaster.

At the behest of his older brother, John, Henry abandoned his lumber business and his law practice as well and got into railroading. The brothers built a railroad to connect Portland, Maine, and Montreal. For the rest of his life, railroads remained his primary interest. Though best known today as the father of stock analysis (which he was not, incidentally), in his own day he was famous as a railroad statistician, and that was the world in which he moved.

The interest may have come about from his boyhood

isolation. To people on the remote Maine frontier, the first snowflakes of winter were like a descending curtain, sealing off the outside world for months. Railroads were more than a convenience; they kept them from starvation.

In 1849, sensing he could do more to promote railroads by writing about them than by actually building them, Poor went to New York to become editor of the *American Railroad Journal*. To someone who loved railroading and who loved to write, it was an ideal position, and he gave vent in his editorials to his feeling that his was an almost sacred purpose:

> *By the new application of steam and electro-*
> *magnetism to the arts of life, the present age will*
> *be signalized by a more rapid change in the order*
> *of society and in the progress of the race, than*
> *any former one . . . Tradition is fast losing its*
> *power over the mind of man."*

He imputed "magical powers" to the railroads and called them the "great apostle of human progress." Note the Transcendental influence: the optimistic tone, the disavowal of tradition, the implication that humankind is fundamentally good and thus capable of creating an orderly society. Railroading was part of that vision, binding the nation together.

The most important barrier in the way of that dream was the hazardous and deceptive way railroads were financed. As Poor pursued his inquiry into railroad finance, he became disgusted with the misrepresentations the railroads were making. Investors were losing fortunes because the owners were exaggerating the worth of their roads. He began a string of disconcerting revelations by disclosing in 1852 that the Erie Railroad's 7 percent dividend had been issued with borrowed money. He continued by revealing the shaky finances of several other railroads.

Predictably, he was not well liked by railroad executives. When Poor sent them requests for information on their accounts, virtually all refused, many of them rudely. But Poor got the data he needed one way or another, and the value of his reports was recognized by investors. Sensing that Poor was a man to be reckoned with, the railroads became more cooperative, and information started coming in. He compiled a manual for railroad investors in 1860. The second manual didn't appear until after the Civil War, but beginning in 1868, it has been published annually ever since. The 2000 *Standard & Poor Manual* is the 133rd edition of that work.

The manual was an immediate success and sold fifteen hundred copies at five dollars apiece its first year. It quickly gained a reputation as the standard manual for business statistics and, except for two short-lived imitators, had the field to itself until 1900, when John Moody began his security analysis reports.

In his writings, Poor made significant contributions to business management theory as well as to railroad finance. Railroad management posed a unique set of problems. There had never been enterprises approaching the scale of railroads—either in the amount of capital required or in their sheer geographic scope. And the companies they formed were physically unwieldy—thread-thin empires a few yards wide and hundreds of miles long, at a time when communication technology was primitive. Management of the finances and the day-to-day operations of these huge and strange businesses posed major problems for the executives. Poor's work in this area remains a classic. Among his interests was developing standardized time zones.

By 1861, he had developed an interest in broader issues—banking, monetary policy, and Civil War finance—and he sold the railroad journal and took a job as an editorial writer for *The New York Times*. He argued against tariffs that increased the cost of steel rails, and against government controls on rail rates. He favored the gold standard. He also went to Washington to become a lobbyist to promote policies favorable to the railroads.

If not for his other accomplishments, he might be remembered primarily as a historian. He coauthored *History of Railroads and Canals in the United States of America,* which he probably would have finished had the Civil War not taken place.

All this hyperactivity did not go unrewarded. As if to defy their family name, the Poors were becoming remarkably wealthy. Henry used his knowledge of company finances before they became publicly available to make wise investments. "Insider information" they call it now, and its use in Poor's day was perfectly legal, and profoundly rewarding. He also speculated in gold during the war years and made so much money that he planned to retire at age fifty-two and move to Brookline, Massachusetts. For a man destined to live to age ninety-three, it would have been a nice long retirement, but in 1864, he suffered a sharp reversal of fortune during a financial panic, lost a fortune, and nearly lost the house he had just bought in Brookline. Even Henry Varnum Poor, the reputed father of investment analysis, was not immune to an occasional disastrous lapse of judgment.

His financial reverses forced him back to work, and he became a broker on Wall Street with a partner, Henry Fitch, but the firm went bankrupt in 1867, further dragging his fortunes down. Next, he and his son Will entered into a partnership to sell railroad insurance. That and the resumption of the publication of the manual the next year kept him afloat, and Henry could now begin his long-postponed retirement in Brookline. The Poor home, a rambling three-story white house with green shutters at 389 Walnut Street, is still standing, with many of Mary's plantings still blooming each spring. But he did not enjoy the life of ease the setting implied, and besides, Henry was congenitally incapable of leisure. He made himself a senior partner with his son and founded Poor and Company, which became a leading Wall Street brokerage, and he continued work on his manual.

In 1877, he purchased the Merrill House, his mother's family home in Andover, as a summer home. Built by his grandfather in the mid-1790s, this structure, which figured so prominently in Henry's life as a child and later as a refuge in his distinguished old age, is still standing, with rooms and gardens the Poors added on. The rooms were designed by Stanford White (architect of Madison Square Garden), and the gardens were laid out by Frederick Law Ohmsted (architect of Central Park), both of whom were friends of the Poors.

Mary's interests in later years turned to prison reform, especially for women.

The Poors had six children over the years. The oldest son, Henry William, called Will, was bright, charming, and garrulous, but lacked scholastic motivation. His father was rather disgusted by his lack of seriousness, but after he joined his father in business, he became assiduous and successful. Even more than his father, he prospered on his father's advice, and lived an opulent life in a Renaissance palace he built in Gramercy Park. He married a stunning young woman, Constance, who soon became lame and later was chronically bedridden with arthritis. The Will Poors reached the pinnacle of New York society and were both guests of and hosts to J. P. Morgan, Jay Gould, and Theodore Roosevelt.

Not much is known of the second son. The youngest boy, Charlie, died at age seven from a fall down a staircase at school.

Agnes, the oldest girl, became an artist and writer, with two published novels, considered by some to be comparable to those of Louisa Mae Alcott and Henry James. Though she never attended college, she became fluent in several languages, including (one wonders why) Danish. She died a spinster at seventy-nine. Daughter Lucy also never married, and in her entire life never wrote of any romantic interest. Having survived a mysterious disease, never diagnosed, that she contracted in England, she lived with Agnes in later life. Eva died of rheumatic heart failure at seventeen.

The careful reader may have noticed familiar names in the account of Poor's life. His mother and his wife were both named Mary. His mother's maiden name was Merrill, and his wife's was Pierce. Any relation to the principals of Merrill, Lynch, Pierce, Fenner & Smith? It would make a nice story if it turned out that Mr. Poor of Standard & Poor and Mr. Merrill of Merrill Lynch were cousins, but, alas, that is not the case.

Starbucks

> *"What has he in his hand there?"* cried Starbuck,
> pointing to something wavingly held by the German.
> *"Impossible!—a lamp feeder!"*
>
> *"Not that,"* said Stubb, *"no, no, it's a coffee pot,
> Mr. Starbuck; he's coming off to make us our coffee."*
>
> —Herman Melville, Moby-Dick

Mr. Starbuck (ca. 1810–1840, if he had been a real
person) was Captain Ahab's first mate in Melville's *Moby-Dick*. He was one of a number of comparatively "normal guys" that stood in strange contrast to the
dorky, obsessed Ahab.

Starbuck, like Ahab, seems not to have had a first
name.

Starbuck came from Nantucket and was a Quaker by
descent. He was unusually superstitious and sensitive to
the spirit world. He is described by his author-creator as
"a long, earnest man, and though born of an icy coast,
seemed well adapted to endure hot latitudes, his flesh being hard as twice-baked biscuit."

He "had seen thirty summers" before he embarked on
the *Pequod* to hunt the great white whale.

He had a wife and young child, living somewhere on
Cape Cod. His brother had apparently been killed whaling, for at one point Melville asks, "Where in the bottom-
less deeps, could he [Starbuck] find the torn limbs of his
brother?"

"He was by no means ill-looking," Melville continues,

"quite the contrary. His pure tight skin was an excellent fit; and closely wrapped up in it and embalmed with inner health and strength, like the revivified Egyptian, this Starbuck seemed prepared to endure for long ages to come . . . his interior vitality was warranted to do well in all climates."

He was "as careful a man as you will find," testified second mate Stubb (also first-nameless), "but his caution should not be confused with cowardice." Melville had Starbuck saying, "I will have no man in my boat who is afraid of a whale." Melville explains, "By this he seemed to mean that the most reliable and useful courage was that which arises from the fair estimation of the encountered peril . . . an utterly fearless man is a far more dangerous comrade than a coward."

Starbuck, as everyone knows, underestimated his peril and perished at sea.

ACCORDING to Howard Schultz, CEO of the famous coffee chain, the name "Starbucks" was chosen because it evokes the mystique of the sea, with which the coffee trade had been long associated. He might have added that the character Starbuck's blend of courage and caution, his adaptability to all climates, his flesh like a twice-baked biscuit, and his potential for enduring for all ages to come are good qualities for an aggressive coffee and biscuit company, too.

Steinway & Sons

Heinrich Engelhardt Steinweg was born in 1797 in Wolfshagen, Germany. His birth couldn't have been at a worse place or time. Wolfshagen was part of the area of fiercest fighting at the height of the Napoleonic Wars, and his mother and several siblings froze or starved to death in the mountains as war refugees. Several more siblings died in actual battle; Heinrich himself fought in the Battle of Waterloo, where he received a commendation for rallying the troops as the regiment's bugle boy. So deeply was music embedded into Heinrich's soul that it blared out, with never a false note, even in the midst of war.

After the war, he and his surviving brothers worked for his father, who was a forester for the Duke of Brunswick, building roads and planting trees. During a thunderstorm, a hut in which they had taken shelter was hit by lightning and collapsed, killing everyone except Heinrich. This was the culminating tragedy of his youth. Within the span of a few years, he had lost his mother, father, and all eleven of his siblings; now, with no skills and no "connections," and not even able to read or write, he was forced to somehow eke out a living in the still-smoldering countryside of post-Napoleonic Europe.

Fortunately, this homeless, illiterate waif, who signed his documents with an *X* to his dying day, found a friendly cabinetmaker, to whom he was apprenticed. He became sufficiently skilled to survive, and even found time to become the village bandmaster of Seesen, where he had settled. He was also the church organist and organ builder. There is now a park named for him, and Steinway pride fills his native village.

It was in Seesen that he met and married a glove maker's daughter, Julianne Theimer, in 1825. It was a unique wedding ceremony: with her to pump the bellows and Heinrich to work the keys, the couple played the organ at their own wedding. According to legend, he gave her a labor of love as a wedding present: his first piano, now on display at the New York Metropolitan Museum of Art. Others (almost everyone, actually) dispute the account, but the Met's piano is certainly among his very first, going back possibly to 1830. Incidentally, another owner of one of the alleged first Steinways was comedian Phil Silvers, whose wife bid for it at an auction, and "thought it might be worth something."

Heinrich and Julianne had ten children, all but one of whom survived childhood, and the family was prospering, having made about four hundred pianos by 1848. The business suffered greatly during the 1848 Time of Troubles that figures so prominently in so many of the stories in this book. Heinrich's son Carl was a leader in the anti-Hapsberg insurgency movement. One of his compatriots, the composer Richard Wagner, was imprisoned for his role, but Carl escaped to America.

In 1851, with the European economy continuing to be in a depression, Heinrich and Julianne, with all their children (except for one son), moved to join Carl in New York. They set up housekeeping on East Fifty-second Street, at a site now occupied by a Mostly Roses flower shop. They Anglicized their name to Steinway; "Henry" (as Heinrich now called himself) and four of his sons found work with established piano makers in New York. Four years later, they felt confident enough to set up their own factory, and were very successful. By 1860, 350 people were on the payroll, assembling two thousand pianos a year.

The Steinways were gaining a reputation for quality, as well as quantity, but they were still just one of a number of piano makers. The "Henry Ford" of the American piano business was Jonas Chickering. You still see Chickering pianos around here and there. Although out of business now, the company operated in a factory that was said to be the nation's second-largest *building*. (Only the U.S. Capitol was larger.) The Chickering-Steinway contest for supremacy became a *cause célèbre* in its day.

During the Civil War, when the Steinway factory came close to being destroyed in the 1863 draft riots, the company was prospering. Mr. Steinway, pushing seventy now, gave increasing control to the next generation—Carl, Albert, Henry Jr., Theodor, and William—the "Sons" of Steinway & Sons. In addition to contributing energy and labor, each son had unique gifts that he offered his father's enterprise.

Carl (later changed to Charles) we have already met as the hot-blooded revolutionary who brought the family to the States. In addition to serving Steinway & Sons well, he was the Union Army's New York paymaster in the Civil War. He died young, in 1865, from typhoid fever.

Henry Jr.'s greatest asset was piano design. This was the Victorian era, and some of the early Steinways were elaborately carved and brightly painted. It was also Henry Jr. who developed a cast-iron frame capable of withstanding the nearly forty tons of force exerted by the strings. This allowed a far more stable string tuning than the wooden frames, which swelled and shrank with weather changes. He also invented the "bass overstring" feature. Lift up the lid of a piano and you will see that the long bass strings pass over the strings of the higher-pitched keys. This makes it possible to have long, resonant bass tones within a comparatively compact string frame. No one, except perhaps his brother Theodor, knew better how to fabricate and assemble the ten thousand parts (if you include nails and screws) that make up a modern concert grand.

Though a brilliant engineer, Henry Jr. had attitude problems that did not endear him to the firm's workforce. During labor disturbances, when a strike seemed imminent, he called the company's four hundred workers "swine" and ordered them fired and replaced with four hundred other "swine" who were willing to work for the wages he offered. He was not the most tactful or generous of the sons. He also had health problems. He went to Cuba in 1865 for his health, but died of tuberculosis, less than a month after Charles.

The loss of two sons within such a short time must have taken a terrible toll on the old man. On many nights, he must have awakened in a cold sweat, having flashbacks to the days of his youth, when the world was also convulsed in war, and death claimed his loved ones so frequently and unremittingly.

Albert, the youngest of the sons, had the interpersonal skills that Henry Jr. lacked, but the war kept him away from much involvement with the company. He served in the Union Army and fought in the Battle of Arlington Heights. A natural leader, he rose rapidly through the ranks. He was a colonel by the time he marched in Lincoln's funeral cortege in 1865, and was a brigadier general at the time of his death in 1877. He had crammed a lot of life into his thirty-six years.

Theodor was the oldest son. He had stayed behind to manage the family business in Germany, and came over to help his father after Charles and Henry Jr. died and Albert had become a career soldier. Theodor made the move with the greatest reluctance: his business was finally thriving after years of struggle, and his wife, Johanna, hated New York.

Theodor was perhaps the most talented musician in the family, and it was he whom his father had used at age fourteen to demonstrate how good his pianos sounded when played well. He had a degree in engineering and acoustics, and was an associate of Hermann von Helmholtz, famous for his law of the conservation of energy. Theodor's talents in acoustics enabled him to select the woods, adhesives, and coatings to give a piano its optimal resonance. He was also the Steinway son who gave us the current string design: three strings for the high notes, two strings for the middle notes, and one string for the low notes.

Theodor had something of a mean streak. He was especially caustic toward his late brother Henry. Speaking of Henry's piano, he said, "The frame is so atrociously ugly that I really fear the grands from the sixties will all go to the devil." Comments like this must have stung like another bullet into the aging flesh of poor Mr. Steinway. They were not a happy family, and he didn't need comments like this to remind him.

The gregarious, affable William was the salesman of the family. He established dealerships throughout the country, and made aggressive use of advertising, which was considered unseemly and even shocking at the time for the rather staid piano business. William also was the nation's Music Man, seeking to bring great music to a culturally barren land. In 1866, against Theodor's objections, he built Steinway Hall, a two-thousand-seat concert hall on Fourteenth Street that became the home of the New York Philharmonic.

He also got involved in completely unrelated ventures:

• He was the first chairman of the Rapid Transit Commission, which built New York's first subways.

• In 1888, even before the Duryea brothers ushered in the automobile age, William had secured the rights to produce Daimler-Benz automobiles in the United States.

• He was a delegate to the 1888 Democratic Convention, which nominated his friend Grover Cleveland for president.

William did not get a great deal of "press" from these ventures, but his domestic life was to gain considerable notoriety. Perhaps prompted by his absorption with work and his frequent absences, Regina, the lonely wife, became involved over the years with a long succession of paramours, whom she invited to the luxurious Long Island estate to be "entertained" when William was away on business. It became a tradition for Regina to dress her lover of the evening in William's bedclothes, and for the butler to bring a service of ice cream and champagne to the couple.

Even after he found out about her liaisons—and even after the realization that all his children might not really be his—he continued to love his wife. He didn't seek a divorce until he found out about "the cruise," the most scandalous episode in this drama. Regina and her niece Reinel took a cruise to England, during which aunt and niece engaged in *ménages à trois* with a succession of men. On reading the love letters from two of the men, William wrote, "No language can describe the mental tortures I endured." But what really may have gotten to him was the effect of the scandal on the family name. Steinway—a name that had evoked nothing but veneration and awe—was now eliciting giggles and smirks.

Henry Steinway, this Job who had survived Waterloo, lightning, economic hardship, draft riots, depressions, and the loss of two sons, died in 1871, before the scandal broke, mercifully sparing him from what would have been his most unbearable affliction.

Uncle Ben's

U ncle Ben was a Texas farmer. When Forrest Mars
and Gordon Harwell started their converted-rice company in the early 1940s, the local rice growers tried to
sell them their rice. They claimed that theirs was "just as
good as Uncle Ben's." Since Uncle Ben set the standard
for rice quality in the area, Mars and Harwell decided to
name the product after him.

Nothing is known about him, and he may not really
have existed, the company says. The picture on Uncle
Ben's rice packages is actually the image of a man named
Frank Brown, once the maître d' of a restaurant in Chicago, who agreed to pose for the portrait.

Proving that you never know when or how your face
may be immortalized.

Walgreens

Drugstores at the turn of the century were not warm, inviting places. They typically sold only medicines, bandages, and closely related merchandise, all available only behind a counter. By the thirties and forties, drugstores had become well lit, with merchandise neatly arranged on open display. Typically, they had a soda fountain or lunch counter that served as a social center and teenage hangout.

During recent years, a second—some would say far less wholesome—revolution in drug merchandising has occurred, with the growth of super-stores, offering thousands of items of general merchandise—and no lunch counters.

The leader of both of these revolutions was the same man, Charles Rudolph Walgreen (1873–1939). The son of Swedish immigrants, Charles and Ellen Olson Walgreen, he was born in Galesburg, Illinois, and raised in nearby Dixon (incidentally, Ronald Reagan's birthplace). Young Charles became a bookkeeper for a while, then worked in a shoe factory, until an injury cost him his job.

Acting on his doctor's recommendation, he became a pharmacist, working in a drugstore and studying pharmacy at night. In 1903, he and a partner bought the store at 4134 Cottage Grove Avenue in Chicago. The store no longer exists, but there is a replica in Chicago's Museum of Science and Industry. Six years later, Charles bought out his partner and called the store Walgreens. People liked the place, and it was so successful that he was able to expand to seven new stores by 1916. The chain continued to grow, even during the Depression, and in the early thirties, the Walgreen Company declared its first dividend.

Walgreen developed modern soda-fountain equipment, reportedly invented the malted-milk shake, built the first super-drugstore (in Tampa, Florida, in 1934), and manufactured his own merchandise under his own label. By its owner's death in 1939, Walgreens manufactured twenty-five thousand store-brand items.

Revolutionary as Walgreen was, he would not like being described that way: he was distinctly right of center in his politics. He pulled his wife's niece out of the University of Chicago because he regarded the curriculum as too liberal and gave the university $550,000 to endow a conservative foundation for what he considered the "proper" study of American institutions.

Walgreen died at age sixty. He was never robust, always suffering from the lingering effects of malaria and yellow fever that he had contracted as a soldier during the Spanish-American War.

He and his wife, Myrtle, whom he had married in 1902, had two children, Charlotte and Charles Jr. Charlotte enrolled at Northwestern University and married Justin Whitlock Dart, who started as a stock boy at a Walgreens store and ended up as president of Dart Industries, which now owns Tupperware, West Bend kitchen appliances, and Duracell batteries.

Charles Jr. (1904–) succeeded his father as president of the business in 1939 and remained until 1971. He is still very much alive. In 1998, at age ninety-four, he wanted to be the oldest man ever to go to the North Pole. He got as far as Alaska and was not permitted to continue, because he didn't have medical clearance. He was livid.

Charles Jr. was succeeded in turn by his son, Charles III (1935–), who served as the company's president until late 1998, when, after eighty-nine years of continuous management by a Charles R. Walgreen, the chain was finally passed on to other hands.

Warner Bros.

If the Warner brothers had made their lives into a film, it would have been a classic. Their story had it all: a rags-to-riches plot, fierce power struggles, abrupt changes in fortune, graphic violence, steamy sex, even a fiery car crash—everything perhaps but comic relief. The Warner brothers—Harry, Jack, Sam, and Abe were their names—regrettably never filmed their amazing story, but they changed the world of entertainment forever.

They were four of the twelve children of Ben and Pearl Warner, and their story began in 1883, when Father Ben came over on a cattle boat from Poland. Immigration officials changed the family name to Warner; from what, no one knows. Ben was so intent on leaving his past behind that he went to his grave without ever revealing his old-world name.

He went to Baltimore, where his life was to change very little, except for the absence of a family. He was a cobbler, as he'd been before, and the streets were as muddy as those of his old village of Krasnaskiosk. But he was free, and he worked hard and made enough money to bring his family to join him two years later.

Ben's wife, Pearl, and the two eldest sons, Harry and Abe, arrived on our shores in 1885, but Sam and Jack (Jacob, actually) weren't born until the family was already in the New World, and had moved to Canada, where, drawn by a horse named Bob, they lived out of a wagon and went from town to town trading with the Indians—household goods for beaver pelts. After two years of work, traipsing along rutted, muddy trails and being exposed to nature at its iciest and cruelest—Ben found that his furs, which he'd periodically transported for storage in Montreal, had been stolen.

The disheartened Warners moved to Youngstown, Ohio, a smoky and strike-plagued town that was as tough and hard as the steel it produced, where the family eked out a living repairing shoes and selling groceries. Later, they moved to New Castle, Pennsylvania, where the brothers, then in their teens and early twenties, developed an interest in a curious new fad, moving pictures. Abe, who was a soap salesman at the time, and Sam were the first to be sucked in; then Harry, who was working in an Armour meatpacking plant, and finally Jack. Using their own money and somehow convincing their stubborn father to pawn a treasured family watch and their beloved horse Bob, they bought a projector for an incredible $1,000 and started showing films on a screen in a darkened room. They called their theater the Cascade, and they opened for business on May 28, 1905. Located on South Mill Street, it was the first permanent movie house in the United States. The theater is long gone, but the building that housed it is still standing and (mercifully) is scheduled for restoration.

A film, *The Great Train Robbery,* was included in the projector deal. The first American film to tell an entire story, it contains the classic scene in which an innocent heroine is tied down to a railroad track and rescued by her hero seconds before the arrival of a speeding train.

Sam was the Cascade's projectionist; advertising and overall management were under the control of Abe and Harry. A sister, Rose, was in charge of ticket sales; she also accompanied Jack on the piano when he did song-and-dance routines while the film was being spliced together after breaking.

The Cascade may have sounded like kids' play, but it was serious business. The Warners had quit their "day jobs" to risk poverty on what seemed a mere novelty. In retrospect, of course, we know that their venture would give the brothers international fame and unimaginable wealth, but at the time, their father hoped that it would merely give the kids something to do to keep them from squabbling. But instead of harmony, the new projector became a machine of the devil that initiated a sequence of events that would tear the family apart, just as it tore apart the fragile celluloid film that displayed the film's flickering story on the screen.

Like most satanic deals, the hefty investment payed off, and the Cascade was a sensational success. In 1905, no one had ever seen anything like a motion picture, and the public was enthralled. They ducked in their seats at the seeming approach of an onrushing train, and thrilled to special effects we laugh at today. Some resolutely refused to leave after the performance, insisting on seeing the show again. Business boomed, and the Warner Brothers—and Sister—soon accumulated enough buffalo nickels to retrieve Dad's watch and poor Bob from the pawnshop, with plenty of nickels left over.

There were two problems, though. For one thing, to seat people, they had to borrow chairs from the local mortician, so whenever there was a funeral, they couldn't show any films. A more important problem was getting good-quality films (or sometimes, just *any* films). They decided there was only one way to solve it: become distributors themselves. So the brothers (sister Rose had dropped by the wayside) founded the Duquesne Amusement Company to distribute films to theaters throughout the East. It was the first business of its kind, and it was a gold mine. The $2,500 they made per week(!) allowed them to sell the Cascade and pocket $40,000 in the process. But fortune was to turn again: the next year—1908—they were driven out of business, because Edison, who had invented the projector, declared that he had exclusive rights to all films produced in the U.S. and France and created a trust to buy out or force out all independent distributors.

In 1912, the courts broke up the Edison Trust, allowing the Warners to get into film distribution again, but by this time they had moved on. They were now in a dusty, unknown, isolated town near Los Angeles called Hollywood, where they were actually making films. In 1917, they produced a documentary, *My Four Years in Germany*. With its horrific realism, it was the *Saving Private Ryan* of its day. It fed on the rabid anti-German feelings of the period, and it received a standing ovation at its New York premiere. It grossed $800,000, and made $130,000 profit for the brothers. More important, this was the film that established WB's distinctive style: hard-hitting, realistic films, bleak commentaries on all that was ugly and lurid in American life—poverty, black oppression, violence against women, and "untouchable" subjects like venereal disease.

They used their windfall to buy a studio on fabled Sunset Boulevard. The cost of that and three years of money-losing films left them nearly broke by 1920, but by 1925, they were again out of the hole and risking it all on technical-cutting-edge ventures, notably sound and color.

The brothers worked with people at Bell Labs to make "Vitagraph" sound pictures. These were movies that ran in sync with disks that resembled phonograph records, but played from the center out to the edge. The first Vitagraph movie was *Don Juan,* with John Barrymore. It was not a "talkie"—the sound track featured only music and sound effects of clashing swords—but it was preceded by demonstration shorts in which the lips of singers and speakers moved in sync with the sound. (The first speaker was Will Hays, a former postmaster general, who later became the movie industry's first censor.) At its New York premiere, the enthralled audience of a thousand, who had paid eleven dollars a ticket, rose to their feet and showed studio moguls, who up to then, curiously, had been resistant to sound films, that the Warners were onto something. Two years later, WB released *The Jazz Singer,* the story of a cantor who leaves his synagogue to marry a showgirl and become a cabaret singer, and later returns as a penitent. Its most memorable line, "You ain't heard nothin' yet," is (erroneously but poignantly) considered filmdom's first words. Its most memorable scene showed Al Jolson singing "Mammy" in blackface, with clasped hands, on bended knee. The film also received thunderous applause, and still causes people watching it on video to reach for their Kleenex.

Though reputed to be the first talkie, *The Jazz Singer* was basically a silent film with only four brief sound sequences. The first *true* talkie was *Lights of New York,* which followed the next year, also by Warner Brothers. And the year after that, the studio released the first talking *color* movie—*On With the Show.*

The Warners were indeed technical innovators, but they were original in the way they did business, too. Under Abe's direction, they pioneered "vertical integration" and bought and built movie theaters. This was partly to make money from ticket sales, but mostly to guarantee that WB movies would be showcased. They built one hundred of these theaters; often they were the grandest, most opulent structures in town. Sadly, only five remain.

What doomed these theaters was television, ironically an invention of Lee DeForest, the same person who had made possible the Warners' success by inventing the film sound track. Jack felt so threatened by TV that he wouldn't allow a set to be shown in any WB movie, and (only half-jokingly) he even banned the mention of the word in his presence. Harry, in contrast, saw potential in making films for the new medium and even thought of quitting the movies and focusing on it, but he was old and tired of fighting.

They were different, these brothers. All four of them, in fact. Like so many brother sets we have met in this book, it's hard to believe they came from the same family. It was 1950 now, not 1905, but in a sense nothing had changed for forty-five years. Harry was still the guy in charge, Sam remained the technician, Abe was still a kind of manager, and Jack was the boy who never grew up. More about the personal lives of these remarkable men:

Abe. Abe was treasurer of the company and was also in charge of distribution. He was a big, ham-handed man, whose gruff exterior belied a genuinely good nature. He married twice, both times to a woman named Bessie. He was always defensive about his lack of education, though actually he was the only one of the brothers who had any college at all. Ever a gambler, he liked to play the horses and held all-night gin parties with his buddies. He was down-to-earth, even crude, no doubt to the consternation of the second Bessie, who was a refined, educated woman. They lived on a luxurious estate in Rye, New York, on Long Island Sound.

Sam. Sam was the friendliest and best liked of the brothers. In 1934, he married an eighteen-year-old former child star, Lina Basquette, "the Shirley Temple of the Silents," who later became a Ziegfeld Follies dancer. They had one daughter, Lita.

Sam, you may remember, was the Cascade's projectionist and was the "technician" of the group. He never stopped innovating. Harry glowingly said of him, "He gave us . . . the gift of music and the spoken word on film." He was the one who worked with Western Electric engineers to develop this technology, in the face of unreasoning resistance and ridicule from most of the industry. At first, even Harry questioned the feasibility of talkies. *The Jazz Singer* vindicated him, but he didn't live to see it: the man who "gave us the gift of music and the spoken word on film" died the night before its premiere.

While Sam's death was a moment of bitter irony, sadness and shock, it was to have more lasting effects. Sam was the mediator who kept Harry and Jack from tearing each other apart. The man who spliced together broken film at the Cascade took upon himself the more difficult task of mending the broken family in their Hollywood years. Harry and Jack were such implacable foes that there was talk that they paid off the doctors to make sure that Sam died. "They killed Sam," William Demarest, costar of *The Jazz Singer,* reportedly said to the family, though few believed him.

After Sam's death, an ugly sequence of events ensued. Harry had his widow, Lina, declared unfit and took custody of daughter Lita. The Darling of the Silents had squandered her inheritance from Sam, remarried, quickly divorced, and the next year attempted suicide. She was consorting with bad-girl sextresses like Clara Bow and Carole Lombard, and Harry, by most accounts, did the right thing, though it is a cruel fate for any mother to have a child taken away from her. Lina was to see her daughter only twice during the next twenty years.

Harry was the oldest of the brothers, and he was head of the company then just as much as he had been at the Cascade. He was a slave driver who kept his brothers, particularly Jack, on a tight leash. And the studio as well. Actors rose at five and often worked from eight A.M. to midnight—except on Saturdays, when WB cameras did not stop filming until dawn the next day, under torrid carbon arc lamps. During the Depression, he forced workers to work at half pay, but he himself welcomed the industry's periodic downturns. It enabled him to buy WB stock at depressed prices and sell it for a hefty profit when good fortune returned. In one year alone, he made $9 million by such shenanigans, all thoroughly legal at the time.

Harry and his wife, Rea Levinson, who came from an upper-class family in Manchester, England, had three children, Lewis, Betty, and Doris. Lewis was being groomed to take over WB when the founders had passed on, but he died in 1931, from complications that resulted from an infected wisdom tooth. Harry and Rea bought a ranch, and Harry spent more and more time there. Though not entirely cold and pitiless, he rode in a chauffeured limousine even during the darkest days of the Depression. His colossally poor judgment provoked full-scale riots and caused Hollywood to become a hotbed of Communist sympathizers.

Jack was the most colorful of the brothers. He was the

only one to actually perform in a film (*Open Your Eyes,* 1917). In 1914, he married Irma Salomon, to whom he had been introduced by Sid Grauman, who later founded the Chinese Theater. The marriage was not happy. Jack was an unabashed philanderer, and he and Harry had hot and repeated arguments over Jack's incessant starletizing. Jack finally divorced Irma to marry a starlet named Ann Paige. The divorce saddened and enraged Harry even more than Jack's affairs and his trips to the south of France to gamble and whore. At times, their top-of-the-lungs arguments could be heard throughout the studio. There was even physical violence, culminating in a chase scene famous in company lore. Shouting, "I'll kill you, you son of a bitch!" Harry pursued Jack around the studio with a lead pipe. He threw it at him, hard enough to kill him if it had landed right, but it missed.

Sometime later, Jack cheated death once again. He fell asleep at the wheel, and in a fiery Bruce Willisesque crash scene, was thrown forty feet out of his flaming car and nearly died.

Jack's brushes with death did not have the softening effect such occurrences sometimes have on gentler souls. During the Cold War, he became an avid anti-Communist and led right-wing studio moguls in supporting Joe McCarthy and his blacklisting campaign.

In his dealings with his family, he was just as hard. Abruptly and without real cause, he fired his son, Jack Jr. The only son of any of the Warner brothers who had anything to do with the business, young Jack was trying to get the studio into television and by all accounts was doing a decent job. As we know, Jack Sr. hated TV. But more important, Son reminded Dad of the part of his life that he'd spent with Irma, and he was determined to rid himself of that unpleasantness and move on. Characteristically, he didn't have the courage to do the dirty deed himself, and left it to his lawyer to bring his son the news.

The firing of young Jack might have been termed the "Great Betrayal," but it was not; that term would be reserved for an even sorrier episode: Jack suggested to his brothers that they all sell out and spend their retirement years at leisure while they still had their health. Because the studio was his life, Harry signed only with greatest reluctance. A few weeks later, Harry learned that Jack had in fact not sold out at all, but had arranged a behind-the-scenes buyback that made Jack a major stockholder and the company's president. It was one of the great coups in American corporate history, and a blot on the already well-blood-sullied cloak of Jacob Warner.

Harry must have wanted to kill his usurping brother, but his life went on, and he and Rea were celebrating their fiftieth wedding anniversary the next year when Jack entered the scene once again. Uninvited, he ridiculed his brother for staying with one woman for fifty years, and then left Harry to die after a series of strokes during the next two years.

"Harry didn't die," said Rea. "Jack killed him."

Jack did not attend the funeral. He was gambling and womanizing in the south of France.

Welch's

Thomas Bramwell Welch (1825–1903), who gave grape juice to the world, was the sixth of fifteen children of Abraham and Mary Welch. Born in Glastonbury, England, on New Year's Eve of 1826, he came to the New World at age six, where his father became a farmer-shopkeeper in a village in upstate New York.

Young Tom was deeply religious and in 1844 became a minister in the Wesleyan Methodist church. It was a strong abolitionist church, and Tom and his parishioners were active in the Underground Railroad.

In 1847, he married Lucy Hutt, a shopgirl in his mother's hat store. Eventually, Tom and Lucy had seven children, one of whom, Charles, was to make Welch's Grape Juice a world-class company.

Throat problems made preaching difficult for Tom. Besides, he wanted to change his profession, so he went to Syracuse Medical College, graduating in 1852. He opened up a medical practice in Penn Yan, New York, the next year.

After four years, Tom tired of doctoring and decided to become a dentist. He also tired of New York and moved to Winona, in the Minnesota Territory. Lucy found the winters there hard to take, so the family moved once again, this time to Vineland, New Jersey, where for the first time in their lives they entered into a somewhat settled existence. They stayed in Vineland for twenty-five years. Tom practiced dentistry and also invented and marketed his own dental amalgams, which, until recent years, were still in common use.

But for the restless Tom, dentistry became a bore, and it was again time to move on. The next project: grape juice. In the years following the Civil War, the temperance movement was growing, and Tom, a fervent teetotaler, opposed the use of wine even in a church sacrament. He wanted to develop a nonalcoholic grape juice as a substitute.

One would think that grape juice wouldn't have to be "invented": you just crush grapes and there it is. But it's not that simple. Left by itself, grape juice ferments from yeasts on the grape's surface. Tom came up with the idea of pasteurizing the juice to kill the yeast. He tried bottling the juice and submerging the bottles in boiling water. It worked, and in 1869, he began marketing his product, "Dr. Welch's Unfermented Wine."

In his retirement years, this remarkable and restless man went on to yet another totally unrelated venture. He produced a "Sistem of Simplified Spelling," later championed by Franklin Roosevelt, to make it easier for immigrants to learn English, but it never caught on.

Wells Fargo

Wells Fargo stagecoaches, so familiar to us as museum pieces and props in bad Gabby Hayes movies, played an important and largely unrecognized role in the development of our country. They were the UPS and Greyhound of their day. But more than that: they changed commerce, public works, and banking in ways that may surprise you.

The "Wells" of Wells Fargo was Henry Wells (1805–1878), born in Thetford, Vermont. His father, named Shipley, was a farmer who also made bricks and served as the local Presbyterian preacher. When Henry was nine, the family moved to Seneca Falls, in the scenic Finger Lakes region of New York, where Henry was to become a leather worker and shoemaker, and to take a bride, Sarah Daggett. In 1836, in a move that determined the principal direction of his future life, he took a job handling freight on the Erie Canal.

In 1840, a man named William F. Harnden walked up to young Henry and offered him a job in a new type of business. Harnden is scarcely remembered today, but he made a huge contribution to the history of American commerce. The post office's Parcel Post, and private carriers like UPS, Federal Express, and dozens of others that have come and gone—all can trace their ancestry to him, for he was the founder of the parcel delivery business; and Wells seems to have been his first employee.

Before the advent of express services like Harnden's, if you wanted a package delivered to your aunt in St. Louis, you would find a friend, acquaintance, or even a respectable-looking stranger who was going there and entrust the parcel to their care. Though this arrangement actually worked better than you might suppose, it sometimes had disappointing results, so there was a great market for Harnden's express service, especially in the fast-growing Great Lakes region. Wells and Harnden used the railroads, quickly expanding at the time, for rapid delivery. The telegraph was another recent and rapidly developing technology, and Wells financed several of the country's earliest telegraph lines.

Harnden and Wells did a booming business in express delivery of parcels and also letters. In violation of the law, he and Harnden issued their own stamps and offered delivery of letters for *one-fifth* the price the post office was charging. Many of his couriers were arrested, but Henry was credited with forcing postage rates down to affordable levels.

In Harnden's eyes, Wells was a model employee. Two years after being taken on, he made him a partner with authority to "hire and fire." One of Wells's first moves was to hire an agent for the company's Albany office. He chose an ex-mailman from Pompey, New York, named William George Fargo.

William George Fargo (1818–1881) was the eldest of the twelve children of William Fargo, a farmer who lived near Pompey. William's mom, for someone born probably in the 1790s, had the jarringly modern name Tracy.

Young Will got an early start in the "express" business, becoming Pompey's mailman at age thirteen. He then tried his hand at the grocery business and innkeeping, but didn't care for either and became an agent for the Auburn & Syracuse Railroad. That's where he was when Wells found him. At that time, he and his wife, Anna H. Williams Fargo, were newlyweds.

When Harnden died in 1845, Fargo and Wells "inherited" the business, and they went into partnership with guys named Livingston and Pomeroy to run stages between Buffalo, Chicago, and Detroit. By 1849, the express business had grown by a hundredfold, and Hank, Bill, and their partners were already wealthy men.

Henry Wells and William Fargo, the faces behind those famous stagecoach names.

As with all lucrative businesses in the Wild West, theirs attracted rivals, donning black hats and riding black horses. Their nemesis was John Butterfield, who actually looked something like a stereotypic Western villain. Like Wells and Fargo, Butterfield almost totally lacked formal education but had ambition and a natural business flair. After engaging in a nearly disastrous price war, the two companies called a truce, called the "Buffalo Truce" in company lore. They formed a new company, which they called "American Express." Long after the founders had passed on, it was to become famous for its travelers' checks and credit cards.

Butterfield and Fargo were headstrong, irascible personalities, and they found it so hard to agree on a structure for the company that Wells left in disgust to travel for several months in Europe. In this interim, the company's charter finally took form, and it was one of the most curious in history. Under it, American Express would be composed of two distinct operating units, both accountable to a single governing board. There would be a Butterfield "half" and a Fargo "half" to keep the combatants separated. It would not be a corporation, but an "unincorporated joint stock association," meaning that 1) the personal assets of stockholders could be seized to pay for the company's debts, 2) the partners could operate in virtual secrecy, and 3) the board would not be accountable to stockholders. Another curious feature was a sunset provision: after ten years, the company was to dissolve, with no option for renewal. One might wonder who would ever be enticed to invest in such an enterprise, but amazingly, some were.

The vacationing Wells was appointed president in absentia. It was a good choice. He was the only one capable of mediating between Butterfield and Fargo. Moreover, he *looked* the part—over six feet tall and broad-shouldered, he was handsome, distinguished looking, and elegantly outfitted. With his ruffled shirts and a gold-tasseled beret, this flashy gentleman stood far above the common man. But he was not standoffish; he was friendly and natural, despite having a severe stutter, an unfortunate impediment for such a communicative individual.

There's an old business joke: never miss a meeting; they might appoint you to something. It was not a joke, or at least a very funny one, to Henry Wells. When he returned from his travels, he learned of his appointment. At the board's first meeting in the New York's Astor House, he was welcomed home with open arms, but after less than a month, he once again left in apparent disgust and—without even resigning—retreated to the wilds of upstate New York, where he built a lovely Italianate villa for Sarah and their four children (Charles, Mary, Oscar, and Edward) and founded a college for women. Clearly, Henry was less than pleased with the way things had developed at American Express, and he acted as if his chief interests were elsewhere, as they almost certainly were.

Despite his dislike of his duties, and his insistence on living a two days' journey from New York City, he remained president for another eighteen years.

Meanwhile, there were other exciting developments.

One was the California gold rush. In February 1852, Fargo suggested to the board that the company extend its stagecoach service to California, to capitalize on the demand created by the "49ers." All but Wells and Fargo voted no. Frustrated with the intransigence of the American Express board, they developed their own independent company, which they called Wells Fargo. Soon the dusty, bandit-ridden trails of the West were being traversed by Wells Fargo stages. The gold rush, though three years old, was still going strong, and the partners, far luckier than all but a few of the gold panners they carried, prospered. Even after the rush, thousands remained in San Francisco in more conventional pursuits, so demand for Wells Fargo remained, and even came to be thought of as a California company. They expanded into the banking business. Meanwhile, by 1857, American Express was prosperous enough to build a lavish new corporate headquarters at the corner of Jay and Hudson streets in New York.

American Express was re-formed after its mandatory tenth-birthday dissolution. Wells remained as its president—even more unwillingly than before, because of a fall from a carriage that left him almost unable to walk even a year afterward.

With the coming of the Civil War, the already prosperous express business was further enriched. Soldiers, starved for news from families and sweethearts, and anxious to let their loved ones know they were still alive, paid almost anything to anyone who could bring them letters or take them for safe delivery. American Express couriers rode through the hottest, most bullet-infested fields of the war. Some came to succor the wounded and dying with news from home; others greedily extracted all they could from the desperately homesick men. Either way, the couriers involved in the perilous and macabre enterprise made fortunes for their bosses. American Express stock shot through the roof, dividends were sometimes actually in excess of the value of the stock, and executive salaries exploded like powder magazines in Virginia forts.

During this period of upheaval, the rather laid-back Wells was forced out, in favor of the more aggressive Fargo. At age sixty-three, Henry retired to Aurora, to live with his new wife, Mary Prentice, whom he had married two years after Sarah's death in 1859. He knew the value of education and was among the pioneers in promoting education for women. His college, now called Wells College, was only the second women's college in the country. He also had an interest in speech therapy, and built several schools for the speech-impaired. He died ten years after his return to Aurora while on vacation in Glasgow, Scotland.

Fargo stayed on as president of both Wells Fargo and American Express. He also served as mayor of Buffalo, where he was succeeded in office by Grover Cleveland, and held that office even when he was heading his business and raising a family of eight. He also owned the local newspaper, the *Buffalo Courier*. This busy man also had a controlling interest in the New York Central Railroad and, with Jay Cooke, built the Northern Pacific. One of the station stops on the Northern Pacific—Fargo, North Dakota—was named for him.

Wendy's

M elinda Lou Thomas (1961–) was born in Fort
Wayne, Indiana, where her father, R. David Thomas, was the assistant manager of a restaurant called the "Hobby Ranch House with Barbecue." Her toddler siblings had difficulty pronouncing "Melinda Lou"—they made it sound something like "Wenda"—so the family altered it slightly to an actual name and came to call her Wendy. The name has stuck to this day.

At age one, she moved to Columbus, Ohio, taking her family with her. Her father (called Dave by his friends) is of course a familiar face to TV viewers; her mom, Lorraine Buskirk, was a waitress when she met Dave, but became a full-time mother-homemaker after their marriage. Wendy has a sister Pam (1955–), six years old at the time of the move to Columbus; another sister, Molly; and a brother, Kenny, (birth dates unknown). Later, there would be a third sister, Lori.

Wendy's father came to Columbus to assume the responsibilities (and the considerable debts) of an ailing Kentucky Fried Chicken franchise, consisting of four stores. Colonel Sanders himself was a friend of Dave's, and he had warned him about the Columbus franchise. With Wendy perhaps listening from her playpen and wondering who the strange-looking goateed man in the white suit and string tie was, the Colonel expressed his displeasure: "That operation is ⚡✗☆✱ , and you're going to uproot your wife and kids and make a G.D. fool of yourself. Wise up, boy . . . It's a one-way street going nowhere."

Wendy's dad took the franchise anyway, and to everyone's surprise made it so successful that the Colonel offered him a job as supervisor of all three hundred KFC stores east of the Mississippi. He took that offer, too, for a big salary, but there was a downside: it meant five days a week on the road, and Wendy didn't see him often.

Later, her dad had a falling-out with Colonel Sanders. The issue: how to properly drain the grease off chicken when it's come out of the fryer. The two hardly spoke afterward.

Dave had legal problems, too: a conflict with John Y. Brown, who with a partner had bought out the Colonel. This is the same John Y. Brown who later married Miss America Phyllis George and became governor of Kentucky. Dave retained F. Lee Bailey as his lawyer. He won their case, and Wendy's parents found themselves millionaires.

After a brief flirtation with Arthur Treacher's Fish 'n Chips, Dave used his money to open his own hamburger restaurant. He chose "Wendy's" as its name to give it a wholesome, family image, which he reinforced with a caricature of the freckle-faced redhead as the company's logo.

At the dedication of the first Wendy's, in November 1969, in Columbus, eight-year-old Wendy complained about having to smile so much, but performed her duties well.

In 1979, she enrolled at the University of Florida. She and her husband, Paul, have one daughter, Amanda. Paul and Wendy operate a Wendy's franchise, so it's possible to go to a Wendy's somewhere (they won't tell me where it is) and get served by Wendy herself.

Weyerhaeuser

❦

T he Weyerhaeuser Company did not just become the
nation's leading lumber business; it also changed the
way the industry operated, from a mow-down-and-move-
on to a harvest-and-replant mentality.

Forest businesses have a way of maintaining themselves as well as the forests that sustain them. George H.
Weyerhaeuser (1926–), the current chairman of the Weyerhaeuser Company, is the fourth generation to head the
family business, founded in 1858. His company does not
hold the record for longevity, however: in Kittery, Maine,
Mr. Weyerhaeuser reports, there is a sawmill founded in
1633 that is now being operated by eleventh-generation
descendants of its founder. Nevertheless, with its 140-year
history, the Weyerhaeuser Company is the longest-lived
family-operated business described in this book.

Its founder was Frederick Weyerhaeuser (1834–1914),
born in Niedersaulheim, Germany. His father, John, was
a hardworking farmer and vintner who died young, leaving the twelve-year-old Frederick with onerous family responsibilities. He was one of thirteen children, but the
only male to survive to adulthood.

Like at least five others in this book, he fled Europe
during the disorder of the late 1840s. And like some of
them, he worked in a brewery, but only briefly. He tried
farming, also briefly, and then migrated to Rock Island,
Illinois, where he worked on the fabled-in-song "Rock
Island Line," the first railroad to cross the Mississippi and
open the West. Amtrak uses this line, and if you take the
train, you may ride over rail lines surveyed by Mr. Weyerhaeuser.

Frederick was a robust and affable young man. He took

pride in his newly learned German-tinged English by quoting sayings in *Poor Richard's Almanac*. He took up beekeeping as a sideline and began drinking a quart of buttermilk daily, a habit that he said sustained his health throughout his eighty years.

In 1854, there were two major charges in young Frederick's life—his entry into the lumber business (as a night fireman at a local sawmill) and his marriage to Sarah Bloedel, the daughter of an ax maker from his own hometown of Niedersaulheim.

Frederick advanced in the company and soon became its general manager. In 1860, when the mill went bankrupt, he entered into a partnership with his brother-in-law to buy it. Frederick and his partner, F.C.A. Denkmann, made $3,000 their first year, and nearly double that the next, and eleven years later, they bought a second lumberyard, also in Rock Island.

Photo courtesy Weyerhaeuser Archives.

Frederick "Dutch Fred" Weyerhaeuser made wood a renewable resource and changed forestry practice forever.

They felt rich, and the lumber business certainly seemed like the place to be. The nation was growing fast and needed timber, and the days of the make-your-own-log-cabin were coming to a close.

In a way, the business was too good. Dozens of companies felled trees and floated their logs down the river, in and out of logjams, and at the river mouth tried to figure out whose logs were whose. First, they had a scheme of "brailling" the logs with identifying notches (sort of like cattle branding), but the notches were subject to confusion and "alteration," and many a fistfight broke out among the tallymen, to the entertainment of the lumberjacks.

To bring order, "Dutch Fred," as Weyerhaeuser was called, formed the Mississippi River Logging Company, a cooperative in which every member had a share in the profits of all logs floated down the Chippewa River to the Mississippi. Each individual member company's share was proportionate to the number of logs it floated.

While taking a leadership role in the development of his industry, he worked for many years developing the pine forests of the northern Midwest. He and Sarah Elizabeth moved to Minnesota, the land of ten thousand lakes—an appropriate place for a man whose family name means "one who dwells in a house among lakes." In St. Paul, they became neighbors of J. J. Hill, founder of the Great Northern Railway, which ran from Chicago to Seattle. It was Hill who enticed Weyerhaeuser and fourteen others to buy almost a million acres of forest land in Washington State. It was the largest private real estate sale in U.S. history to that date. Weyerhaeuser, the first among the partners, suggested calling their partnership the Universal Timber Company, but the others insisted on calling it the Weyerhaeuser Company, in recognition of his leadership and integrity.

Dutch Fred was in fact different from the others. In contrast to most foresters, who slashed and moved on, Weyerhaeuser saw timber as a resource that should be maintained. He reportedly said, "This is not for us, nor for our children—but for our grandchildren." He established a policy of tree planting, and led in the forest-fire protection movement.

In 1911, the company built its own eleven-story office building, in Tacoma. Still in use, it was the company's headquarters until 1971.

In 1911, Frederick and Sarah Elizabeth bought a retirement home in Pasadena. Mrs. Weyerhaeuser died without ever occupying it, but Mr. Weyerhaeuser moved there and kept busy gardening—poppies and oranges mostly.

He died three years into his California retirement, with

his three daughters and two sons at his bedside. He was buried in Rock Island.

His eldest son, John P. Weyerhaeuser (1858–1944), took over the business and moved to Tacoma, but he left the work of the company to its general manager, George Long. During John's tenure, the company continued to growth, with the Panama Canal offering new opportunities for overseas expansion.

In 1931, the company got into the pulp paper business to make use of hemlock, almost a nuisance tree with no use as lumber. Paper was ultimately to become more profitable than lumber. It also allowed greater utilization of the company's land. Only about 18 percent of the mass of a tree is usable as lumber; but when the waste portion is pulped as paper, the percentage increases to 30. When portions are used as a component of pressed lumber, like wall paneling and plywood (developed in the 1940s) and particleboard (introduced in 1955), over 50 percent of the biomass is used.

In 1933, J. P. Weyerhaeuser (1899–1956), John's son, took over the business. "Phil," as he was known, had experience in running sawmills in Idaho. He made major contributions to the company during his tenure, which lasted until he died of leukemia in 1956. During his years, the reforestation program was greatly expanded, thanks to the Civilian Conservation Corps, and the company diversified into a number of lumber-based products. His brother, F. K., took over the reins for a short time.

In 1935, the Weyerhaeuser family became a household name—not because of its forest products, but because of a celebrated kidnapping. Phil's nine-year-old son was walking home from school for lunch when he was kidnapped and held for ransom by a woman and two men. It rivaled the Lindbergh kidnapping of 1932 in terms of media interest, but fortunately the child was returned unharmed and the kidnappers were apprehended. The child was George Weyerhaeuser, the company's current chairman.

Wrigley's

❧≈❧

William Wrigley Jr. (1861–1932) gave his name to the world's leading chewing gum, but he was a multifaceted individual who made fortunes in mining, resort development, and sports promotion.

He was the first of the nine children born to William and Mary Ladley Wrigley, of Philadelphia. His father, a Civil War veteran, ran a modestly successful soap factory.

Son Will was a difficult youth. At age eleven, he ran away to New York, where he stayed for months with no contact with the rest of his family. Shortly after his return, the youngster, no doubt still teary-eyed and red-butted from his welcome home, was put to work in Dad's soap factory, stirring heavy kettles of viscous lye and fat with broad paddles. Doing so made him develop an upper-body musculature that he never lost, and physical fitness was ever after a passion with him. But his real forte was sales, and at age thirteen, he started peddling his father's soap in towns within a wagon's-ride distance of the city. His persistence led a Quaker lady to say, "Thee will be a rich man someday."

But life wasn't all work. One day on a steamboat ride in 1883, he met a petite, sixteen-year-old named Ada Foote, whom he married two years later. So childlike and delicate were her features that years later Mrs. Wrigley was once accidentally herded in with a group of Sunday-school kids on an excursion until rescued by her valiant husband. The couple were to have two children of their own, Dorothy and Philip.

In 1891, Will, then thirty, and Ada left for Chicago, where he made and sold Wrigley Scouring Soap. How he got into the gum business is lost to history. At first, it was a way to entice people to buy his soap, and it wasn't until 1895 that he saw himself primarily as a gum maker.

In fact, he didn't actually make the gum. Manufacturing was contracted out. The contractor, a company with a most peculiar combination of product lines—chewing gum and paint—made two now forgotten brands for Mr. Wrigley, but soon replaced them with "Juicy Fruit" and "Spearmint," which became instant successes. The wrappers, which Wrigley designed himself, have changed little through the years. The recipes for the gums haven't changed either, and neither did the price, at least until 1972, when inflation finally took its toll, and the company raised the price for the first time in fifty-five years.

In 1911, Wrigley and his manufacturer merged, giving Wrigley tighter control of manufacturing operations.

Will built his empire by traveling throughout the country, selling one stick at a time. He was successful wherever he went, but at great cost of time and energy: one year he spent 137 nights sleeping sitting up on trains. As business grew, he took on a force of salesmen and distributors but still worked routinely every day, usually even on Sundays.

At one time he considered selling out to his principal rival, American Chicle. He asked son Philip, then six, if he wanted to take over the business someday. Philip said, "Yes, Dad, of course I do." That decided the matter for him, and he didn't sell.

By 1920, twenty-nine years after coming to Chicago with thirty-two dollars in his pocket, William Wrigley Jr. had become a wealthy man and world leader, incredibly all by selling a product with a unit price of one cent. On November 11, 1920, the tenth anniversary of the company's incorporation, son Philip laid the foundation stone for the Wrigley Building, then Chicago's tallest structure. "A tribute to the power of human jaws," one headline called it, but it really owed its existence to the tenacity and talent of a remarkable man, who, true to form, ignored the advice of everyone in building his shining tower. He used a white marble that cost $65,000 more than the stone everybody else was using. He had it floodlit. He insisted on a foundation on bedrock, even though it would increase the cost enormously. And he chose as a site a rat- and thug-infested area near the Chicago River wharves.

Still the crown jewel of Chicago's Loop and called America's most beautiful art deco structure, the unique tower with its alabaster city's gleam fixed the future development of the City of Broad Shoulders, and the once-seedy stretch on Michigan Avenue too dangerous to walk down became its "Miracle Mile." The building so impressed Stalin that some say he used it as the model for the main building at the University of Moscow.

How does one account for the Wrigley story's happy ending? Will attributed his success to advertising. "Tell 'em quick and tell 'em often," he said. During the depression of 1907, he purchased advertising at bargain-basement prices (about one-sixth of its value the previous year). At a time when his competitors were eliminating their advertising, all you saw, gum-wise, was Wrigley ads. He also gave boxes of free gum to stores that agreed to stock Wrigley's gum. When the economy improved, he increased his sales by a factor of ten.

His philosophy on sales was reported to be: "Be always pleasant, always patient, always on time, and never . . . argue." Good advice for nonsalesmen as well.

Another technique was premiums. Umbrellas, cuspidors, fairy boudoir lamps, and "baby carriages with laced edge satinet parasols" were some of the hundred or so inducements he offered storekeepers to stock his gum. Not all of them worked, and his office was cluttered with bicycles, Smyrna rugs, and "ladies' eiderdown dressing sacques" that nobody wanted. Many times in the lean 1890s, creditors huffed and puffed at his door. "Jack," he said to his bookkeeper melodramatically, "I guess we're through. The sheriff will be here on Monday morning. I've got just twenty dollars in the world. Here's half of it for you." During this incident, supposedly the only time the man ever evinced despondency in his business dealings, he still was willing to give away half of what he had.

But his most basic key to success was that he refused to accept failure. "He had no use for the man who tried, who did his best," one biographer says. "No Wrigley salesman ever said, 'I'll do the best I can.' If he had . . . he would have been (in a favorite Wrigley phrase) 'all washed up.' "

The stubborn streak that made him a success got him into trouble as well. For fourteen years, he was tied up in trademark infringement suits and countersuits with a guy named Larson, a rival gum maker. It was a dramatic story, with vanishing documents, private detectives tailing jurors, and the death of a key witness. Wrigley, who could have settled out of court for $75,000, ended up paying out nearly $2 million. This was in 1928. The company's annual report mentions the loss and concludes, "We anticipate a favorable . . . 1929." Ever the optimist was William Wrigley Jr.

Rotund and chubby-cheeked, with dark wavy hair, Bill, as he was thought of by most, but never called, was a jolly, ever-smiling man, whose door was always open to employee and client alike. Fashionably attired, often in diamond-studded Ascot ties and wing collars, he was clean-shaven, except in his youth, when he wore a barbershop mustache.

He admired Teddy Roosevelt and, like John Dodge, was a delegate to the 1916 Republican Convention. When TR launched the Progressive party, Wrigley was its first major contributor. Four years later, there was an attempt to draft him as Harding's running mate, until he made it clear he wasn't interested in being vice-president. If he'd accepted, he would have become president, for Harding died in office.

The Wrigleys led an unsettled, peripatetic existence. The family changed residences frequently and usually lived in hotels. It wasn't until he was forty-five that he finally bought the family a house, and even then, he moved on to another after only five years.

Until 1912, Wrigley had never taken a vacation. Now, thought his family, it was time for the fifty-one-year-old executive to get some well-deserved R&R. He, Ada, and Philip, then seventeen, embarked on a three-month world cruise. But "Wrig," as one of his aides called him, was not exactly a natural traveler, and his patience quickly wore thin. Anxious about business matters, he left the tour in Cairo and took passage on a mail boat, whose only virtue was speed and whose vices were cholera-infected seamen, an utter absence of amenities, and a want of sea-worthiness. After the ship barely limped into port with a crew that had nearly lost all hope in one of the worst storms in Mediterranean history, he stepped ashore to attend promptly to business in the company's newly established London operations.

Back in Chicago, he pursued his routine. He began each day, even in the worst weather, at six o'clock with a horseback ride in Lincoln Park with his long-suffering man Friday, Joe Patrick. Afternoons, when his schedule permitted, he swam and boxed at the Chicago Athletic Club, the same club where Dr. Scholl lived. He read very little, but enjoyed being read to, and Joe performed that duty faithfully.

Wrigley's interest in the challenge of sport led him to become one of ten investors who bought the Chicago Cubs, then owned by a Cincinnati newspaper publisher, Charles P. Taft, brother of President William Howard Taft. By 1921, Wrigley had accumulated a controlling interest in the team. Greats like Grover Cleveland Alexander and Rogers Hornsby were among his star players.

The team won the National League pennant in 1929 and nearly won the World Series, against the Philadelphia Athletics. In the deciding game, the Cubs were up by eight and seemed sure to win, until the seventh inning, when the A's scored ten runs, and the Cubs couldn't recover.

In the succeeding seventy years, the team was never to be in serious contention again.

It was a heartbreaking moment for the man who loved the sport, and his team. He treated his players better than any other owner in baseball. He sent them on first-class trains, put them up in the best accommodations, and paid them top dollar. This was in stunning contrast to the White Sox owner, Charlie Comisky, a man so cheap that he even refused paying to have his players' uniforms washed.

Because Wrigley had little concern with profit, he did things that he knew would cut into ticket sales. He broadcast his games on the radio. He originated Ladies' Day, when women were admitted free. He gave thousands of free tickets to youngsters from low-income families. All these altruistic gestures that businessmen-owners would never make, in the end made good business sense, since they created an enthusiasm for the game and the team and brought women and a whole new generation of youth into the bleachers. The immaculate maintenance of his stadium attracted fans, and the loyalty went both ways. Even today, the Cubs crowd is the best in the league: when a fan catches a home run hit by an opposing team, tradition requires that he or she throw it back onto the field, as if it were something ritually unclean.

His love for Chicago was also shown by his becoming a benefactor of the Lincoln Park Zoo. He donated money for a female hippo, named Princess Spearmint.

In 1914, he went to Pasadena, California, to buy an estate not far, incidentally, from where Mr. Weyerhaeuser was living. But after only a few weeks, he and Ada sailed "twenty-six miles across the sea" to Santa Catalina. In those days, there was little there. A sleepy fishing village and a seedy hotel. A few "diminutive boats" chugged back and forth occasionally, carrying visitors, most of whom tented out, but a few of whom stayed in the seedy hotel, the St. Catherine (English for Santa Catalina).

The Wrigleys fell in love with the rugged but enchanted isle. Ada said, "I should like to live here." Years later, he recalled his response: "Right then and there I determined that the island should never pass out of my hands." He made it the spring training grounds for the Cubs, and later into a major resort and tourist attraction, which boasted, among other things, the world's largest cafeteria. He took a great interest in birds and built one of the largest and most exotic aviaries in the country. Later, he built the Hotel Atwater, named after Philip's wife's maiden name. He made a sawmill and furniture factory, installed diesel generators, dug wells, and made the island self-sustaining. The million dollars he poured into the island each year paid off: in 1919, there were ninety thousand visitors; ten years later there were eight times that number. Discovery of a silver mine that he named the "Black Jack" Mine was an unexpected bonus. Gravel deposits gave him even more mining income.

He also had a farm on Lake Geneva in Wisconsin, where he raised pigs.

When Wrigley died in 1932, Philip kept the promise he'd made at age six and took over the business; he remained its president until his own death in 1977. Before William's death, Philip and his wife, Helen, blessed him with two granddaughters, but William didn't live to see the birth of his grandson and namesake, William, who became the CEO of the company until his death in 1999. The current CEO is his son (1963–). His name, William Wrigley, Jr., is the same as his great-grandfather's, but is written with the comma.

Afterword

🎀

I hope you've enjoyed getting to know some of the people who made the stuff in your "grocery cart," so to speak. Now when you're in the store, you can point to cans on the shelf and impress your fellow shoppers by recounting amusing or poignant anecdotes about the people on the labels.

If you browsed through the book and passed over some people that didn't seem interesting at first, or weren't "your type"—maybe you skipped Harley-Davidson, because you don't ride a chopper—take a second look. Those guys, too, lived good lives while creating part of the American dream.

Perhaps you were surprised to discover, as I was, how entrepreneurs played important roles outside their business lives. We saw Pierre Du Pont whispering the suggestion that the U.S. purchase the Louisiana Territory in Jefferson's ear; we saw Gail Borden play a major role in the settlement of Texas and R. S. Reynolds of Reynolds Wrap fame possibly making a difference in the outcome of World War II; and we noted young immigrant "Chef Boyardee" serving Woodrow Wilson meals on his honeymoon. So in ways momentous and trivial, the subjects in this book sometimes wove the threads of their lives into America's tapestry, affecting its color and texture in important and surprising ways.

Sometimes the threads cross, and we find several of our subjects at the same place at the same time. At the Philadelphia Centennial in 1876, where Robert Wood Johnson attended the Lister lecture that set the direction of his life's journey, Milton Bradley received his award for his work in the kindergarten movement. Milton Hershey was there, too, selling his first caramel candies, and H. J. Heinz was peddling his pickles. At the Chicago World's Fair in 1893, where Busch lost the Blue Ribbon to Captain Pabst, Caleb Chase and James Sanborn were making coffee. It was there that Milton Hershey (there he was again!) decided that he would make chocolate, and Henry Ford decided he would make cars. Could it be that these people passed in the halls, or casually chatted, never imagining each would someday become a household name?

Perhaps you noticed that sometimes the threads of their stories crossed your own, or your family's. I found to my surprise that several of them worked where I once visited or lived.

Another observation, though hardly a surprise, is that nearly all of America's entrepreneurs came from humble origins. Of the 116 people written about in this book, only two—Du Pont and Monsanto—came from a privileged background. Only a few others came from what could even be described as "comfortable" circumstances. Almost all started with virtually nothing and probably hadn't the faintest notion that they would become wealthy, and many in fact failed repeatedly before "making it." Yet, driven by blind hope and straining with tireless effort, often against the advice of nearly everyone, they built thriving businesses, and even empires. Virtually all of them—so extraordinarily diverse in almost every way—shared one common trait: an obsession with excellence and a willingness to pour heart and fortune into making their companies work and their products become the best they could be. By doing so, whether they intended it or not, and whether they knew it or not, they laid the foundations for a national prosperity that most of them would never have imagined possible.

Maybe you noticed, too, how many of them thought far beyond the limits of their enterprises, and believed in grandiose world-changing visions. The Warner brothers exposed injustice in their hard-hitting films in much the way Dickens had done in his novels the century before. In striking contrast, H. J. Heinz saw the world Sunday-school movement as the key to brotherhood and peace. Hershey's self-contained "industrial commune" more or less succeeded as an ideal become reality, but we saw its *reductio ad absurdum* in the outrageous utopian vision of King Gillette and his hundred-million-soul World Corporation.

Though sometimes misguided, these were people with expansive vision who ignored the "doses of reality" and pressed on to change the world. And the great majority of them (with some pretty glaring exceptions) were people of self-discipline and high moral character. Rather than lay off his workers during the Depression, Hershey put them to work building a town. Procter paid debts to people in England who could never have hoped to collect from him. Paul Newman has given to charity $100 million in profits from his food-products venture.

These entrepreneurs have scattered their less worthy and scrupulous competition to the wind. It seems that the invisible hand that Adam Smith writes of in his *Wealth of Nations* does not just guide; it also shakes, and vigorously winnows out dishonest dealing, shoddy products, and ungenerous souls. Left to itself, the capitalist economy, for all its faults, does not let the snake-oil salesman prosper long. It treats most kindly those who make the best widgets, represent them the most honestly, charge the fairest price, and have the most expansive civic spirit. So much for Thorstein Veblen's notion of entrepreneur as robber baron; usually the nice guys finish first, and for me, this was my biggest surprise.

But there was also a second surprise, alas, as disheartening as the first was uplifting: our shameful neglect of our commercial heritage. I found that time and again, proud family-owned companies have been taken over by new management or by conglomerates that have little interest in their histories. Figuratively, or maybe literally, company archives are stuffed into boxes and carted to the basement for storage—or worse. Several no doubt worthy individuals missed inclusion in this book because their stories lie moldering in their cardboard graves.

But it's not just the conglomerates; "the enemy is us," too. Inexplicably, we don't commemorate our business history the way we do other aspects of our national life. We laud entrepreneurs as authentic American heroes, but there are only a few sites where an important event in our commercial heritage is acknowledged. There are historical markers everywhere. Sometimes you can hardly see the scenery for all the signs honoring founders of schools, writers of songs, and fighters in some Civil War skirmish at some creek. But where is the plaque on the building where Otis's first elevator was installed, or where the first Lionel trains were made, or where the first Chevrolet rolled out the door? As much as on its battlegrounds and schools, these were places where the world was changed.

Writing this book has changed me as well. Now when I'm in a shopping line, I ignore the tabloids entirely and instead look down at all those packages and cans—no longer wondering about the people who made them, because I know something about them now, but amazed at what I see. The coffee in the sealed tin, the sterile bandages in the little box, the soup in the can, the neatly rolled aluminum foil—none of that even existed before the people in this book had lived their lives and done their work.

None of these products is miraculous, of course, and you may even call them trivial advances in the progress of humankind, yet the cumulative effect of their presence is the American life we live.

Now that I know something about the people who bore the familiar names in my shopping cart, how hard they worked and how much they risked, I remain bemused, but no longer with idle curiosity; rather it's with admiration and gratitude, as I think what my life would be like if they hadn't lived theirs.

References

Adams, Russell. *King Gillette: The Man and His Wonderful Shaving Device*. 1978.

Alberts, Robert C. *The Good Provider: H. J. Heinz and His 57 Varieties*. 1973.

American Heritage. December 1972.

American Lumbermen.

Brandon, Ruth. *A Capitalistic Romance: Singer and the Sewing Machine*. J. P. Lippincott, 1977.

Brenner, Joël Glenn. *The Emperors of Chocolate: Inside the Secret World of Hershey and Mars*. 1999.

Brooks, John. *The Autobiography of American Business*.

Brown, Henry D., et al. *Cadillac and the Founding of Detroit*. 1976.

Cavanaugh, Joe. Dr Pepper Museum.

Chandler, Alfred D. *Henry Varnum Poor: Business Editor, Analyst, Reformer*. 1956.

Chandler, Robert J. "Banking and Finance to 1913," in *Encyclopedia of American Business History and Biography*.

Chase & Sanborn company literature.

Chazanof, William. *Welch's Grape Juice: From Corporation to Cooperative*.

Chrysler, Walter. *Life of an American Workman*. 1937.

Cleary, David Powers. *Great American Brands*.

Collier, Peter, and David Horowitz. *The Fords: An American Epic*. 1987.

Collins, Douglas. *America's Favorite Food: The Story of Campbell Soup Company*. 1994.

Cray, Ed. *Levi's: The Shrink-to-Fit Business That Stretched to Cover the World*. 1978.

Duke, Marc. *The Du Ponts: Portrait of a Dynasty*. 1976.

Dutton, William S. *Du Pont: One Hundred and Forty Years*. 1942.

The Editors of *News Front Year. The Fifty Great Pioneers of American Industry.* 1965.

Encyclopedia Britannica.

Eveready Battery Company. "The Eveready Battery Story." 1995.

Fanning, Leonard M. "Gail Borden, Father of the Modern Dairy Industry." A company publication.

Fields, Debbi, and Alan Furst. *One Smart Cookie.* New York: Simon & Schuster, 1987.

Forrestal, Dan J. *Faith, Hope, and $5,000: The Story of Monsanto.*

Foster, Lawrence. *Johnson & Johnson: A Company That Cares.* 1986.

Frantz, Joe B. *Gail Borden, Dairyman to a Nation.* 1951.

Gallo, Ernest, and Julio Gallo. *Our Story.* 1976.

General Mills. "The Story of Betty Crocker."

Gerber Products company literature.

Gillette, King. *The Human Drift.* 1976.

Gilmore, C. P. "William Lear: Two Hundred Million Dollars," in *The Very, Very Rich and How They Got That Way,* edited by Max Gunther.

Goldwasser, Thomas. *Family Pride.*

Gould, William. *McDonald's.* From the VMG Business Portraits series, 1996.

Gross, Daniel. *Forbes' Greatest Business Stories of All Time.*

Grossman, Peter C. *American Express.* 1987.

Hallett, Anthony, and Diane Hallett. *Entrepreneur Magazine's Encyclopedia of Entrepreneurs.*

Hambleton, Ronald. *The Branding of America.*

Hatcher, Harlan, and Erich Walter. *A Pictorial History of the Great Lakes.*

Hawkes, Ellen. *Blood and Wine: The Unauthorized Story of the Gallo Wine Empire.* 1993.

Hecht, Henry, ed. *A Legacy of Leadership—Merrill Lynch 1885–1985.*

Hencey, Robert T. *Empires.* 1995.

Hernon, Peter, and Terry Ganey. *Under the Influence: The Unauthorized Story of the Anheuser-Busch Dynasty.*

Hershey Company. "The Man Behind the Chocolate Bar."

Higham, Charles. *Warner Brothers*. 1975.

Hollander, Ron. *All Aboard, the Marvelous Toy Electric Trains and the Man Who Made Them*. 1981.

Hoover company literature.

Hoover, Frank. *The Fabulous Dustpan*. 1955.

Hormel Company. "The Hormel Legacy, 100 Years of Quality." 1991.

Ingrham, John N. *Biographical Dictionary of American Business Leaders*.

International Foods Corp. "The History of Chef Boyardee."

JCPenney. "James Cash Penney, His Life and Legacy."

Jensen, Amy LaFollette. *The White House and Its Thirty-five Families*.

Jinks, Roy G. *History of Smith & Wesson*. 1977.

Johnson & Johnson. "Brief History of Johnson & Johnson."

Katz, Donald R. *The Big Store*.

Kogan, Rick. *Brunswick: The Story of an American Company*. 1995.

Kroger Company. "Barney Builds a Business: The Story of the Kroger Company."

Lager, Fred "Chico." *Ben & Jerry's: The Inside Scoop*. 1994.

Langworth, Richard, and Jay P. Norbye. *Chevrolet, 1911–1985*.

Lavine, Sigmund A. *Famous Merchants*.

Levine, Peter. *A. G. Spalding and the Rise of Baseball*. 1985.

Lewis, Alfred Allan, and Constance Woodworth. *Miss Elizabeth Arden, an Unretouched Portrait*.

Lieberman, Richard K. *Steinway & Sons*. 1995.

Loomis, Noel M. *Wells Fargo*. 1968.

Love, John F. *McDonald's—Behind the Arches*. 1986.

Major, Lettie Leitch. *C. W. Post: The Hour and the Man*. 1963.

Margolick, David. *Undue Influence: The Epic Battle for the Johnson & Johnson Fortune*. 1993.

Maytag Company. "The Spirit of Maytag, 100 Years of Dependability." 1993.

McCormick company literature.

McGovern, James R. *Yankee Family*. 1975.

McMahon, James D., Jr. *Built on Chocolate: The Story of the Hershey Chocolate Company*. 1998.

Miller, William. *Men in Business: Essays in the History of Entrepreneurship.*

Milton Bradley Company. "Interesting Facts and Highlights on the Life of Milton Bradley."

Nevins, Allan. *Grover Cleveland: A Study in Courage.*

New Yorker, The. 6 September 1947.

Otis company literature.

Oumano, Elena. *Paul Newman.* 1989.

Packard, David. *The HP Way: How Bill Hewlett and I Built Our Company.* 1994.

Pillsbury, Philip W. *The Pioneering Pillsburys.* 1950.

Pitrone, Jean Maddern, and Joan Potter Elart. *The Dodges.* 1981.

Powell, Horace B. *The Original Has This Signature: W. K. Kellogg.* 1956.

Procter & Gamble Company. "Our Founding Fathers." 1997.

Rae, John B. *Henry Ford.*

Ratcliffe, Ronald. *Steinway.*

Regli, Adolph C. *Rubber's Goodyear: The Story of a Man's Perseverance.* 1941.

Richards, Bart. *Warner Brothers.* 1973.

Rodengen, Jeffrey L. *The Legend of Dr Pepper/7-UP.* 1995.

Sadler, Christine. *Children in the White House.*

Saladini, A., and P. Szymezak. *Harley Davidson: History, Meetings, New Models, Custom Bikes.* A company publication.

Sanborn, Elmer. Interviews with a proud sixth cousin twice removed of James Sanborn.

Sanborn, Helen J. *A Winter in Central America.* 1886.

Schissgall, Arthur. *Eyes on Tomorrow: The Evolution of Procter & Gamble.* 1981.

Scholl, William H. *Dr. Scholl, Foot Doctor to the World.*

Sears Roebuck Company. "Sears Yesterday and Today."

Shay, James J., and Carl Mercer. *It's All in the Game.* New York: G. P. Putnam's Sons, 1960.

Shippen, Katherine, and Paul Wallace. *Milton S. Hershey.* 1959.

Spalding Company. "Spalding Fact Book."

Spector, Robert. *Shared Values: A History of Kimberly Clark.* 1997.

Sperling, Cass Warner, and Cork Millner. *Hollywood Be Thy Name*. 1994.

Szudarek, Robert. *How Detroit Became the Automotive Capital*.

Thomas, Dave. *Dave's Way*. 1992.

Tilly, Nannie M. *The R. J. Reynolds Tobacco Company*. 1985.

Uncle Ben's, Inc. "The Story of Uncle Ben's Converted Rice."

Van Tasel, David, and John Grabowski. *Dictionary of Cleveland Biography*. 1996.

Walls, Don. "The McCormick Story." *Baltimore Daily Record*, May 22–24, 1962.

Weil, Gordon L. *Sears Roebuck USA*. Stein & Day, 1977.

Wendt, Lloyd. *The Wall Street Journal*. Rand McNally, 1982.

Weyerhaeuser company literature.

Weyerhaeuser, George F. "Forest of the Future." Newcomen Society Tract, 1981.

Wright, David K. *The Harley-Davidson Motor Company: An Official Eighty Year History*. 1987.

Wrigley's. "The Story of Gum."

Zimmerman, William. *William Wrigley, Jr.: The Man and His Business*. 1935.